Voices For The Future

Voices For The Future

Essays On Major Science Fiction Writers

Volume Two

Thomas D. Clareson

Bowling Green University Popular Press
Bowling Green, Ohio 43403

Library of Congress Catalog Card Number: 78-61202

ISBN:0-87972-135-9 CB
    0-87972-136-7 PB

Cover design by Michael Gurtzweiler

CONTENTS

Introduction

Volume two of *Voices for the Future* continues the series of essays dealing with major writers of science fiction. For the most part, it gives attention to individuals whose careers began in the 1950s, although no attempt has been made to impose a chronological order on the sequence of essays.

Just as those authors dealt with in volume one made significant contributions to the development of the genre during the 1930s and 1940s in particular, so the authors examined here have done much to shape science fiction as it has evolved within the past quarter century. As always with such a collection as this, some readers may ask why certain favorites did not receive consideration. Perhaps the best answer may take the form of an example: at the time of his unfortunate death, James Blish was working on an evaluation of the fiction of Brian Aldiss. (A study of Aldiss, incidentally, has already been scheduled for volume three.)

The contributors have had complete freedom to develop their subjects as they saw fit. I would not have it otherwise. Not surprisingly, by and large each has sought to give some insight into the body of the individual writer's work. Although I do not think of the collection as being aimed exclusively at an academic audience, because an enthusiast of science fiction is also its student, I hope the essays will be of value to teacher and student alike, both in the classroom and in their individual study and reading.

Wooster, Ohio

February, 1979

Thomas D. Clareson

The Fictions of Robert Silverberg

Because of Philip Jose' Farmer's use of the Riverworld, Wolff-Kickaha, and the Wold Newton families, one thinks of his work, at least in part, in terms of elaborate frameworks to which he may return time and again in order to sustain his readers' interests by elaborating upon previously established settings and story-lines.[1] Not so Robert Silverberg. One senses that for him particularly each narrative has a uniqueness which must be worked out in its own terms. With him one must therefore trace the ways in which he has varied his explorations of pervasive themes; or again, one must notice the relationships between stories and novels—not necessarily written during the same period—because, for example, he frequently manipulates some element of plot attractive to him in order to gain very different results.

In addition, the reader must be constantly aware of the changes in the manner in which he has handled his material technically. He has always been a first-class craftsman and story-teller: *Invaders from Earth* (1957), *Recalled to Life* (1957, rewritten 1971), *The Gate of Worlds* (1967), *Those Who Watch* (1967), and *Across a Billion Years* (1969), as well as a legion of early short stories, attest to that. But increasingly, during the past decade especially, he has abandoned the straightforward, beginning-middle-and-end narrative frame, a staple of so much science fiction, in favor of technical experimentation. As early as "The Songs of Summer" (1956) he employed fragmented, overlapping monologues to gain a more complex perspective of a simple tale. He used that same technique perhaps most effectively in *The Book of Skulls* (1972), in which four contemporary young Americans quest for immortality. A measure of his artistry and sense of aesthetic rightness lies in the inability of the reader to imagine a given story told in a different

1

fashion. *The Book of Skulls*, for example, would lose much of its emotional and intellectual force had only one of the youths "told" the story or had Silverberg attempted an omniscient point of view. Indeed, experiment with point of view is a trademark of Silverberg's method. His finest achievement undoubtedly occurred in "Sundance" (1969). A second characteristic of his style has become a reliance upon the present tense, as exemplified in "Passengers" (1968)—winner of a Nebula Award—and portions of "Born with the Dead" (1974). Not only does he gain a greater sense of immediacy and dramatic impact, but frequently his use of the device also forces his reader to grow aware of different levels of reality.

In short, by the 1970s Silverberg was writing science fiction much as such of his contemporaries as Barth, Reed, Barthelme, and Coover were presenting their renditions of everyday American life. For example, the delightfully comic "Many Mansions" (1973)— which plays with the paradoxes of time travel and the notion of eliminating one's spouse—calls to mind Robert Coover's "Babysitter." Although for different reasons, both stories are constructed of brief sequences—external scene or internal thought—some no more than a paragraph in length, depicting various possible courses of action. By the end of both the reader does not know who has done what to whom, if anything; that is to say, the authors' games have completely befuddled the readers' sense of what is real.

From the same year two other stories warrant attention. "Some Notes from the Pre-Dynastic Epoch" (1973) purports to be a first-person account by an archaeologist of the future as he describes fragments of poetry and other artifacts of the late twentieth century. Abruptly the narrator exclaims: "None of the aforegoing is true. I take pleasure in deceiving. I am an extremely unreliable witness."[2] Without further hesitation, however, he tells how he and his professional colleagues have journeyed to the past through a gate of dreams. The story becomes a lament and a warning; the narrator feels a unity with all people of all times ("All time converges on this point of now."); ostensibly the climax occurs when he cites the judgment from the Book of Daniel (5:25—"...Mene. Mene. Tekel. Upharsin"). Yet once more the unreliable narrator abruptly shifts the tone:

Let me unmask myself. Let me confess everything. There is no Center for Pre-Dynastic Studies. I am no Metalinguistic Archaeologist, Third Grade, living in a remote and idyllic era far in your future and passing my days in pondering the wreckage of the Twentieth Century. The time of the Dynast may be coming, but he does not yet rule. I am your contemporary. I am your brother. These notes are the work of a pre-dynastic man like yourself, a native of the so-called Twentieth Century, who, like you, has lived through dark hours and may live to see darker ones. That much is true. All the rest is fantasy of my own invention. Do you believe that? Do I

seem reliable now? Can you trust me just this once?
All time converges on this point of now (p.44).

A similar ending governs "Ms. Found in an Abandoned Time Machine" (1973), but the tone differs, for the narrator is overcome emotionally by his fictions. The story blends together items which might come from the contemporary press items underscoring social injustice and ecological disaster—and the first-person narrative of "Thomas C___," a militant young idealist who demands to be heard:

> ...Listen to me. Just listen. Suppose you had a machine that would enable you to fix everything that's wrong in the world. Let's say that it draws on all the resources of modern technology, not to mention the powers of a rich, well-stocked imagination and a highly developed ethical sense. The machine can do anything.... It's all done with the aid of a lot of science fiction gadgetry. I won't apologize for that part of it. Apologies just aren't necessary.... The aim is to eradicate the well-known evils of our society, and if we have to get there by means of time machine, thought-amplification headbands, anti-uptightness rays, molecular interpenetrator beams, superheterodyning levitator rods, and all the rest of that gaudy comic-book paraphernalia, so be it. It's the results that count.[3]

Thomas' accomplishments include saving Lincoln from Booth so that the racial problem may be solved and confronting the current President ("Dicky"), who is persuaded to initiate all of the desired reforms. True, Thomas must resort to a ray gun and "zap" him, but the president does agree, and "the rest is history." At that point Thomas breaks off; he cries out:

> Oh.Oh.Oh.Oh, God. If it could only be that easy. One, two, three, zap. But it doesn't work like that. I don't have any magic wand. What makes you think I did? How was I able to trick you into a suspension of disbelief? You, reader, sitting there on your rear end, what do you think I really am? A miracle man? Some kind of superbeing from Galaxy Ten? I'll tell you what I really am, me, Thomas C___ I'm a bunch of symbols on a piece of paper. I'm just something abstract trapped within a mere fiction. A "hero" in a "story." Helpless, disembodied, unreal. UNREAL! Whereas you out there—you have eyes, lungs, feet, arms, a brain, a mouth, all that good stuff. You can function. You can move. You can act. Work for the Revolution! Strive for change! You're operating in the real world; you can do it if anybody can! Struggle toward...umph...glub...Hey, get your filthy hands off me—Power to the people! Down with the fascist pigs...hey—help—HELP! (p.54)

In these stories Silverberg has made use of those techniques reminiscent of Barth's *Lost In the Fun House* and Effinger's *What Entropy Means to Me*. Fiction is not reality; it is an artificial construct in which author and reader participate. Perhaps one need say little more except to point out how effectively Silverberg uses the final intrusion in "Ms. Found in an Abandoned Time Machine" as a call to action, thereby reinforcing his theme, however didactically. Then, too, by reminding his readers—almost angrily—that the narrative is but an artifice, he undercuts a long-established, escapist convention of science fiction: the appearance at precisely the right moment of a superman or alien who saves mankind from its dreadful woes and goes on to establish an earthly paradise. But Silverberg is not yet satisfied; the nicest irony occurs when the narrator slips back into the "reality" of the narrative and is overwhelmed by the very readers whom he has implored to take action. Theme and form have been fused effectively.

Because Silverberg has written here openly of the paraphernalia of science fiction, one should consider a companion piece, so to speak, "The Science Fiction Hall of Fame" (1973). He juxtaposes scenes containing many of the cliches' of content and style characteristic of earlier magazine science fiction with the first-person narrator's reflections upon the role of sf in his own life and its worth as a literary form.

Nor should one forget that Silverberg—with a background in comparative literature and a wide knowledge of literary criticism—strengthens his work with a sub-structure of literary allusion. Faust and the Bible have become central to much of his fiction, while references to such figures as Yeats and Dostoevsky abound. In "Breckenridge and the Continuum" (1973) he achieved something of a tour de force when he deliberately garbled the classic myths. In that same story he introduced "Some possible structural hypotheses"[4] to guide his readers to various levels of meaning—and, by inference, delighted in an ending which fuses together those various levels in the here-and-now. Another, "After the Myths Went Home" (1969) emphasizes how vital myth is in shaping and giving meaning to a culture. A less obvious use of literary sources occurs in "When We Went to See the End of the World" (1972), in which a number of young couples succumbs briefly to the latest fad in tourism. Yet for none of them is the end of the world the same. So inured are they to the chaos of their everyday culture (as reported on television) that they can speak casually of the physical end of the Earth; the irony, of course, lies in their seeming inability to realize that their own world/civilization is destroying itself—partly, at least, because of their blasé indifference to it. The issues and their effects, so to speak, go in one ear and come out the other. One of the descriptions of the world's end includes the crab and red sun figuring in H.G. Wells's *The Time Machine*. One suspects that many, if not all, of the final scenes draw upon earlier science fiction. Such a body of allusions not only adds to the texture of the individual stories but ties Silverberg's works firmly to the wider body of Western fiction.

To date, since completing *Shadrach in the Furnace* in the spring of 1975, Silverberg has written no new fiction. In a recent introduction to a reprint edition of his first collection of short stories, he explained that "none of those early good stories sold of their own merit"[5] and that as a result he "slipped into the tradition of the action story: strong plots, swift stripped-down style, direct conflict of man against man and man against environment. It was a good way for a beginning writer to learn the essentials of his craft...[6] In describing the stages of his career, he has said that after the period 1955-1959, when he produced "hundreds of science fiction stories," he abandoned the field "for a variety of reasons, of which the most pressing were financial and artistic."[7] For a time he turned almost exclusively to non-fiction, but after Fred Pohl accepted "To See The Invisible Man" (1962), Silverberg submitted stories to Pohl with increasing frequency. By 1967-1968 he was again active, ready to undertake those stories and major novels upon which his reputation as one of the outstanding talents in the field must finally rest. Yet such a three-part division of his career oversimplifies, for during the first half of the 1960s a number of his earlier titles were being issued in book form, while such non-fiction as *The Realm of Prester John* appeared as late as 1972. And there were those occasional stories for Pohl. In short, from the mid-1950s onward there never was a time when the name Silverberg was completely absent from science fiction.

Another way of describing his career is to say that a skilled craftsman and story-teller increasingly rejected "machine-made formula fiction" as he consciously sought to find new and more significant uses of science fiction materials. This is not to imply that he was alone in such an effort, but it does mean to suggest that he abandoned the literal action story in favor of the metaphorical as a basis for commentary upon the condition of man in the twentieth century. Perhaps the most intriguing proposal would emphasize that his career has encompassed the intellectual history of science fiction—moving at will back and forth through its entire spectrum from the stance of the Enlightenment to the romantic and the absurd.

Speaking more specifically in a 1977 introduction to a reprint of *To Open the Sky* (1967)—a "suite" novel made up of five episodes published separately in *Galaxy* by Pohl in 1964-1965—Russell Letson has declared that "It now seems to be the book that signals the full emergence of the 'new' Silverberg...not only because of its use of characteristic images and motifs and its superior literary control; it also announces the themes that will dominate his work hereafter."[8] Despite the initial qualification, such a judgment is convenient but—at least—somewhat arbitrary, for it seems to ignore what Silverberg was doing in other narratives during the last half of the 1960s. Moreover, despite its implication, there has been no distinct, linear development to Silverberg's fiction. All of the complex moods, the concern for artistry, and certain pervasive themes have been present from the beginning when he wrote "Road to Nightfall" in 1954. Two years later the story remained unpublished; Harlan Ellison campaigned on its behalf; finally in July 1958 it appeared in *Fantastic Universe*. Ironically, two years earlier at the Worldcon in 1956 Robert Silverberg had received a Hugo as the most promising new writer of the year.

In view of the innumerable post-holocaust stories so popular since World War Two, the reception of "Road to Nightfall" seems puzzling, although if one reads it without knowing the date of composition, he can easily place it somewhere in the 1960s. It portrays a ruined America in which New York, Trenton, and Baltimore survive as oases in a radioactive desert. The explanation may rest in this: however dire the visions of most other authors in the late 1940s and early 1950s, they left some room for hope— perhaps for a rational decision which would prevent the extinction of civilization and mankind, as in Theodore Sturgeon's classic "Thunder and Roses" (1947). Not so Silverberg. Starvation haunts New York. What food supplies have come from the Trenton oasis have been cut off because of conditions there. Vandals hunt dogs in Manhattan; no person is safe alone in the streets after dark or in an unfamiliar neighborhood. The protagonist, Katterson—specifically described as a giant among his contemporaries ("...the biggest man alive...Appetite like an ox."9)—rejects the offer of Malory, who would recruit the ex-soldier to supply him with meat. Katterson also refuses the meat offered him by the girl with whom he lives, a gift to her from an admirer. But after hunger gnaws at him, Katterson, like his contemporaries, succumbs to cannibalism. First he tries unsuccessfully to possess a corpse lying in the snow, but others take it from him. Then he goes to Malory, collapsing on his doorstep.

Here is an example of those stories which Lester del Rey denounced during the 1960s, proclaiming that their writers had lost faith in the future. At one point Katterson declares, "This whole world is dead—we've spent the last thirty years committing suicide."10 Although Silverberg's only full-blown dystopian portrait of society was to be *The World Inside* (1971), increasingly, as in titles already cited, he was to sketch backdrops whose vivid details (often presented as though they were news reports from contemporary media) emphasize the social and political injustices, the ecological disasters of a mindless society in the midst of self-destruction.

The dark vision of "Road to Nightfall" continued in those stories which Silverberg has said deal with "psychic cannibalism." The potential from which he developed that theme made a notable early appearance in "Warm Man" (1957). Into the typical suburb of New Brewster comes the solitary Mr. Hallinan, a most sympathetic individual always ready to listen to the troubles of his companions. He immediately becomes "a fixture at any important community gathering," for many of his emotionally crippled neighbors delight—indeed, find relief in telling to him "whatever secret hungers and terrors"[11] dominate their lives. Thus is introduced a second theme essential to Silverberg: the necessity of communication, however painful. Soon, however, the adults cut Hallinan, resenting his "goody-goody warmness" and suspecting that he is gathering material for a novel. In his isolation he turns to Lonny, a strangely silent boy. Finding him pummelled by classmates and crying, Hallinan asks if he can be of help; Lonny pours forth accumulated grievances—telepathically. The outburst—"like a high voltage wire"— kills Hallinan, who was an empath/receiver, while the boy is a sender. As he dies, Hallinan gasps, "*I...was...a...leech*" (p.45).

Within a few months the short story, "The Winds of Siros" (1957) appeared. Silverberg soon expanded it into a novel which was not published for several years, *The Seed of Earth* (1962), a tale of one effort in Earth's colonization of the galaxy. The story coincides essentially with the final seven chapters of the novel. Aliens abduct two couples from the new colony and place them—otherwise unrestricted—in a cave, caring for them and observing them closely. The protagonist realizes that they "listen to our emotions, soak them up, feed on them."[12] The Earthlings provide "a circus...a kind of entertainment" (p.157) as the aliens watch tensions and hatreds build among them. At this period in Silverberg's career, however, the situation merely presents the characters with a problem to solve. Reason prevails; the Enlightenment breaks through. Despite personal animosities which lead to a switching of partners, the four cooperate, build a rope ladder, and simply hike back to the colony without interference from the aliens. There they learn that hatred and bloodshed have flared among the men desiring power, but now there is hope of peace and success.

The tone had changed by "The Pain Peddlers" (1963), a straightforward account of the manner in which TV networks feed their audience's insatiable demand for vicarious pain. Technology—in this case an EEG amplifier—permits the viewers to share the brain waves of those in pain, whether during an operation on a gangrenous leg or after an eventually fatal wound. In "Flies" (1967), written expressly for Harlan Ellison's *Dangerous Visions*, alien surgeons give a dead starman new life, reconstructing him from fragments surviving his accident. They give him a greater sensitivity to others—"new hungers...certain abilities"[13]—and return him to Earth so that he can transmit the emotions of those whom he encounters. At best the aliens' motivation remains ambiguous, although implication suggests that out of curiosity they only seek data. But something goes wrong with their handiwork; wantonly, brutally, the protagonist inflicts pain upon his three ex-wives. He basks in their agonies. Appalled, the aliens recall him for adjustment; they restore his conscience and reverse the process so that he can transmit only his own emotions. Then they release him: "*nailed to his cross*" (p.91).

The importance of "Flies" to Silverberg may be measured by his use of the basic incident—the operation on the starman by aliens—as a point of departure for two major novels of the late 1960s. The action of *Thorns* (1967) is manipulated by Duncan Chalk, "a pain-responsive, pain-fed eater of emotion, depending on his intake of raw anguish as others did on their intake of bread and meat."[14] He decides to feast upon a man and a woman and, more than that, to sell them to a world-wide audience as star-crossed lovers. The man chosen is Minner Burris, who has been operated on—mutilated—by aliens interested solely in the "secrets of human construction" (p.48). He lives, something other than human, in endless pain. The woman chosen is Lona Kelvin, from whom several hundred fertile but immature eggs have been taken in another deliberate experiment. Once she had supplied the ova, she was forgotten, not even allowed to carry one of her babies. Chalk enlists Burris by promising surgery which will end his pain and correct his physical differences (besides internal changes, he has tentacles and a strange skin). Chalk promises Lona that she may raise two of her babies. Of the project before its inception, he remarks to a colleague: "Bring them together. Who knows? We might generate some pain...we can learn lessons from pain. It teaches us that we're alive" (p.17). His promise causes Burris to leave the room where he had isolated himself; "...it was something like being born" (p.62). He later refers to that isolation as "That dark night of the soul" (p.83).

As Lona watches Burris suffer during "the full celebrity treatment," she demands to know why he submitted himself to the ordeal if he wanted no one to see him; he replies, "As a penance. As a deliberately chosen atonement for my withdrawal from the world. For the sake of discipline" (p.169). Throughout his later fiction atonement and redemption more and more become central motifs. *Thorns* may be considered his fullest exploration of the redemptive power of pain in a natural world—an existential world outside the Christian tradition. Yet increasingly, he has given much of his fiction a sub-structure of Christian allusion—oftentimes explicit, sometimes not—which heightens his ironies and sharpens his consideration of a theme. Burris' fascination for thorns thus achieves a complex symbolic value because "The thorn is merely a highly evolved form of leaf. An adaptation to a harsh environment. Cacti can't afford to transpire the way leafy plants do. So they adapt. I'm sorry you regard such an elegant adaptation as ugly" (p.83). In short, the novel becomes a study of Burris' spiritual adaptation to the grotesque situation in which his consciousness finds itself.

That adaptation is difficult, to say the least. Burris and Lona are not star-crossed lovers. They quarrel; they goad one another; they separate. And Chalk feeds upon them. Only after they realize that he knew that they would loathe each other and only after they realize that they cannot change what they are—mutilated starman and mother of a hundred babies—do they understand that there can be "No more hatred" (p.219). Together—aware of their new sympathy, if not love—they flood Chalk with their shared emotion and kill him in a passage in which Silverberg evokes the images of Melville's White Whale and Marlowe's Faustus (p.220). Although they have defeated Chalk, they know that they cannot overcome a world which regards them as freaks, so they choose to return to the planet where Burris was mutilated physically. As they go, in a sequence echoing Chalk's initial view and implying, seemingly, that stoic resignation is all that is possible, Burris tells Lona "To be alive—to feel, even to feel pain—how important that is..." He presses thorns into her hand:

"We bleed," she said. "We live. We feel."
"Pain is instructive," said Burris, and they walked more quickly (p.222).

Just as Burris and Lona retreat from Earth, so, too, does Richard Muller, protagonist of *The Man in the Maze* (1969). At some time in the past, given the opportunity of going alone or heading a team, he chose to act as the sole emissary to the only aliens yet found in a galaxy where a "curious blight of extinction had come upon all...other intelligent races."[15] Despite the aliens' apparent indifference to him—he did not communicate with them—they did operate on his mind. Not until he returned to Earth, however, did he learn that they had fixed him so that he could not suppress his emotions: "What came forth was this gush of self: a torrent of raw despair, a river of regrets and sorrows, all the sewage of a soul. He could not hold it back" (p.113). So sickening was the aura that even his fiancee' could not bear to be with him.

In anger and despair he had fled to a distant planet, exiling himself in the ruins of an ancient city perhaps as much as five million years old—a city of "inconceivable machinery—imperishable caretaker devices" (p.25), the so-called maze of Lemnos. Now, "in a time of system-wide crisis" (p.31), an expedition of Earthmen arrives and seeks to persuade him to leave the maze in order to act once more as an emissary to a recently-discovered, second race of aliens—"colossal, unimaginable beasts...superwhales...forging a captive society" in which men "make outstanding slaves" (pp.166, 167). Attempts at communication have failed because they are non-verbal. At one level the novel proves to be a classic example of science fiction as puzzle in that the narrative closely follows the efforts first of robots and then of men to penetrate—solve—the booby-trapped maze. But that action simply affords a necessary backdrop for Muller's reflections about what has happened to him and for his dialogues with young Rawlins, who has been sent in to deceive Muller and persuade him to come out voluntarily.

At one point Muller cries out, "...Kill the stranger: it's the law of the universe. And if you don't kill him, at least screw him up a little" (p.110). Again he speaks of his sin of pride in choosing to go alone among the aliens and of thinking of himself as a god in their mythology—a mutilated god (p.110). Of Rawlins' reaction to him and the aura he exudes, Silverberg explains:

...Muller's sorrows were not unique to himself; what he offered was nothing more than an awareness of the punishments the universe devises for its inhabitants. At that moment Rawlins had felt that he was tuned to every discord in creation: the missed chances, the failed loves, the hasty words, the unfair griefs, the hungers, the greeds, the lusts, the knife of envy, the acid of frustration, the fang of time, the death of small insects in winter, the tears of things. He had known aging, loss, impotence, fury, helplessness, loneliness, desolation, self-contempt, and madness. It was a silent shriek of cosmic anger (p.114).

When Muller speaks for himself, he translates that "awareness of the punishments the universe devises"—that "shriek of cosmic anger"—into a description of the natural basis of the human condition:

"No. I belong to the human race. I'm the most human being there is, because I'm the only one who can't hide his humanity. You feel it? You pick up the ugliness? What's inside me is also inside you....I speak for man. I tell the truth. I'm the skull beneath the face....I'm all the garbage we pretend isn't there, all the filthy animal stuff, the lusts, the little hates, the sicknesses, the envies. And I'm the one who posed as god. *Hybris*. I was reminded of what I really am" (p.124).

Rawlins underscores Muller's verdict by accusing him of "blaming humanity for being human" (p.150).

Silverberg's dark vision remains one of the tensions throughout his fictions, achieving perhaps its finest artistry in "Passengers" (1968) and *Dying Inside* (1972). It stems from the continuing concern which he shares with those writers identified with literary naturalism: namely, that man is controlled by—the victim of--a hostile, deterministic universe having no comprehensible meaning. His work takes on an existential quality, as does so much of the significant fiction of the twentieth century, because it tries to discover how man can conduct himself, what he can learn in such a universe. In speaking of what his niece has learned from the destruction of the trees in "The Fangs of the Trees" (1968), the protagonist puts the question succinctly: "What had she learned in Sector C today? That the universe often offers only brutal choices?"[16] He gives fullest expression to the problem in the opening paragraph of *The Stochastic Man* (1975):

We are born by accident into a purely random universe. Our lives are determined by entirely fortuitous combinations of genes. Whatever happens happens by chance. The concepts of cause and effect are fallacies. There are only *seemingly* causes leading to *apparent* effects. Since nothing truly follows from anything else, we swim each day through seas of chaos, and nothing is predictable, not even the events of the very next instant.[17]

The narrator seems to dismiss such disorder by asking immediately, "Do you believe that? If you do, I pity you, because yours must be a bleak and terrifying and comfortless life. I think I once believed something very much like that..." The irony of the novel occurs because one comes to question the reliability of that narrator. One learns that he heads an institution, "a community dedicated to the abolition of uncertainty, the absolute elimination of doubt":

Ultimately we will lead mankind into a universe in which nothing is random, nothing is unknown, all is predictable on every level from the microcosmic to the macrocosmic, from the twitching of an electron to the journeys of the galactic nebulae. We'll teach humanity to taste the sweet comfort of the foreordained. And in that way we'll become as gods.... We will *see*, we will understand, we will comprehend the inevitability of the inevitable, we will accept every turn of the script gladly and without regret. There will be no surprises; therefore there will be no pain. We will live in beauty, knowing that we are aspects of the one great Plan (pp.239-240).

That the narrator's language makes one recall views of earlier utopian societies adds to the irony, because, of course, the universe he envisions is a static mechanism in which man has been reduced to automaton, like Martin Carvajal in the novel, who makes no attempt to avoid his murder as he has foreseen it. It is a version of that bleak universe which has shaped so much of twentieth century literature.

Be that as it may, in *The Man in the Maze* Muller would identify himself as Everyman. The potential of that image is lost in an ending which some may well judge unsatisfactory because it seems hurried and contrived. After a flurry of melodramatic action— Muller is first held at gunpoint by members of the expedition threatening to remove him forcibly and then has the opportunity to kill them or himself—he leaves the maze voluntarily to face the aliens. He realizes that they probe his mind. He feels "his soul escaping through his pores" (p.185), surrenders gladly, tells them to drink deep, and senses that he is being altered. The effect of this encounter upon the future of mankind is dismissed—unknown. As for himself he learns from Rawlins that he no longer possesses the aura which isolated him. Reminded that he is thus free to return to Earth, he asks, "But is humanity fit to consort with me?" (p.187) and retreats to Lemnos. Rawlins concludes that Muller "is beyond hate. Somehow. He's at peace. Whatever he is" and explains that one reason has governed all of his actions: "He loved mankind" (pp.191,192).

If the insistence that Muller acted out of love provides some sense of affirmation, it contrasts sharply with the final emptiness of the story "Passengers" (1968), in which parasitic aliens seize their human hosts at will and without warning so that human life has no continuity of action or memory. Once again aliens use mankind for their sport. While possessed, the protagonist and a young woman have been manipulated as sexual partners. By some "fluke" he remembers and, despite her anger and revulsion, pleads that because they have so little time, they must attempt to establish a meaningful relationship while they are "free." She agrees, hesitantly; he is taken suddenly, abandons her coldly, and enters into a homosexual liaison.

Nowhere else does the motif of psychic cannibalism—or Silverberg's gnawing worry about determinism—achieve so terrible a dramatization symbolizing the irrationality of a universe where man is mere creature overwhelmed by forces completely beyond his control. As a result, like so many contemporary writers, Silverberg has been drawn to the dilemma of man's tortured consciousness marooned in a world without meaning for the individual.

For example, the protagonist of "Schwartz Between the Galaxies" (1974) rebels against the "International homogeneity. Worldwide uniformity...the same universal pseudo-American sensibility..."[18] A world-famous anthropologist flying about the world on lecture tour, he seeks escape through his fantasies of intergalactic travel with a diversity of aliens, a journey which gives him a sense of belonging—of unity—perhaps attainable only through death. Whatever the story, Silverberg has employed man's encounter with nonhuman intelligence to heighten the dramatic impact of his themes. Increasingly for him, as he has turned from a reliance upon melodramatic action, the need for communication— that is, for understanding—has served as the starting point. Schwartz must fantasize. In his most obviously Freudian tale, "One-Way Journey" (1957), the ship's commander destroys the protagonist by forcing him through a psychotherapy session because the officer cannot imagine or condone the idea that a *man* could love an alien. He rejects all aliens as inferior. Nor can the reader miss the element of pathos in "Ishmael in Love" (1970), in which the fair Lisabeth cannot recognize nor accept the love offered her by the porpoise. Here again, as in many of the stories already cited, the failure of sentient beings to communicate gives rise to the dramatic conflicts of the stories.

In contrast there is the comedy of "Something Wild Is Loose" (1971), the story of the alien Vsiir, brought inadvertently to the hostile environment of Earth, who is able at last to make arrangements to go home. After many frustrations he manages to "speak" with a neuropathologist who, during a teletherapy session, has entered the mind of a young woman deep in a coma. Once again it is a mark of Silverberg's ability that he can adapt the same incident to opposite ends, as in "A Sea of Faces" (1974). He uses the experimental "Consciousness-penetration treatment"—a fusion of the two personalities, therapist and patient—to dramatize the entrapment of the doctor within the disordered universe of the patient's mind. (Early in "A Sea of Faces," incidentally, while discussing the possibility of such a treatment, he intrudes to suggest, "Suppose there is a way. Let's pretend there is a way. Is that an acceptable hypothesis? Let's pretend. Let's just pretend, and see what happens."[19])

But the act of communication itself, without understanding, as in "Ishmael in Love" does not guarantee a 'happy' ending. As early as "The Man Who Came Back" (1961), he builds upon the cliché-ridden plot of a man's returning to claim the girl who spurned him in his youth. For eighteen years Burkhardt served as an indentured colonist on a distant planet to which he fled. At last he has purchased his freedom in order to return for Lily Leigh—queen of the solidofils for a decade-and-a-half, five-times married, completely selfish, and carefully preserved as a teen-age beauty by her physicians. To these time-worn conventions, Silverberg added the alien, Donnai, who instructed Burkhardt that "*Any creature that thinks can assert its will. Give me your hand, and I will show you....It is all a matter of channelling your desires....Any creature that thinks can learn how to assert its will.*"[20]

Scoffing at his proposal at first, Lily succumbs for no apparent reason, agreeing to marry him, give up her wealth, and return to the planet as a colonist. Burkhardt reflects:

...Control was possible. He had channelled desire eighteen years, and now Lily was his. Perhaps she was no longer Lily as men had known her, but what did that matter? She was the Lily of his lonely dreams. He had created her in a tingling moment of a handshake, from the raw material of her old self (p.189).

There is an irony in the perverted use which Burkhardt has made of the knowledge Donnai entrusted him with. One cannot help but think of Levin's *The Stepford Wives*, even as he recognizes in Burkhardt something of those aliens who operated on Burris and the protagonist of "Flies."

In contrast to Burkhardt, the protagonist of *Invaders from Earth* (1957) gained a deeper understanding as a result of his encounter with the alien culture of Ganymede. If it were it not for the ending, a reader might well place that novel considerably later in the sequence of his works because of its social and political criticism. The basic plot line grows out of the discovery by the Corporation's Research and Development Section, Ganymede Division, that that moon is both rich in needed radioactive materials and inhabited by intelligent but primitive aliens. The Corporation hires a public relations firm to persuade the people of Earth that the United Nations must underwrite the cost of military occupation, if not a hot war, while mining operations proceed. To accomplish this, the protagonist is instructed to create an imaginary colony, complete with women and children, so that the public may be roused emotionally against the depredations of savage natives.

When the protagonist goes to Ganymede to gain local color in order to give his deception greater authenticity, he observes the brutality of the Corporation men, especially their leader, toward the natives and anyone voicing sympathy for them. He learns that non-violence is essential to the aliens' philosophy and that they accept the harsh conditions of their world stoically, learning to live as a part of nature. They preach the need to respect all life—to understand the "currents of beingness." Here is the essential kernel of the basic role which aliens will play throughout all but the dark side of Silverberg's fiction. They are *people*; they have intelligence and a cultural tradition meriting as much respect as that of Earth; they provide a perspective from which to measure the conduct of man; and they can teach man what he has ignored or forgotten. In 1957, however, the young Silverberg had yet to recognize this potential fully. Instead he turned back to a fast-moving plot. Of course the protagonist made public the dirty linen of the Corporation after overcoming its schemes to silence him; of course he returned to Ganymede (with the bride he dearly loved) as a special envoy of the United Nations.

While *Invaders from Earth* indicated the direction of his later work, his other early novels dealing with aliens manipulated the stuff of space opera. In *The Silent Invaders* (1957), two alien races, contending between themselves for control of the universe, send agents in human form to Earth (yes, the protagonist is a handsome young man, while among the opposition is a beautiful young woman with whom he falls in love). The protagonist switches loyalties after induced telepathic insight shows him that his people are "the killers of the dream" while the other race is characterized by "faith and honesty...a devotion to the truth...dogged courage."[21] When he learns that humanity is evolving into the first telepathic species in the universe, he chooses to remain, "serving a godlike race in its uncertain infancy" (p.132). A debt to Clarke's *Childhood's End* seems obvious. The following year *Stepsons of Terra* (1958)—highly important because in it Silverberg played extensively with the paradoxes of time travel which have fascinated him intellectually— destroys an invading alien horde by casting it five million years into the past. In *Collision Course* (1959) humans encounter a race equally intent upon colonizing the galaxy. A plan to split the universe between them stalls when mankind is informed that it may retain only those planets which it now occupies. Potential warfare is averted after the discovery and intervention of a second race of aliens who are so wise that they consider both Earthmen and Norglen to be "children."[22] *The Seed of Earth* (1962) and Silverberg's dark vision followed.

Those Who Watch (1967) is a transitional novel in terms of his development as an artist, while *Across a Billion Years* (1969) voices important, recurrent themes and introduces several topics to which he was to give ever more attention during the 1970's. Although the basic premise of both *The Silent Invaders* and *Those Who Watch* is that antagonistic alien races maintain constant surveillance of Earth, the novels differ sharply. The story-line of *Those Who Watch* develops after the three-member crew escapes the explosion of one of the patrol ships, landing in the region of Albuquerque. Because the aliens have agreed not to intrude into mundane affairs, both sides launch searches for the survivors, but the reader is immediately aware that Silverberg attempted to keep this potentially melodramatic action to a minimum. His interests lay in portraying the relationships between the three survivors and the humans they met. Two lines of the plot focus upon love affairs; the third, upon the intellectual awakening of an Indian boy.

Like so much of science fiction, *Across a Billion Years* (1969) takes the form of a quest. Tom Rice, the first-person narrator, accompanies a team of archaeologists to a dig in search of artifacts of the Mirt Korp Ahm, the so-called High Ones, whose civilization once flourished throughout the galaxy. An episodic plot leads to their home planet; there Rice finds a quantity of what he calls a "thought-amplifier," a device which may be used not only by men but by "*all* organic lifeforms."[23] When it permits him to communicate telepathically—"our minds met and became one"—he understands that its discovery means "the end of secrecy and suspicion, of misunderstanding, of quarrels, of isolation, of flawed communications, of separation" (p.247). Besides stating so explicitly what one may argue is the central problem of Silverberg's later fiction, for a moment at least Rice epitomizes the anguish and indeed frenzy of innumerable of Silverberg's protagonists, among them, for example, Minner Burris, Richard Muller, Edmund Gundersen of *Downward to the Earth* (1969), Simeon Krug of *Tower of Glass* (1970), and David Selig of *Dying Inside* (1972), as well as such figures as Genghis II Mao IV of *Shadrach in the Furnace*

(1977). After Rice removes the thought-amplifier, thereby breaking his telepathic union, he realizes: "I was alone, terribly alone, once more locked into my skull" (p.246).

In addition to its theme, the novel has importance because it reveals how Silverberg's imagination stayed with materials which he used again and again. For example, the seeming fixation with organ transplants and complex life-support systems characteristic of much of his fiction of the 1970's, including *Shadrach in the Furnace* (1977), is present in the sequence in which Rice and his companions face one of the High Ones—"frighteningly old...the prisoner of its own hunger to survive...an insane vegetable" (pp.240-241). In an incidental scene Rice converses with Kelly, a beautiful android woman, in a manner that places before the reader one of the principal themes of *Tower of Glass* (1970). When he tries to explain that "Making life in a laboratory vat is...almost godlike," she replies, "And so...you godlike ones show your godlike natures by feeling superior to the artifical humans you create....Why must you be so concerned about superiority and inferiority? Why not simply accept all distinctions and concentrate on matters of real importance?" (pp.145-146).

If one goes beyond *Across a Billion Years*, one finds that "The Man Who Never Forgot" (1958) may be thought of as *Dying Inside* (1972) with a happy ending, while "Push No More" (1972) reports an adolescent's simultaneous loss of his virginity and his telekinetic powers so that, once loved, he must fight back the tears as he descends "numbly into the quicksand, into the first moments of the long colorless years ahead."[24] Despite the at times comic tone, his fate resembles that of David Selig in *Dying Inside*. In *To Open the Sky* (1967) Noel Vorst's loss of his pre-cognitive powers also anticipates the fate of David Selig, just as his final ascension to the stars has its parallel in Simeon Krug's obsessive flight to NGC 7293 in *Tower of Glass*. Again, from *To Open the Sky* Vorst's unquestioning belief in what he glimpses from the future duplicates Martin Carvajal's surrender to his visions in *The Stochastic Man* (1975). The list could continue. The attention given genetic manipulation and immortality in *To Open the Sky* looks forward first to *Nightwings* (1968, 1969) and then to the 1970s.

Yet such a cataloguing cannot of itself convey the complexity or the diversity of Silverberg's fictions. Unless reminded, one may well forget that *Those Who Watch* (1967), "Flies" (1967), *Thorns* (1967), "Passengers" (1968), *The Man in the Maze* (1969), and *Across a Billion Years* (1969) were published within a three-year span. During the same period he produced three novels dealing with time travel. The early story "Hopper" (1956) was expanded into *The Time Hoppers* (1967), whose protagonist Quellen escapes from the "hellish...crowded world"[25] of A.D. 2490 to the wilderness of

America before the advent of the white man. In *Hawksbill Station* (1967), first a novella and then a novel, given the opportunity to return to a world which had earlier banished him as a political undesirable, the protagonist chooses to remain in the late Cambrian age. *Up the Line* (1969), surely one of the most delightfully comic novels in all of science fiction, follows the misadventures of Judson Daniel Elliott III, a time courier guiding sightseers to various periods of Byzantine history, who ensnares himself in all of the pardoxes of time travel after falling in love with his many-times-great grandmother, the lovely Pulcheria. In addition, in *To Open the Sky* (1967), he traced the growth of Noel Vorst's new religion, while in *The Masks of Time* (1968), he brought Vornan-19 from the future to Rome on December 25, 1998, and involved him in the spiritual turmoil occurring on the eve of the millenium.

Were this not enough, he completed two major novels which remain among his most significant works, both thematically and artistically. In very different ways *Nightwings* (1968,1969) and *Downward to the Earth* (1969,1970) make use of the encounter with aliens in dramatizing similar quests for redemption and transcendence. Through the consciousness of the first-person narrator—called simply Watcher in the original novella-*Nightwings* thrusts the reader into Earth's Third Cycle of civilization. It is a ruined world, victim of the "foolish arrogance [and] excessive confidence"[26] of the Second Cycle, during which man had "spread out to the stars" and "created a paradise on Earth" (p.96). As the Watcher and his companions, Avleula the Flier and Gormon the Changeling, enter the imperial city of Roum, one calls up images from the medieval world, for this society is organized in terms of guilds; the travelers seek and are refused shelter in the hostelry of the Watchers, and they are told to throw themselves upon the mercy of the Prince of Roum. Other details create a tension, however, for they indicate not only that Roum has fallen from some previous height but that it still remains part of a galactic scene:

> The environs of Roum showed vestiges of antiquity: isolated columns, the fragments of an aqueduct transporting nothing from nowhere to nowhere, the portals of a vanished temple. That was the oldest Roum we saw, but there were accretions of the later Roums of subsequent cycles: the huts of peasants, the domes of power drains, the hulls of dwelling-towers. Infrequently we met with the burned-out shell of some ancient airship (p.18).

> We saw the line of fusion-pylons built early in the Third Cycle to draw energy from the world's core; they were still functioning, although stained and corroded. We saw the shattered stump of a Second Cycle weather machine, still a mighy column at least twenty men high... We viewed a market where visitors from the stars haggled with peasants for excavated fragments of antiquity (p.41).

> ...In the plaza we were accosted by mendicants of many sorts, some not even

Earthborn; something with ropy tendrils and a corrugated, noseless face thrust itself
at me and jabbered for alms...(p.25).

Silverberg carefully constructs a backdrop of such contradictions
and adds to the effect by referring to such geographical changes as
the Land Bridge across the Mediterranean basin and by including
variations of familiar names: Agupt, Talya, Jorslem, Perris. In the
first part of the novel he does so without explanation so that the
narrative loses much of the weight of exposition so common to
science fiction.

The action develops in three sequences. The function of the
guild of Watchers is to alert the world to any threat of invasion, for,
as Gormon explains, "...another race covets Earth and owns it by
treaty, and will some day come to collect" (p.37). During his
ritualistic Watching, the protagonist literally projects his
consciousness outward into the galaxy; he later refers to that act as
one kind of "transcending of self" (p.144). The invaders come; Roum
falls; in the company of the blinded Prince of Roum, Watcher starts
for Perris, where he would join the guild of Rememberers, for he
wishes to learn of Earth's past.

In Perris from the data banks of the Rememberers, he finds that
"the fortunate ones of the Second Cycle overreached themselves and
committed two misdeeds" (p.97). First, because they came to regard
all aliens as inferiors, for a thousand years they maintained "study
compounds" on Earth initially for purposes of scholarship and then
for purposes of amusement when the compounds were opened to the
general public. "These supposedly scientific compounds were, in
fact, zoos for other intelligent species" (p.98). At last they discovered
a race of humanoids and caged a "breeding colony" of them. Under
proper tutelage from Earth's opponents, the humanoids protested;
when nothing was accomplished diplomatically, they threatened
that one day they would conquer Earth. The second mistake gave
them their opportunity. When man tried to control the weather
through shifting the magnetic poles and changing the geography of
the continents, the resultant devastation reduced the civilization of
the Second Cycle to chaos. Powerful alien races intervened to
salvage what they could; the Third Cycle began; the humanoids
reimbursed those who had saved Earth "in return for an assignment
of all rights and claims..." (p.103), reserving the right to take
possession at some future date. Now they have done so. As a result of
his research, in exchange for the promise that the Prince of Roum
will be given amnesty, the protagonist gives the invaders "an image
recording of the compound in which your kidnapped ancestors lived
while they were prisoners on Earth. It shows their sufferings in
poignant detail. It is a superb justification for the conquest..."
(pp.113-114).

Expelled from the guild of the Rememberers and driven by a

sense of guilt at having betrayed his "Earthborn heritage" (p.117), the protagonist becomes a Pilgrim to Jorslem. During the journey he learns that such variant forms as the Fliers and the Changelings were the product of genetic manipulation. On another occasion he uses a starstone as a substitute for the "ecstasy" he knew while Watching; he feels a summons and yields himself to it:

> And slipped down through the layers of my life, through my youth and middle years, my wanderings, my old loves, my torments, my joys, my troubled later years, my treasons, my insufficiencies, my griefs, my imperfections.
>
> And freed myself of myself. And shed my selfness. And merged. And became one of thousands of Pilgrims, not merely Olmayne nearby, but others trekking the mountains of Hind and the sands of Arba, Pilgrims at their devotions in Ais and Palash and Stralya, Pilgrims moving toward Jorselm on the journey that some complete in months, some in years, and some never at all. And shared with all of them the instant of submergence into the Will. And saw in the darkness a deep purple glow on the horizon—which grew in intensity until it became an all-encompassing red brilliance. And went into it, though unworthy, unclean, flesh-trapped, accepting fully the communion offered and wishing no other state of being than this divorce from self.
>
> And was purified (p.145).

After he arrives in Jorslem and acknowledges that he seeks "Renewal. Redemption" (p.170), he experiences another moment of transcendence when he senses a link with the mind of the individual who examines him to learn if he is worthy of renewal. He is made young again in the renewal tanks—one thinks of *Downward to the Earth*—and becomes a member of the new guild of Redeemers. The voices of all his companions in the guild speak to him telepathically:

> "When all mankind is enrolled in our guild, we will be conquered no longer. When each of us is part of every other one of us, our sufferings will end. There is no need for us to struggle against our conquerors, for we will absorb them, once we are all Redeemed. Enter us, Tomis who was Watcher Wuellig" (p.186).

The experience of transcendence takes place:

> And I entered.
>
> And I became the Surgeon and the Flier and the Renewer and the Changeling and the Servitor and the rest. And they became me. And so long as my hands gripped the starstones we were of one soul and one mind.... I knew this was something wholly new on Earth, not merely the founding of a new guild but the initiation of a new cycle of human existence, the birth of the Fourth Cycle upon this defeated planet....They put a vision before me of a transformed planet.... They showed me an Earth that had been purged of its ancient sins (pp.186-187).

No previous fiction, not even *Across a Billion Years*, had taken so affirmative a stance. Together with *Downward to the Earth* — which was being issued serially even as *Nightwings* saw publication in book form—it may well mark the high point of the romantic impulse in Silverberg's fiction.

In contrast to the panorama of *Nightwings*, *Downward to the Earth* focuses closely upon the restless Edmund Gundersen, who returns to the planet Belzagor, where he formerly served as a colonial administrator. He is haunted by memories of the elephantine Nildoror and the baboon-like Sulidoror, the dominant species whom men had used as servants and beasts of burden. For Gundersen the basic problem has been that common to so many of Silverberg's Earthmen:

"...I put through new regulations about maximum labor. I insisted that my men respect their rights as the dominant indigenous culture. I—"
"You treated them like very intelligent animals. Not like intelligent alien *people*. Maybe you didn't even realize it yourself, Gundy, but I did, and God knows they did. You talked down to them. You were kind to them in the wrong way. All your interest in uplifting them, in improving them—crap, Gundy, they have their own culture. They didn't want yours!"
"It was my duty to guide them." Gundersen said stiffly. "Futile though it was to think that a bunch of animals who don't have a written language, who don't—" He stopped, horrified.
"Animals..."[27]

The novel is the story of his quest. Guilt-ridden because he once forced a group of Nildoror into a work detail so that they could not continue on their way to the Land of Mist in the interior to undergo their mysterious "rebirth," he gains permission to join a group of Nildoror journeying inland. Some compulsion drives him to undertake the experience, even after he sees his friend Jeff Kurtz, left a grotesque monstrosity mumbling incoherently after he failed to achieve the transformation. Told that he will no longer be human should he go through the process of rebirth, Gundersen replies, "I've tried being human for quite a while. Maybe it's time to try something else" (p.118)--the most explicit condemnation of man made by any of Silverberg's protagonists. After he learns that through the cyclic change of Nildor to Sulidor to Nildor "for those who merit it, life will have no end" (p.166), he asks for transformation, although he cannot know what will happen to him since man has no complementary species. Alone in his cell after the process of rebirth has been initiated, he achieves transcendence:

He partakes of the biological wisdom of the cosmos.
He tunes his soul to the essence of what is and what must be.
He is without limits. He can reach out and touch any soul. ...He perceives his own monstrous isolation, the walls that cut him off from other men, that cut off man from man, each a prisoner in his own skull. He sees what it is like to live among people who have learned to liberate the prisoner in the skull.
That knowledge dwindles and crushes him. He thinks, We made them slaves, we called them beasts, and all the time they were linked, they spoke in their minds without words, they transmitted the music of the soul one to one to one. We were alone, and they were not, and instead of kneeling before them and begging to share the miracle we gave them work to do.

Gundersen weeps for Gundersen.

Na-sinisul says, This is no time for sorrow, and Srin' gahar says, The past is past, and Vol'himyor says, Through remorse you are redeemed, and all of them speak with one voice and at one time, and he understands. He understands (pp.171,173-174).

He has been reborn.

Silverberg does all things well in *Downward to the Earth,* but its emotional and intellectual impact rises largely from its ability to call up other works which reinforce Silverberg's theme. Within science fiction, for example, to some extent at least, Gundersen brings to mind Fowler, Simak's protagonist in "Desertion," the fourth tale of *City,* who denounces the limitations and inadequacies of man. Yet it is the name of Kurtz, lying ill and deformed and recalling the "horror" (p.116), which provides the key opening up the novel. That name alone unlocks all of Conrad's *Heart of Darkness:* the enigmatic jungle which is beyond European experience; Conrad's Kurtz himself, dying and crazed; the Blacks who have been made slaves and beasts of burden; the ethnocentricity of the Europeans who see no values but their own; and the symbolic journey deep into the alien world of Africa. Silverberg has acknowledged his admiration for Conrad, and in *Downward to the Earth* he has adapted the framework provided by *Heart of Darkness* to his own ends. But he has remained his own man, both thematically and artistically. In this regard the tourists visiting Belzagor—a typical cross-section of humanity—fuse the comic and the absurd as they wander even into the Mist Country. To say the least, for them Belzagor is a zoo—a place of entertainment—not a source of profound knowledge.

In both novels Silverberg has suggested that communication leads to a transcendence which fuses all sentient beings into a oneness and thereby gives the universe the only meaning it has. Yet as noted earlier, to say that he has progressed to such a position is in error. If there can be understanding, there can also be chaos, as illustrated in "Sundance" (1969), published in the same year as the book form of *Nightwings* and the serialization of *Downward to the Earth.* "Sundance" takes as its point of departure the familiar premise that should mankind colonize the galaxy, distant worlds will have to be prepared for "human agriculturalists,"[28] because the availability of a food supply may well mean the survival of any colony. Thus the planets will have to be terraformed, or teams will be sent in to exterminate pests, "ecology wreckers" (p.175). On a nameless world such a team is destroying the so-called Eaters who feed on oxygen-liberating plants. It is a time for quick decision, a time of possible error: "...how would you feel about this if it turned out that the Eaters weren't just animal pests? That they were *people,* say, with a language and rites and a history and all?" (p.174). The choice of protagonist and narrative perspective becomes crucial.

The man who originally asked the question can dismiss it as a "speculative hypothesis. To make conversation" (p.181), but for Tom Two Ribbons, the American Indian, the possibility becomes an obsession. Through Tom, Silverberg develops the analogy of the Eaters and the Plains Indians; yet he skillfully adds to the dilemma by emphasizing the difference "between the elimination of the Plains Indians...and the destruction of the bison.... One feels a little wistful about the slaughter of the thundering herds; one regrets the butchering of millions of the noble brown wooly beasts, yes. But one feels outrage, not mere wistful regret, at what was done to the Sioux. There's a difference. Reserve your passions for the proper cause" (p.176). Later Tom watches as the Eaters move through the fields "in a straggling herd, nibbling delicately" (p.179). Indian or bison?

To exploit the dilemma effectively, Silverberg had to solve several technical problems. No character other than Tom Two Ribbons can properly develop the potential of the story; he must be the protagonist. On the other hand, no single perspective of him— especially the first-person—can save the tale from becoming another 'Lo! the poor Indian' cliche rising out of the mood of the late 1960s. As a result Silverberg focuses closely on Tom, but varies the point of view from scene to scene. He begins the story: "*Today you liquidated* about fifty thousand Eaters in Sector A, and now you are spending an uneasy night. You and Herndon flew east at dawn..." He thus gives an immediacy to the action, but more importantly, he forces the reader into close psychological association with Tom. What happens thus happens to *you* and Tom. Necessary description and exposition he objectifies in the omniscient third-person, but he renders in first-person those scenes in which Tom observes the Eaters, takes part in their rituals, and becomes convinced that they are people. He first tries to prevent them from eating the neural pellets, and then he dances with them until he sees "no Eaters now, only my own people, my father's fathers across the centuries..." (p.189). Indian or bison?

There remains yet another way of sharpening the dilemma. His companions inform Tom that he has suffered from a delusion which has been a part of his therapy, his personality reconstruct:

...."It was done to reconcile you to mankind, you see. You had this terrible resentment of the displacement of your people in the nineteenth century. You were unable to forgive the industrial society for scattering the Sioux, and you were terribly full of hate. Your therapist thought that if you could be made to participate in an imaginary modern extermination, if you could come to see it as a necessary operation, you'd be purged of your resentment and able to take your place in society as—" (p.188)

As what? Having so closely shared Tom's experience, the reader is once again jolted: which is more outrageous—to subject Tom Two

Ribbons (you) to such a therapy or to disguise the extermination of an alien culture behind such a lie, such hypocrisy? At the end Tom/ you cannot be certain of any position, any meaning. You "fall through" from one level of belief to the other. What is the reality? There is only uncertainty, madness.

As suggested several times, because of the diversity of his work, one cannot place Silverberg into a fixed position thematically (as one can, for example, with Isaac Asimov because of his fundamental optimism), one does notice that increasingly he used the encounter with aliens to dramatize the problem of "the prisoner in the skull." Significantly, however, he chose to bring these motifs together, for from the outset he has worked with the complex of expanded awareness, multiple consciousness, transcendence, and —finally—immortality in a group of works dealing exclusively with mundane society. Just as the alien stories cover a broad spectrum ranging from "Flies," "Passengers," and "Sundance," so, too, does the latter group range from *Recalled to Life* (1957, rewritten 1971) and *Son of Man* (1971) to *Dying Inside* (1972) and "Thomas the Proclaimer" (1972).

The early novel *Recalled to Life* gives an essentially traditional science fiction treatment to the theme, even to its deep-seated annoyance with death (one hesitates to speak of this as Silverberg's reaction to death, although one recalls his attitude toward determinism). A laboratory has discovered a process whereby it can reanimate persons who have been dead for less than twenty-four hours, if those persons have suffered no brain damage (six of seventy-one restorations have been zombies). James Harker, the protagonist, has been hired to sell the idea to government, church, and public, but obstacles arise: certain scientists make a premature announcement in order to win the glory; the church is uncertain what occurs to the soul in such a situation; and the government orders a committee investigation. Harker solves these problems by volunteering to undergo the process himself; immediately, of course, his act sells one and all (the reader is reminded of such stories as Asimov's "Trends," in which the *fait accompli* of spaceflight to the moon switches public opinion). Harker contemplates the future which he has brought about:

...This was a new era—an era in which death, the darkest fact of existence, had lost much of its dread finality. Staggering tasks awaited mankind now. A new code of laws was needed. A new ethics of life and death. The first chapter was over, but the rest of the book was unwritten.[29]

The same kind of affirmation characterizes *To Live Again* (1969), in which the so-called Scheffling Process permits one to have the mind of a deceased person grafted onto one's own consciousness. The plot turns on the struggle to obtain the mind of a financial genius. *Son of Man* (1971), surely his most lyrical and formless novel, projects the protagonist Clay into a pastiche of incidents in which he shares the consciousness of the varied forms of those who have taken man's place. At the climax he encompasses all time as he "is caught in a sea of shapes, prehuman and human and posthuman, coming and going, smothering him, demanding comfort from him, seeking redemption, chattering, laughing, weeping—":

...."Give me your sorrows," he whispers. "Give me your failures and your errors and your fears. Give me your boredom. Give me your loneliness." They give. He writhes. He has never known such pain. His soul is a white sheet of agony. Yet there is a core of strength within it that he had not known was there. He drains the sufferings of the millenia; he dispenses redemption in crimson spurts.... He embraces them. "I am Clay. I am love." The pain is rising within him; he feels a white pinpoint of anguish in the middle of his skull... And he says, "Do you need death? What can you learn from it? Let me. Let me. My time is over; yours is still beginning." He reaches into them and sees that they throb with pity and love.[30]

In such works as *The Man in the Maze* and *Thorns*, Silverberg's protagonists seek redemption; in *Nightwings* and *Downward to the Earth* Tomis and Gundersen achieve redemption; for the first time, in *Son of Man* the protagonist acts as redeemer.

Yet once again such affirmation is momentary. *The Second Trip* (1972) becomes his variation of the Jekyll and Hyde confrontation as two men—Nat Hamlin, the genius psychol-sculptor, whose consciousness has been obliterated because he was a rapist, and Paul Macy, whose consciousness was manufactured by the Rehabilitation Center and has been substituted for Hamlin's-struggle for control of their shared body. (Hamlin is called back to existence accidentally by a girl having telepathic powers who finally kills him at the cost of losing her powers and destroying her own personality.)

Except for telepathy, Silverberg abandoned all science fiction paraphernalia in *Dying Inside* (1972), his most realistic novel in the traditional sense. A novel of everyday life here-and-now in New York City, it traces the story of David Selig, one of the finely drawn anti-heroes of contemporary fiction, who survives by ghosting term papers for Columbia students. As science fiction, it becomes one of Silverberg's most effective symbolic statements, for it dramatizes Selig's loss of the telepathic powers which he has had since childhood. Like Hallinan in "Warm Man," he has only been able to receive; a "voyeur," he calls himself.[31] He explains that since the gift has left him "wide open to everyone's innermost thoughts," he has grown incapable of love because "he doesn't much trust his fellow human beings" (p.52). The narrative develops through a three-fold technique. First, in first-person sequences Selig recreates, primarily through flashbacks, accounts of his relationships with various the thematic center of the novel. For him "this adventure is a dark version of Pascal's gamble, an existentialist all-or-nothing trip" (p.12) in a world where "There's no mystery left in modern life. The scientific generation killed it all. The rationalist purge, driving out the unlikely and inexplicable. Look how hollow religion has become in the last hundred years. God's dead, they say. Sure he is: murdered, assassinated" (p.55). At the end, "joyously, expectantly, undoubtingly," he gives himself "anew to the Skull and its Keepers" (p.222). He cannot, of course, be finally certain; his is a desperate act of faith growing out of his own needs.

Just as "Born with the Dead" (1974) denies the ecstatic hope of Eli, so, too, does it ironically undercut Harker's vision of a new era for a humanity gifted with immortality in *Recalled to Life*. Its plot line grows out of the efforts of Jorge Klein to communicate with his dead wife, Sybille, who has returned to life through the process of "rekindling."[34] For years he pursues her; his memory of her and his desire to be with her become a consuming passion. He follows her and her companions to Zanzibar and later to Zion Cold Town in Utah, one of the cities of the "Deads." He is continually rejected, her companions telling him that he bores them and must "climb" (p.82) to their level. Significantly, although they keep to themselves, the Deads retain mortal interests, Sybille, for example, continuing her historical research and taking a lover. They fill their time with amusements and festivals and journeys, going frequently to Africa to hunt such extinct animals as the quagga, the passenger pigeon, the dodo, the aurochs—creatures whom "genetic necromancers" (p.49) have called forth solely for the entertainment of the Deads.

One of the early important clues to their state occurs when in a holographic cube Jorge views an image of her hunting a dodo:

..When he had last seen her, lying in her casket, she had seemed to be a flawless marble image of herself, and she had that same surreal statuary appearance now. Her face was an expressionless mask, calm, remote, aloof; her eyes were glossy mysteries; her lips registered a faint, enigmatic smile. It frightened him to behold her this way, so alien, so unfamiliar (p.39).

Later after she had told Jorge an anecdote which she may have invented simply to trifle with him, he reconstructs an imaginary conversation with her, realizing that he has put the words into her mouth and therefore has learned nothing about her. The speech he assigns her thus becomes the key to the irony of the story:

..*Everything is quiet where I am, Jorge. There's a peace that passeth all understanding. Like swimming under a sheet of glass. The way it is, is that one no longer is affected by the unnecessary. Little things stand revealed as Little things. Die and be with us, and you'll understand* (p.73).

Jorge is finally poisoned by her companions. He is then "rekindled," individuals, chief among them a mistress and his foster-sister Judith. There is an emotional intensity about them as he reveals how he has been dissatisfied and rebuffed. Secondly, he includes the texts of papers he has written at various times. Thirdly, he speaks objectively of himself—of Selig—as he reflects upon the meaning of the loss of his powers. One of the chief images developed is that of entropy, for he sees himself as "casualty of the entropic wars" (p.205). Very early in the novel, after mentioning in an essay on Kafka "the impossibility of human communication" (p.22), he voices the essential irony of his situation:

> But why does David Selig want his power to come back? Why not let it fade? It's always been a curse to him, hasn't it? It's cut him off from his fellow men and doomed him to a loveless life. Leave well enough alone, Duvid. Let it fade. Let it fade. On the other hand, without the power, what are you? Without that one faltering unpredictable unsatisfactory means of contact with them, how will you be able to touch them at all? (p.30)

Thus, by the time silence falls thick upon him and he cries out, "Until I die again, hello, hello, hello, hello," Silverberg has achieved one of the most effective symbols of man's separateness and isolation. What is equally important, is that he has done so through the use of one of the most time-worn devices in all of science fiction gadgetry: telepathy.

In the same year he turned explicitly to the issue of immortality in *The Book of Skulls* (1972), which Barry Malzberg insists is his finest novel, a work which is "not under any definition" science fiction.[32] Yet Silverberg makes specific reference to Haggard— "Thank you, H. Rider Haggard"[33]—and adapts most of the conventions of the so-called lost race novel to the contemporary scene. Four young Americans journey deep into the Arizona desert to find a secluded sect called the Keepers of the Skull, whose manuscript, found in a university library by one of the youths, promises immortality. Candidates must present themselves in groups of four to undergo the trial because one must die by his own hand and one at the hands of his companions so that the other two may gain eternal life. A forgotten manuscript, an unknown society possessing secrets which transcend the knowledge of the everyday world, the quest, the unworldly setting—all the ingredients are present, and once again Silverberg's ability to adapt traditional materials asserts itself.

It is his technical skill which makes the book, for the narrative is presented in four overlapping, fragmented interior monologues so that ambiguities of value and motivation give rise to the dramatic conflicts. The speakers are a young Jewish scholar, a homosexual an ex-Kansas farm boy, and a member of the New England aristocracy. Nevertheless, Eli, the young Jewish scholar, stands at and on the third day after his awakening, Sybille and her friends come to him, talking animatedly of their immediate activities and the need to plan their "winter's amusements." He realizes then that "they are mere dancing puppets jerking about a badly painted stage, they are droning insects..." (p.96). Far from gaining "a peace that passeth all understanding," they cavort emotionlessly in a meaningless life-in-death. Perhaps out of fear, they could not accept the facts of death and eternity; consequently, they demanded an empty immortality made up of unnecessary little things. Jorge has no interest in them, for he believes he has been "freed of old chains"; yet he is one of them, even though he does not join their "set" and years pass before he sees Sybille again. "But they spent the last days of '99 together, shooting dodos under the shadow of mighty Kilimanjaro" (p.97)—a vivid and ironic final image.

Recalling Eli's denunciation of modern religion in *The Book of Skulls*, "Thomas the Proclaimer" (1972) portrays the outcome of another act of faith. Once more entropy affords a central image describing a world where disorder has passed the point of no return. In 1999 Apocalyptists (they made their first appearance as a cult in *The Masks of Time*) declare that the world will end with the millenium. Out of Nevada comes Thomas, a reprobate, who has been instructed by God to go forth unto the people, telling them of his wasted life and bidding them "to gather and pray and restore their faith and ask for a Sign from on high."[35] The day following a "worldwide program of simultaneous prayer" (p.103), a Sign comes: the sun stands still for a period of twenty-four hours. The narrative opens as that period ends and Thomas exhorts his followers to put away their fears. When next he preaches, however, he laments:

Where is that new world of faith? Where is that new dream of hope? Where is mankind shoulder to shoulder, praising Him and working together to reach the light? (p.129)

On all sides he sees "new madnesses take form" in the face of "the cancer of doubt...the virus of confusion." With increased frenzy leading to rioting and bloodshed, the Apocalyptists intensify their outcry warning of the end of the world, while a tendency develops in "certain ecclesiastical quarters toward supporting a mechanistic or rationalistic causation..." (p.133). Eventually, although the Pope acknowledges that he does not understand what power was responsible for the Sign, he "thinks it would be rash to attribute the event to God's direct intervention without some further evidence" (p.167). An archbishop of the Church of England, speaking as an individual, theorizes that one cannot rule out the possibility of "a manipulation of the Earth's movements by superior beings native to another planet" (p.133) as they prepare for invasion and conquest. Others warn of a possible sign from Satan. At one point the voice of God seems to command TV, assuring his audience that no apocalypse is intended and reminding them that the problems of the world "can be attributed to the rise and spread of atheistic socialism" (p.168); that revelation proves to be a hoax perpetrated by bored technicians. Thomas plans a Day of Rededication at Atlantic City—"a real old-time total-immersion revival meeting where we'll all get together and denounce the new cults and get things back on the right track again" (p.158); in the resulting mob thousands are drowned in an oil slick.

Such confusion is given order by the manner in which Silverberg handles his narrative. He manipulates point of view in a number of brief chapters, one of them simply the inclusion of Chapter 8 of the Book of Revelation. He balances Thomas' unquestioning faith against the conversion of William F. (Bill) Gifford, who proposes to a group of faculty people mainly from M.I.T. and Harvard—persons "who are in the habit of intellectual activity"—that they "replace credulity and superstition with reason":

An end to cults; an end to theology; an end to blind faith. Let it be our goal to relate the events of that awesome day to some principle of reason, and develop a useful, dynamic, *rational* movement of rebirth and revival—not a religion per se but rather a cluster of belief, based on the concept that a divine plan exists, that we live under the authority of a supreme or at least superior being, and that we must strive to come to some kind of rational relationship with this being (p.145).

Despite his arrogance he is as sincere as Thomas; his "Discerners" and Thomas' followers measure the spectrum of religious belief. Another dimension is added by Saul Kraft, Thomas' business manager. In seclusion, he wonders whether or not Thomas was the wrong "vehicle" for the Crusade of Faith and whether or not the failure of the crusade means that the Lord is displeased with him. The flow of the action is structured around three mob actions. The first, of course, disrupts the Day of Rededication. The second occurs when Gifford leads the Discerners to a city dump, where they build a trench in which to bury their unneeded religious relics as they inaugurate the rule of reason. "Fierce-faced people in gaudy robes" attack the blasphemers and kill them. Finally, Kraft, out of mixed motives, betrays Thomas' identity to a crowd which "swarms" over him. Reason and faith are destroyed; irrationality prevails.

Two other novels demand attention: *Tower of Glass* (1970) and *Shadrach in the Furnace* (1977). The twenty-third century world of *Tower of Glass* is made up of "a small, culturally homogeneous human elite served by computers, mechanical robots, and hordes of obliging androids."[36] As such it is largely the creation of Simeon Krug, who learned to manufacture the androids from chemical vats. The dramatic conflicts rise out of his inability to recognize and accept other sentient beings as equals; of the androids he exclaims,

"...*Things*. Factory-made things. I was building a better kind of robot. I wasn't building men" (p.135). In a sense familiarity has bred contempt, for the narrative becomes a study in the irony between his accomplishment and his obsession. The tower being erected west of Hudson Bay serves as a monument to his dream of communicating with alien intelligence somewhere in the far reaches of the galaxy. When the initial probes to the near stars returned during his fatherless, impoverished youth without "traces of advanced lifeforms out there" (p.96), he disagreed with the new Geocentricism which argued that man was a unique creature and continued "diddling with the nucleic acid" of the vats. Now his obsession has been fed by the reception of signals—numerical patterns—from the planetary nebula NGC 7293 in Aquarius, a system which has gone through something like a nova, whose inhabitants must necessarily take an unimaginable form because of the "fantastically strong radiation" (p.19).

He had envisoned a very different planet—an idyllic, pastoral world whose gentle inhabitants "moved through the groves and vales of their paradise, probing the mysteries of the cosmos, speculating on the existence of other civilizations, at last sending their message to the universe. He had seen them opening their arms to the first visitors from Earth, saying, Welcome, brothers, welcome..." (p.20). Although the thought of "scaly armored monstrosities" has blighted that hope of finding a father-figure, so deep is his passion that he asks, "How can we go to them?... How can we embrace them?" His meglomania has been born of fear and pride: "...We don't go back, we only go forward.... We know who we are. We're man.... We got to answer them. We got to say we're here. We got to reach toward them, because we've been alone long enough.... *we wish no longer to be alone in the cosmos*" (pp.55,13). Later, as he thinks of calling out, "Hello? Hello? Hello, you! This is Simeon Krug!"—he reflects:

In retrospect he saw his whole life as a single shaped process, trending without detour or interruption toward this one goal. If he had not churned with intense, unfocused ambitions, there would have been no androids. Without his androids, there would not have been sufficient skilled labor to build the tower. Without the tower--(p.96)

Whatever else he may be, Simeon Krug is also Silverberg's variation of Frankenstein so that the novel becomes a study of the creator and his creatures. A minority of the androids has formed the Android Equality Party and campaigns both for equal civil rights— the law regards them as property, not persons—and representation in Congress. The parallel to the civil rights movement in the United States at the time is underscored explicitly: "They think it's black slavery all over again" (p.136). The majority, however, worship Krug. One of Silverberg's accomplishments is the creation of the biblical text of the androids:

> In the beginning there was Krug, and He said, Let there be Vats, and there were Vats.
> And Krug looked upon the Vats and found them good.
> Let men come forth from the Vats, said Krug, and let women come forth, and let them live and go among us and be sturdy and useful, and we shall call them Androids.
> And it came to pass.
> And there were Androids, for Krug had created them in His own image, and they walked upon the face of the Earth and did service for mankind.
> And for these things, praise be to Krug (pp.4-5).

From the first one senses the inevitability of tragic confrontation. Through the android Alpha Thor Watchman, supervisor at the tower, the reader learns that the believers expect Krug to deliver them from servitude. Watchman accepts his present status, "knowing that a time of redemption is to come" (p.70) and is badly shaken when Krug does not react more strongly and sympathetically to the accidental murder of a representative of the AEP: "Where was the hope of redemption?" (p.80). To influence Krug, he turns to the lovely Alpha Lilith Meson, who is the lover of Krug's son Manuel. (The symbolism of this affair becomes more apparent and complex. Although Krug has given the androids genitalia, he has kept them sterile; moreover, sexual relationship with an android is regarded as a perversion, even by Krug himself.) Lilith takes Manuel to "Gamma City" beneath Copenhagen, where the androids huddle, keeping with them their rejected "brothers" who have been malformed in the vats. During this descent into the underworld, Manuel learns that the androids worship his father. When first told, Krug replies, "What concern of mine?" (p.159). Yet he takes Watchman with him into the so-called shunt room, where individuals may probe the consciousness of one another.

"The intensity of Krug's refusal to accept godhood was devestating to Watchman" (p.169). In addition, he "found a total dismissal of android aspirations." For Watchman, God is dead. He leaves Krug, who rejects the idea that his creatures worship him out of love, accusing them of self-interest instead. In a flurry of action insurrection begins, Watchman causes the tower to crumple by thawing the tundra, and Krug kills Watchman. Fleeing to the site where his starship waits, Krug is sealed within its freeze unit: "Krug is at peace. He departs forever from Earth. He begins his journey at last" (p.184). And the cities of Earth burn, while Manuel stands seemingly helpless beside the fallen tower. One can belabor the symbolism. Certainly, at least, the climax conjures up the image of an indifferent god abandoning his creation to seek other worlds to toy with. *Tower of Glass* takes its place among Silverberg's dark visions.

His last novel, *Shadrach in the Furnace* (1977), focuses upon the physician Shadrach Mordecai, particularly in terms of his relationship with Genghis II Mao IV Khan, Prince of Princes, Chairman of Chairmen, ruler of a world which "has abdicated; the game of politics is ended; Genghis Mao rules by default, rules because *no one cares*, because in an exhausted, shattered world dying of organ-rot, there is general relief that someone, anyone, is willing to play the role of global dictator."[37] The two men are linked; for Shadrach it is as though he lives in two bodies because several dozen receptor nodes implanted in his body keep him constantly aware of data regarding Genghis Mao's "major bodily functions" (p.2). As personal physician to the Khan, his chief job is to act as a kind of supercomputer—"to monitor, evaluate, and report on the moment-by-moment physiological changes within Genghis Mao's body" (p.24) during the innumerable organ transplants which have kept the old man alive. He realizes that his patient is "deathhaunted, certainly, a man whose grasp on life is so ferocious after nine decades that he will submit to any bodily torment in order to buy another month, another year..." (pp.16-17). Thus the Khan symbolizes the very world he rules, for the terrible eruption of Cotopaxi initiated a "worldwide chaos" of global revolution leading to the virus war which caused the plague of organ-rot. The virus released has become "so intimately entwined with the human genetic machinery" that it is passed from generation to generation and can become lethal at any time (p.185). In this context Shadrach has clarified his own position:

...Of *course* serving an evil dictator is wrong. No job for a nice sincere dedicated black boy from Philadelphia who wants to do good. But is Genghis Mao evil? Are there any alternatives to his rule, other than chaos? If Genghis Mao is inevitable, like some natural force...then no guilt attaches to serving him: one does what seems appropriate, one lives one's life, one accepts one's karma, and if one is a doctor then one heals, without considering the ramifications of one's patient's identity (pp.48-49).

Despite this seeming moral neutrality, however, the Khan observes that Shadrach *"feels such sorrow for the rotting ones. A man of compassion. Childlike"* (p.133).

The dramatic conflict of the novel develops from the efforts of Genghis Mao to find a means of assuring himself greater longevity, if not immortality. Of three state-sponsored projects, the most promising attempts "to develop a personality-transfer technique that will permit...his soul, his spirit, his persona, his anima, but no actual physical part of him—to move to another, younger body" (p.20). He has chosen Mangu, his political heir-apparent, to serve as donor, but when Mangu learns his fate, he commits suicide. The Khan then selects Shadrach, who immediately learns of his danger. Instead of disappearing, as he is advised to do, he tells Genghis Mao that he wishes to leave the capital for a time, although he does not know where he will go.

The narrative is structured around three operations. It opens on the eve of the first, a liver transplant, thereby affording opportunity to establish background, characters, and the necessary exposition. The second one—an abdominal aorta transplant intended to remove the threat of an aneurysm—takes place after Shadrach has learned of the threat to his life. Then he ventures into the world. In Nairobi, free from his ties to the Khan, he tries to explain to an old Hindu, Bhishma Das, that there does exist an antidote for organ-rot and that "one day it will be given to all the people" (p.185). He is accused of optimism when he insists that "Things *will* get better" (p.187). To him the world "seems very beautiful," and he resolves not "to succumb to another man's lust for immortality" (p.190). In Jerusalem, in the company of Meshach Yakov at the Wailing Wall, he admires the strength of the Hindu and the Jew and prays: "Thank you, Lord, for having made this world and for having let me live in it as long as I have.... And show me how I can help make it more like the place you meant it to be" (p.190).

He returns to find Genghis II Mao IV the Khan suffering from severe headaches resulting from intracranial pressure caused by the accumulation of cerebrospinal fluid. The third operation—insertion of a valve to drain away excess fluid—gives him his opportunity. Into the palm of his hand Shadrach inserts a crystal with which he can control the valve; simply by clenching his fist, he can cause the Khan pain and kill him, if he chooses. As Genghis Mao convalesces, Shadrach experiences an induced transcendence; he "drifts across the centuries, moving freely in space and time":

...Yes, yes, the Black Death, and Shadrach goes among them saying, I am Shadrach the healer...and he touches their fiery swellings and lifts them to their feet and sends them forth into life, and they sing hymns to his name. And he moves on to another city, a place of bamboo and silk, of gardens rich with chrysanthemums and junipers and small contorted pines, and in the stillness of the day a fireball bursts in the sky, a great mushroom cloud bellies toward the roof of heaven... and Shadrach, standing like an ebony tower among them, tells them in soft tones not to be afraid, that it is only a dream that afflicts them, that pain and even death may yet be rejected, and he spreads forth his hands to them, soothing them, draining the fire from them.... The howling Assyrian hordes ride through the streets of Jerusalem, slashing without mercy, and Shadrach patiently sews together the sundered bodies of the fallen, saying, Rise, walk, I am the healer....He takes Jesus from the cross when the Roman soldiers go off to the tavern, slinging the limp body over one shoulder and hurrying into a dark hut, where he wipes the blood from the maimed hands and feet, he applies ointments and unguents, he mixes a healing draft of herbs and juices and gives it to Him to drink, telling Him, Go, Walk. Live. Preach. He seines the fragments of Osiris from the Nile...(p.239).

Voices hail him as the "true healer." After demonstrating to the Khan the power which he holds, Shadrach promises to continue in his old capacity; but he does demand a place on the Committee so that he may distribute the antidote and expand research to find a permanent cure for the organ-rot. As did voices in his vision, the Khan salutes him as Genghis III Mao V. In a final gesture Shadrach "touches th tips of his fingers to his lips and blows a kiss to all the world" (p.245).

One may argue that Shadrach comes-to-realize too suddenly, although the potential was early pointed to: "*A man of compassion.*" One may regard the operation as too contrived. Yet *Shadrach in the Furnace* proves to be one of Silverberg's most affirmative statements. Like Clay in *Son of Man*, Shadrach is the redeemer.

Even if he writes nothing more, the scope and diversity of Silverberg's fictions make difficult any brief assessment of his work. One can begin by saying that of those who have worked in the field, none has a more thorough command of science fiction materials. But that of itself is not sufficient. At his best, especially during the past decade or so, he has shown consistently tht science fiction can be used to great effect as a vehicle for the themes and techniques of serious contemporary fiction.

Thomas L. Wymer

Philip Jose' Farmer:
The Trickster as Artist

Philip Jose' Farmer is presently among the most well-established of science fiction writers, although he is among the most difficult to place or type. He first hit the pulps nearly a decade and a half after such grand old men as Asimov, Bradbury, Heinlein, Sturgeon, and van Vogt and would seem to belong to that middle generation of writers who began in the 1950s. But, born in 1918, he is two years older than Asimov and Bradbury, the youngest of the group. On the other hand, his innovations, both sexual and stylistic, have tended to associate him with the generation of the 1960s.

Critical reception has been equally contradictory. Ted White calls Farmer "a classical case of the uneven writer."[1] James Blish has little to say beyond suggesting that "Riders of the Purple Wage" (1967) unfairly split the 1968 Hugo award for novella, "a case of bowling-over of non-readers by daring innovations" which were lifted from 1919 vintage James Joyce.[2] Alfred Bester, on the other hand, extols Farmer's "courage to extrapolate a harmless idea to its terrible conclusion."[3] Sturgeon calls him "one of the most original, one of the most talented, and certainly one of the most fearless writers around."[4] Norman Spinrad sees him as one of a small group of "heroic and windblown martyrs," who held on during the 1950s and early 1960s "leading lives of desperate heroism, still producing meaningful work but at enormous economic and emotional cost."[5]

Academic critics have paid Farmer less attention, but the studies that do exist show a similar division. Leslie Fiedler, while acknowledging that Farmer often writes "hastily, sometimes downright sloppily," insists that "he has an imagination capable of being kindled by the irredeemable mystery of the universe and of the soul, and in turn able to kindle the imagination of others—readers who for a couple of generations have been turning to Science Fiction to keep wonder and ecstasy alive in times apparently uncongenial to

34

those deep psychic experiences."[6] Fiedler goes on to illuminate three of Farmer's major themes as seen through a Freudian glass. Franz Rottensteiner has attacked Farmer's recent work for its exploitation of "the particular method of mass-market SF.... A Kaleidoscope of oddities that is simultaneously derivative, self-perpetuating and incestuous...drawn into the gigantic junk-yard of SF, where everything is but a pretext for another cops-and-robbers story." His creations are "remarkable as fruits of a grotesque imagination," but "never of any importance as speculative thought, as intellectual effort."[7] Finally, Russell Letson, in the most recent study, both supports and corrects Fiedler by pointing out that the Freudian vision in Farmer is balanced by evidence of influence from Jung and Joseph Campbell, among others. Letson also begins the process of refuting Rottensteiner by pointing out the mythic and symbolic significance and the intellectual effort behind several of Farmer's works.[8]

The critics seem like the legendary blind philosophers who, each touching the creature in a different place, bring back conflicting reports of what an elephant is. The fact is that there is a considerable amount of truth in all these responses, and whether or not Farmer criticism has reached a point where a comprehensive view of him can be presented, I would like to suggest, with no pretensions to being any less blind than the others, that a key to these contradictions may be found in what appears to be the image in terms of which Farmer most often presents himself as an artist, the trickster god.

The trickster is among the oldest and most enigmatic of mythological figures. He is to be found among the ancient Greeks, Celts, Chinese, Japanese, Semites, and Amerindians. Many of his traits have been perpetuated in the medieval jester and *festum fatuorum* and in the alchemical figure of Mercurius and have survived to the present in clowns and Punch-and-Judy plays.[9] And at least one recent critic has seen him as a central figure in American literature.[10] The trickster is sometimes a creator god, sometimes opposed to the creator god, but always a taboo breaker, an erotic and scatological rascal. He is also the father of lies, the original teller of tales, the archetypal artist.

And Farmer seems to have a special affinity for Trickster. He calls attention to characters who behave as tricksters, like Tarzan, always ready in his adolescence "to play one of his grisly trickster jokes"[11]; moreover, Farmer has Tarzan reveal in his memoirs that the mangani, the hominid species among whom he was raised, though possessing a primitive language, were without much imagination, so that he was able to perform one of the prototypical trickster deeds, to invent the lie[12]; and again in *Tarzan Alive* (1972) we are told that he independently invented the pun (p.33). Other such characters are the hero of *Lord Tyger* (1970), Kickaha of the Wolff-Kickaha series,[13] and Winnegan Finnegan of "Riders of the Purple Wage" (1967). Farmer also creates a more ominous vision of trickster gods and supermen who manipulate mankind, after the manner of Twain's "Mysterious Stranger," for purposes sometimes benevolent, and sometimes malevolent, but most often arbitrary and mysterious—like the Immortals of *Inside Outside* (1964), the Ethicals of the Riverworld series, or the Lords of the Wolff-Kickaha series. And Farmer plays the trickster himself by placing thinly disguised versions of himself in his fiction, from which he can look mockingly at us and himself—like the PJF's, Peter Jairus Frigate of the Riverworld and Paul Janus Finnegan/Kickaha, or others like Tom Bonder of "Down in the Black Gang" (1969), Tim Howller of "After King Kong Fell" (1974), and Leo Queequeg Tincrowdor of *Stations of the Nightmare* (1974-1975) and "Osiris on Crutches" (1976). He also plays Trickster in his pervasive interest in taboo breaking, especially by means of the erotic and scatological, in his attack on boundaries, especially those between fiction and reality, and in his comic spirit, which manifests itself most often in that most basic and painful form of humor, the pun. The figure is summed up in Farmer's description of his alter ego in the Wolff Kickaha series: "I am Kickaha, the *kickaha*, the tricky one, the maker of fantasies and of realities. I am the man whom boundaries cannot hold. I slip from one to another, in-again-out-again Finnegan. I seem to be killed, yet I pop up again, alive, grinning, and kicking!... Off I go, and where I will appear or what my name will be, few know."[14] Earlier Kickaha had defined his name as it was given to him by the Bear people on the Amerindian tier of the World of Tiers: "In their language, a *kickaha* is a mythological character, a semidivine trickster. Something like the Old Man Coyote of the Plains Indians or Nanabozho of the Ojibway or Wakdjunkaga of the Winnebago" (p.62).

It is significant that Farmer draws his trickster figures primarily from Amerindian mythology, since it is there, especially in the Winnebago cycle, that the archetypal trickster symbol most clearly reveals its positive aspects. But we shall explore the psychological significance of the trickster later; first we need to look at some of his more obvious manifestations in Farmer in order to establish the pervasiveness of the figure and the problems he represents, and the best place to start is through an examination of the ways in which Farmer reveals his opposition to conventional boundaries and definitions.

The Trickster and Boundaries:
The Opposition To Conventional Definitions

The most obvious manifestation in Farmer of the artist as

Trickster is his assault on the distinction between fiction and reality in the Wold Newton series, a group of stories based on the premise that a number of supposedly fictional characters are real. He has written "biographies" of Tarzan, Doc Savage, and Kilgore Trout, which are mammoth pieces of research in themselves and at the same time parodies of scholarship. And these are only parts of the larger scheme of the series, which is based on the premise that radiation from a meteorite which landed in 1795 in Wold Newton, Northumberland, effected genetic changes in a group of fourteen passersby, who spawned a progeny of super heroes and villains. The genealogy of Wold Newton relations includes fictional characters from as far back as Thomas More's Raphael Hythloday, though the Scarlet Pimpernel—who, together with Elizabeth Bennet and Fitzwilliam Darcy from Jane Austen's *Pride and Prejudice,* was among the original fourteen exposed to radiation—on through Phileas Fogg, Allan Quatermain, Wolf Larsen, Sherlock Holmes, Leopold Bloom, and down to Sam Spade, Lord Peter Wimsey, James Bond, and numerous others—and, of course, Trout, Tarzan, and Savage. There are also historical characters worked into the genealogy, such as Ebenezer Cooke, Lord Byron, and Thomas Carlyle, as well as fictional characters originating from Farmer's own works, like Leo Queequeg Tincrowdor from *Stations of the Nightmare* and Kickaha.

So far this premise has resulted in seventeen biographies, short stories, and novels, including a subseries of works Farmer calls his Fictional Authors series, which further confound the common sense distinctions between fiction and reality. One of these stories, "Osiris on Crutches," Farmer "co-authors" with Tincrowdor; the others he "edits" either in his own name or anonymously. Some are stories by established fictional masks like *The Adventure of the Peerless Peer* (1974), a hitherto lost Sherlock Holmes story by, of course, Dr. Watson. Others are stories by author-characters in fiction. The most successful of these is Kilgore Trout's *Venus on the Half-Shell* (1974/1975), which Farmer edited anonymously and which confused readers and apparently angered Kurt Vonnegut, who, many thought, had written the novel.

The paradoxical sense of reality in these fictions is heightened by other factors as well. Tarzan covets his privacy and Farmer has obliged him by continuing to apply the pseudonym "Greystoke" and by withholding or distorting crucial information which protects Tarzan from discovery until he has time to assume a new identity and cover his tracks. In the meantime, Farmer has developed two additional fictional Tarzans, Lord Grandrith and John Gribardsun, who differ in small but significant ways from the "real" Tarzan and from each other but who may also embody important clues to that Tarzan. Moreover, like all scholarly efforts in history and biography, the Wold Newton cycle is an ongoing endeavor in which new information is constantly turning up. In *Doc Savage* (1973), for instance, Farmer retracts the statement made in *Tarzan Alive* that Fu Manchu is wholly fictional and outlines the evidence that led to his discovery of the real Fu Manchu, and the paperback edition of *Doc Savage* contains several corrections and additions to the original hardback. It is an elaborate and self-perpetuating game of concealment, misdirection, and revelation in which we delight in each new discovery but never know for sure exactly where we stand.

The whole Wold Newton undertaking has a typically tricksterish duality about it. We have already noticed the fact that this extraordinary body of research is a parody of scholarship. Farmer in person, in typically Trickster fashion, will sometimes frankly discuss the problems of creating such a cycle, while at other times he will take offense at any implication that Tarzan and Doc Savage are anything less than living persons. Fiedler describes the series as an indication of Farmer's "gargantuan lust to swallow down the whole cosmos, past, present, and to come and to spew it out again," a part of a "larger attempt (at once absurd and beautiful, foredoomed to failure, but once conceived already a success) to subsume in his own words all of the books in the world that have touched or moved him"(p.238).

Farmer calls it an attempt originating in his subconscious "to make order out of chaos. There were these many beloved characters in my mind, apparently unconnected, each in his own wildly eccentric orbit, each a bit in the randomness of a newly created universe. But the real lord of this world, me, I suppose, said, 'Let there be order.' "[15] It is a Whitmanesque attempt to contain multitudes, to perform the god-like task of creating the cosmos and making all parts of it a song of himself. But it is also an attempt which acknowledges at the start the arbitrary and capricious nature of all ordering systems.

In the Wold Newton series, as in all Farmer's work, there is a strong sense of imaginative play engaged in for its own sake at the same time that serious questions are raised about the relation between fiction and reality. We are thus led to see in a special sense something Farmer has said himself: "Literature *is* life because it's part of life, made by living beings. Literature doesn't just exist in print; it proceeds from living beings, is 'bookized,' and then passes back into living beings, through their minds, and influences their thoughts and their actions. It's part of a great cycle—or recycling."[16]

Something of the mystery of that recycling is revealed in the way in which Farmer handles the tension between myth and reality in *Tarzan Alive*. Throughout this "biography" Farmer presents Tarzan as really living out a mythic pattern. When he is adopted by the mangani after his parents' deaths, he is described as entering "the mythic world of the changeling. Though he existed as an entity in the real world, though he was flesh and blood, he was on the road to the superhuman and demigod...one with Romulus and Remus, Oedipus, Hercules, Telephus, and the many other heroes of fairy tale, folklore, legend, and myth... He would be the last hero in a world where the belief in heroes was dying out" (p.30). The point is constantly reiterated: "Tarzan is legendary, but he also exists, and he is bound by the limitations of real existence" (p.44); he is described as "the last of the heroes, the final great son of Mother Nature, her gift to the twentieth century, and her reminder that the demigods were not yet all dead" (p.68); and in the last chapter, an analysis of Tarzan in terms of Campbell's concept of the monomyth, he is called "Nature's last creation of a Golden Age man" (p.203). Farmer, in effect, demonstrates the claims of students of myth like Jung and Campbell that man lives out mythic patterns, but he does so in the typically trickster's way of the pun, by taking the claim literally and asserting total belief in it. Tarzan also becomes the basis for an assertion of faith in the heroic and for a reminder of our savage origins, while at the same time, being the last hero, he is the basis for an expression of a sense of loss, of disappointment with the modern world in which no more heroes are born, and yet a challenge to all of us to maintain some sort of heroic ideal. Thus does Trickster turn us back upon ourselves.

Another excellent example of a work in which the recycling between literature and life is revealed through a play on the reality of fictional characters is "After King Kong Fell." Fifty-five-year-old Timothy Howller, watching the original *King Kong* movie on Saturday morning TV with his six-year-old-granddaughter Jill, is asked by her why the coyote in the Roadrunner cartoon can get up again from a fall while Kong cannot. Howller's answer is that Kong really fell, that Howller at age thirteen had been in New York that night in 1931, had witnessed Kong's escape from the theater, and had been near the Empire State Building when Kong fell. There follows a narration of those events as seen by Howller, told partly through his dialogue with Jill and partly through interior monologue. The result is a dramatic and personal study of how the significance of a figure like Kong passes into living beings.

The meaning of Kong's fall is the central question in the story and for Howller himself:

Since he had been thirteen, he had been trying to equate the great falls in man's myths and legends and to find some sort of intelligence in them. The fall of the tower of Babel, of Lucifer, of Vulcan, of Icarus, and finally of King Kong. But he wasn't equal to the task; he didn't have the genius to perceive what the falls meant, he couldn't screen out the—to use an electronic term—the 'noise.' All he could come up with were folk adages. What goes up must come down. The bigger they are, the harder they fall.[17]

Ironically Howller did not see the actual fall because he was looking back at the crash of an airplane Kong had knocked out of the air. But he contemplates its significance in a passage which recalls attempts by Melville's characters to read symbolic events or objects:

It was, in after years, one of Mr. Howller's greatest regrets that he had not seen the monstrous dark body falling through the beams of the searchlights—blackness, then the flash of blackness through the whiteness of the highest beam, blackness, the flash through the next beam, blackness, the flash through the third beam, blackness, the flash through the lowest beam. Dot, dash, dot, dash, Mr. Howller was to think afterward. A code transmitted unconsciously by the great ape and received unconsciously by those who witnessed the fall. Or by those who would hear of it and think about it. Or was he going too far in conceiving this? Wasn't he always looking for codes? And, when he found them, unable to decipher them? (p.50).

The fall is personalized for young Tim through a secondary plot which Howller does not tell Jill and which Farmer sets up to intersect with the Kong plot. Tim and his parents attend the live Kong performance at the invitation of his Uncle Nate and Aunt Thea, who live in the Empire State Building. Thea, a beautiful woman whom Tim has a passionate adolescent crush on, pleads a headache at the last minute so that Tim and the three adults go to the theater without her. In the events which follow Tim goes through a series of disillusionments, falls from innocence into experience. In the panic and rush for escape when Kong breaks loose, Tim is knocked unconscious and abandoned by his parents. He wakes up wet with the results of his own loss of bladder control. Later around Kong's fallen body he witnesses various human vultures haggling over who will get to exploit Kong even in death: Carl Denham, responsible for capturing Kong, wants to exhibit the body, but it is claimed and suits are already being filed by the owners of the Empire State Building, by the city transit authority which lost the Sixth Avenue Elevated to Kong's rampage, and by the theater owner. Much later, he tells us, he will learn that Ann Redman has sued John Driscoll for breach of promise, their breakup having been inspired by the speculation that Kong may have attempted or even succeeeded in raping her. But the greatest disillusionment, though not chronologically last, is the last one revealed in the story. Back on the street, when Kong's body is lifted by a crane, Tim discovers the smashed, naked bodies of Aunt Thea and an unidentified man, apparently plucked together out of their bed and hurled down as Kong climbed the building, hitting the pavement at the same place where Kong would land a few moments later.

It is not surprising that there should also have appeared on the scene two other mythical figures, modern champions in a struggle against evil: a black limousine drives up with a man standing on the running board, "a giant with bronze hair and strange-looking goldflecked eyes" (p.52)—Doc Savage, of course; another man, tall, thin, with "a hawklike face and eyes that burned," speaks to a beautiful female companion "in a whispering voice that carried a long distance, 'Come on, Margo. I've work to do' " (p.52)—the Shadow, who knows what evil lurks in the hearts of men. For Kong functions as a symbol of human innocence, and his fall expresses Howller's own discovery of human weakness, most especially of the betrayal of love—in short, his discovery of evil. And Kong as dumb and loving animal victim and savage jungle beast expresses, like Howller's name, man's pain and bewilderment before the problem and the mystery of his own good and evil. Farmer demonstrates how King Kong has achieved the stature of myth by making him carry the symbolic weight of innocence and betrayal; and the play on the reality of these fictional events reinforces a major paradox in all fiction and myth, a paradox which reveals also why the archetypal artist is a trickster figure, that an apparent lie can be a vehicle for the profoundest truth and can intensify our sense of reality.

For Farmer the recycling between literature and life is typically a mixture not only of fiction and history but of all literary levels. As he argues in *Doc Savage*, much "great" literature was originally pop lit, and even inferior pop lit has "elements that make [it] psychologically valuable."[18] It is not surprising, therefore, that Farmer should use popular figures like King Kong, Doc Savage, and the Shadow in contexts which give them intense mythological significance, that his works should straddle the boundary between popular and elite literature, between the tradition of action-adventure and cheap pulps and that of seriously extrapolative and symbolic forms of literature, and that criticism knows not quite where to have him. To quote John Layard, a commentator on the Winnebago trickster:

This is in keeping with the topsy-turvy nature of all trickster mythology, the essence of which is to turn things upside-down, to mirror the great under the guise of the little, and so to confuse issues that only the two-way mind can follow the intricacies of its double-thinking activity. When we do so there is a great reward, but in the process we may get as bewildered as Trickster does.[19]

In pursuing Farmer's topsy-turvy world, we will look at some of the thematic concerns and technical devices typical of Farmer and of Trickster. These include his concern for taboos, both testing their limits and breaking them, for exposing the human unconscious and turning us inside out, and for his own function as trickster artist.

The Trickster And Taboos:
The Opposition To Conventional Morality

The best known example of Farmer as taboo breaker is his reputation for bringing sex to sf with *The Lovers* (1952). The most important innovation, however, was his introduction not simply of sex but of the issues of sexual freedom and perversion and the exploration of their relationships with complex cultural problems. The issue of sexual freedom emerges in the story from the social structure of a politically and sexually repressive future Earth governed by the Sturch, a combination state religion and religious state based on science and materialism and established by Isaac Sigmen, the Forerunner. Sigmen's teachings explain history as a movement toward "Timestop," which is a condition of ultimate stasis. Like Nazism it expresses a neurotic desire for security and changelessness. It is puritanical in the extreme, denying both the physical-sexual and the inward life: it refers to intercourse as "the beastly act" which "man and woman should rightly loath"[20] and should perform only for the sake of reproduction, and it identifies man's inwardness with the "dark self...the deepdown crouching horrible Backrunner in them" (p.27). The Backrunner, appropriately enough named Jude Changer, is the Sturch's Satan and the enemy of Sigmen's idea of progress.

These rejections of the self, the body, and the natural world of change result in imperialism—both political and ecological—racism, sexism, neurotic desires for control, and demonic dreams of power. The interrelatedness of these evils is well known now, and it derives from, among others, studies by Jung from as far back as 1928,[21] but in 1952 these were still revolutionary ideas at least fifteen years before their time and not yet part of the popular consciousness. The issue of sexual perversion is even more revolutionary. In *The Lovers* the specific issue is miscegenation, since Hal Yarrow falls in love with a beautiful, human-looking, extraterrestrial creature, a *lalitha* (obviously punning on Lilith) named Jeannette. Through her he comes to discover and accept his own sexuality and feelings. But she is not human, and in the eyes of the Sturch he has "lusted after and lain with an insect," which makes him "an unspeakable degenerate" (pp.145-146). Their love affair ends with Jeannette's tragic death, but in the process Farmer reveals a theme which is repeated throughout his work, that the functions of bodies are rendered perverse only by the hate, cruelty, and fear that may accompany or prevent their conjunction.

"The Captain's Daughter" (1953) further examines the way in which fear of sexuality fosters repression, ignorance, and ultimately self-destruction. Asaph Everlake, captain of the space freighter *Erlking*, and his daughter Debby exhibit a classic case of incest and repression. He keeps her in isolation, forbidding contact between her and any other man, even killing a lover who manages to get past him, yet at the same time avoiding all contact with her himself, apparently fearing his own sexual desires toward her. Both are members of a cult of religious zealots dominated by puritanically repressive beliefs and by the masculine principle—"Everlake was a man who bristled with sharp points."[22] The detective-story-plot reveals that the situation is being created by an endoparasite called an *oners*, native to the planet Melville, which the cult had made its home. The oners extends itself throughout the host body and, in the presence of another host, stimulates the parasympathetic nervous system of its own, "which results in the sex desires of the host—or hostess—being whipped up at once and to an irresistible point" (pp.101-102). Everlake knows that both he and Debby are afflicted with the parasite but keeps it secret, first out of fears that the condition is incurable and that publication of it would lead to a planetary boycott which would ruin Melville, and second out of guilt—he attributes his affliction to suffering for "offenses in this or other lives" that "he or his ancestor had committed" (p.103). The oners is revealed, therefore, as a kind of veneral disease which is encouraged by "the veil of secrecy and ignorance imposed upon the community and the outside world by the Elders of Remoh" (p.103); its "very nature and the means used to conceal it made its spread inevitable" (p.104). Ironically, the parasite is spread not only in intercourse but in an annual ceremonial bathing, a community purification ritual. Indeed, Debby most likely caught it when she participated in this ceremony as "Virgin of the Lake." Also, ironically, Asaph, with all his bristling points, becomes a kind of Ahab trying to slay the monster of his own sexuality and finally killing himself—by drowning in the ceremonial lake; death, of course, is the ultimate purification. The outcome of the story demonstrates the psychological truth which the doctor-detective-hero tells Debby:

Nobody is wholly angel or wholly devil. We all have a touch of Earth in us. Nor is there anything wrong with that unless one is not honest enough to admit it. In which case, the things we refuse to bring out may corrupt us physically or mentally (p.72).

This is a truth which much of Farmer's work seems to argue, often through taboo-threatening situations which force us to face our desires and inhibitions and admit the touch of Earth within us.

An especially effective story with this theme is "My Sister's Brother" (1960). Cardigan Lane, the central character, is a heroic type, as close as one can imagine to an enlightened character, is a heroic type, as close as one can imagine to an enlightened conception of the ideal man: he is deeply religious yet tolerant, strong and courageous yet able to weep, to release his emotions unashamedly; he is even compared to Christ. A member of the first expedition to land on Mars, he is left alone by the disappearance of his companions and risks his life to seek them rather than return alone. He is saved from reenacting their deaths by a creature who turns out to be a humanoid, apparently female, from another solar system, like him the sole survivor of an expedition which had met with a fatal accident. A relationship develops in which Lane constantly has to face an inward struggle between his belly, which tells him to loathe and reject several of her ways that repel and shock him, and his brain, which tells him that "he shouldn't react to her as he would to a Terrestrial."[23] His brain has the best of the battle for most of the time, with some help from his heart, as he discovers that she too is deeply religious and loving and, more, even innocent to the degree of seeming unfallen. His sexual fears, however, finally get the best of him when he discovers that her unisexual reproductive system demands a series of practices that in his mind suggest fellatio, homosexuality, and masturbation. But masturbation is not in fact involved, since the reproductive process does involve an exchange of love between partners, which she offers him. The result is a vicious act on his part of what amounts to infanticide, committed in the name of defending the human race, but done in fact "because he was afraid, not of her, but of himself...because he, too, beneath his disgust, had wanted to commit that act of love" (p.187). Lane's terrible act makes the fear of love appear more perverse than any possible expression of love and reinforces the ironic theme which points to man as the most dangerous and monstrous creature in the universe.

In this case Farmer has taken a model human being and, by testing that man's sense of taboo to the point of destruction, has exposed the flaw which Farmer sees as the most basic to humanity, the fear of oneself. His overriding purpose is to manipulate the reader into facing his own humanity, especially his own inwardness, most especially those aspects of his inner life which he most wants to deny.

The Trickster Inside Out:
The Universe And The Unconscious

Farmer's concern for exploring and exposing the whole of our humanity is manifested in many ways besides taboo breaking, but they all relate in one way or other to metaphors closely associated with "the topsy-turvy nature of all trickster mythology," worlds and psyches turned inside out or upside down. Fiedler and Letson have outlined some of the ways in which Farmer's works reveal Freudian and Campbellean patterns, but it is worth reemphasizing this fact, in order to relate it to the trickster pattern, that Farmer delights in literalizing mythic dreams and fantasies, using sf to provide a semi-realistic means for the psyche to act out its fears and desires.

In *Flesh* (1960/1968), for instance, Peter Stagg, captain of a spaceship which returns to Earth hundreds of years after it left, is transformed by a biologically sophisticated, but otherwise primitive, postapocalyptic Earth culture into an ancient King of the

Wood right out of Frazer's *Golden Bough.* He becomes a creature of Herculean sexual prowess, biologically altered to inseminate the virgins of a nation. It is, of course, the ultimate male sexual wish fulfillment fantasy, but it is handled in a way which comically reveals the curse inherent in the capacity, as well as the extent to which man is controlled by his sexual drives and desires.

Farmer typically tests the inner compulsions of human beings by creating places, like Dante's Joy in *Night of Light* (1957-1966) and the domain of Mahrud in "The God Business" (1954), where people get what they really want. In "Mother" (1953) young Eddie Fetts, rendered impotent by a domineering mother, is shipwrecked with his mother on a strange planet, where he is separated from her by being swallowed by a bizarre sentient creature—female, of course—inside of whom he manages to survive. In adjusting to this situation, he manages to act out his deepest desires, to overcome his inhibitions by raping his "mother" and literally returning to the peace of her womb.

Even more violent opportunities to act out inner drives are offered by *The Image of the Beast* (1968) and *A Feast Unknown* (1969), stories in which Farmer again plays Trickster by exposing the unconscious dreams evoked by popular fiction and by violating the supposed boundaries between pornography and literature through a combination of the explicitness of pornography with the concern for characterization and style of legitimate fiction. He describes the inspiration behind *Image* in the *Luna* interview: "I'd always considered vampire stories, werewolf tales, and in fact the whole Gothic field, as more-or-less disguised sex stories. Pornography of the weird. Why not bring out the hidden stuff into the open?" If stories of vampires sucking blood from victims' necks are subconscious disguises for "other fluids and organs...why not show Dracula for what he really is?" The result is immediately apparent in the opening scene, in which California smog replaces the conventional Gothic fog and "a private eye (this is a parody on the private eye story, too) is losing his penis to the pointed iron dentures of a vampiress"(p.4).

What he does to the Gothic and detective stories in *Image,* he does to pulp action-adventure in *A Feast Unknown*, again rendering consciously and explicitly what is usually unconscious and implicit. Burroughs' Lord Greystoke appeals in a limited way to our desire to release the feral human within us, to throw off the restraints of civilization and freely express our archaic impulses toward violence and dominance. Farmer's Lord Grandrith does so in an unlimited way, showing the Tarzan figure as what Fiedler calls a phallic *ubermensch,* and what is also an archaic warrior god. We see him cutting out and eating the raw liver of a man he has just slain, tasting with satisfaction the semen ejaculated by a lion in its death throes, engaging in all manner of sexual activities—oral, anal, homo-and heterosexual. He is not, however, compulsively cannibalistic, just hungry, and a dead man is handy. Grandrith is simply without inhibitions, and normally this results in some degree of natural but unsentimental virtue. But even Grandrith, the supposedly unneurotic man, has subconscious drives, a fact revealed through a side effect of the immortality elixir which he and Doc Caliban, as servants of the Nine, are permitted to take. That side effect is a psychotic eruption of repressed urges, manifested in Grandrith as an inability to experience orgasm except in the act of killing, a form of compulsive behavior which even he sees as perverse.

Lester Dent's Doc Savage is the other side of the same coin in that he represents the dream of extreme civilization, complete self-control, mastery of all sciences and disciplines; he is the product of the most advanced kind of training and education, a crime fighter who goes to great lengths to avoid killing and who seeks the most humane methods of correction of captured criminals. But Farmer's Caliban reveals the terrible price paid in repression for such control, for Caliban is extremely inhibited sexually, has subconscious urges just as Grandrith does, and under the influence of the elixir discovers that he, too, enjoys killing.

The effect of the exposure of such urges, however, is by no means pornographic, for that exposure both reveals and ridicules the violent and chaotic forces at the roots of man's psyche, whether natural or civilized. And that revelation is made to ring true by Farmer's use of archaic motifs which reveal that these unconscious urges are also rooted in the dark beginnings of human culture. Ithyphallicism, the representation of male figures with oversized, erect penises, is common in rock carvings as far back as the Upper Paleolithic, associating sexual tension, by means of phallic gods, with magic and religion, with hunting and warfare, with the most central of human activities. Appropriately, these figures emerge from the same time out of which Trickster emerges, himself an ithyphallic god or demigod and one of the most archaic of divinities. And in typically tricksterish fashion, Farmer explores the relation between sex and violence in a context which is both comic and serious, even frightening. *Feast* opens with a startling, comic image as Grandrith wakes up and sees the rising sun bisected by his erect penis, an image which recalls ancient carvings in which ithyphallic figures are depicted with sun symbols appended to their penises. The battle between the naked, tumescent Grandrith and Caliban is a comic parody of warfare, an illustration of how crossing swords is as absurd as crossing penises and how killing is really a kind of generative act turned inside out. But it also recalls numerous ancient carvings of ithyphallic warriors, a connection which reveals the ancient and serious psychic momentum behind human violence.[24]

These dark, archaic urges at the base of our humanity are also represented in *Feast* by the Nine, an ancient secret organization which controls the immortality elixir, the most powerful of whom is Anana, a woman thirty millennia old, whom Grandrith describes as, along with three others of the Nine, "the only human beings that ever made me feel touched with fear."[25] They are the comic epitome of the secret, evil organization of comic book and pulp action-adventure, but they also function as symbols of the archaic, unbridled ego that hungers after immortality and still lives in man, even super heroes like Grandrith and Caliban. And they are an outside force as well which corresponds to what Farmer describes in *Doc Savage* as "Chaos and her sister Evil," forces often seen in his work as endemic to the universe: "After all, the universe is entropic, and everything is going downhill, and at the bottom is Hell. Down there, at the bottom of the hill, and often below its surface, Chaos and Evil are breeding" (pp.8-9).

In *Dare* (1965), rather than present action which is a direct externalization of fantasy, Farmer examines this process of externalization as a cultural phenomenon. Externalization on this level is, of course, myth, as Richard Slotkin defines it: a narrative "that dramatizes the world vision and historical sense of a people or culture, reducing centuries of experience into a constellation of compelling metaphors."[26] The special importance of Farmer's examination of this process, as we have seen in his examination of the fantasy of popular fiction, is in the critical approach which he takes to the myth.

The premise of the story is that the lost Roanoke colony had been transported to another planet by a superpowerful race called the Arra, who [left the settlers] after promising to return in four hundred years and judge what men have made of themselves. On the planet the colonists come in contact with seemingly primitive aborigines, humanoid creatures with horse tails, whom they call horstels. Horstels are a non-technological but highly civilized race of worshippers of the Great Mother; they are unified with nature, at peace with themselves, and tolerant of others—idealized versions of Amerindians, although they are also based on the horse-tailed sileni, ancient nature daemons of Greece originating in Asia. The colonists, on the other hand, are types of Western man, neurotic worshipers of a masculine god and of money, afraid of their bodies and emotions, indifferent to nature except insofar as it can be exploited for profit, and intolerant of the native sentients, whom they would be glad to enslave or exterminate if the horstels did not defend themsevles so effectively. Thus Farmer creates an idealized version of the American frontier experience, which, as Richard

Slotkin recently reaffirmed in illuminating detail, has shaped American mythological consciousness.

Like Puritan Americans these colonists project their fears of their own unconscious out into the horstel forest, which becomes demonic rather than daemonic in their eyes, while the horstels themselves, like Amerindians and blacks, become symbolic projections of the colonists' Id, of their own repressed sexuality, which must be exorcised or subdued. In this context we follow the struggle of Jack Cage to cross the boundary between neurotic civilized consciousness and the fertile darkness of the forest of his unconscious and unite the two. To do so he has to break the taboos of his neurotic culture; avoid the destructive and more typically American mythological structures, as Slotkin describes them, of exorcism and regeneration through violence; and instead, act out the mythological structure which Slotkin calls "Sacred Marriage," in which "the human protagonist is united with a female who is the embodiment of the god-spirit immanent in nature and the 'other half' of his own individual nature (anima)" (p.79). Unlike many sf writers, such as Heinlein,[27] Farmer attacks the classic frontier myth and suggests a shift from what Slotkin, following Joseph Campbell's lead, describes as the mythology of the hunter, which "provides the cosmology and ethic for a religion of world heroes, dominators, rulers, exploiters," to the mythology of the shaman, "the saint and seer, the mystic adventurer in consciousness, who experiences and suffers the universe, mastering it through sympathy rather than power" (p.559).

An important source of ambiguity in Farmer, however, is the fact that the problem is not always a projection of psychic disorder. In *Night of Light* (1966), for instance, the major problem at first seems to be internal as public enemy John Carmody experiences the Night on Dante's Joy, is turned inside out, and undergoes a death-rebirth experience. Projections of his inner life help him discover the self-destructive nature of his violence, the potential for creation and compassion which he has long repressed, and the god within himself, which he cooperates in giving birth to. Part II begins twenty-seven years later when Carmody, now a Catholic priest, is sent back to Dante's Joy by the Church, which is alarmed by the spread across the galaxy of the religion of the goddess Boonta. Moreover, the current god, Yess, whom Carmody co-fathered, is planning to force a major change in the ritual of the Night. Normally only volunteers partake—only people, whether good or bad, with the courage to face themselves—while the others retreat into a drugged sleep. The collective projections of their unconscious desires determine whether the good Yess or the evil Algul is born out of the womb of Boonta, an archaic Great Mother, depicted in a colossal statue as giving birth to one child and devouring another,

her face "a study in split personality," one side loving, the other vicious.[28] Yess wants to command all natives of the planet to remain awake so that he can use the Night to create an ultimate conflict between the collective unconscious forces of good and evil in order to end the periodic conflict between them. As a result of the Night, civilization on the planet is all but destroyed, but both Yess and Algul survive, setting the stage for an apocalyptic struggle that promises to engulf the galaxy. Even worse for Carmody is the blow to his faith produced by the accuracy of a whole series of Yess' prophecies: "How could he have seen and not believe in the all-power of Boonta?" (p.160).

Letson argues that the meaning of the story is clear, that Farmer insists on the recognition and acceptance of good and evil:

Although individual purging of evil and selfishness is possible, universal victory of one side over the other is not. The pattern—life itself—requires both, and only by accepting the whole can we transform ourselves.... The burden of Farmer's work is the *recognition* of lust, violence, and irrationally as irreducible and unavoidable parts of the whole. Our capacity for evil will not disappear, but if we face it, we have a chance to rise above it—to be like gods (p.130).

This is, in effect, the mythology of the shaman and unquestionably a central complex of ideas in the novel and in Farmer. Indeed, *Dare* concludes on such a note as R'li tells Cage, "Life is always uncertain; death is around every corner. Let us build our houses, till our soil, and raise children. We will hate no one and hope that no one hates us, knowing full well that there is as much hate as love in this world....It won't be easy. The only easy thing is to give up."[29]

But the model of wise acceptance does not consistently fit Farmer—or the trickster—nor is that response consistently appropriate to his universes. *Night of Light* ends not with the recognition Letson describes, however implicit it may be in the novel, but with a world thrown into chaos by the decision of a supposedly good god and with Carmody in agony, the same Carmody, who, in a series of stories written between the two parts of *Night,* had become one of the most delightful, balanced, whole, compassionate men of all of Farmer's characters. As much as evil may be caused by the individual's own fragmented self, we are also frequently reminded in Farmer of the fact that there seems to be something fundamentally wrong with external conditions—with society, culture, the universe itself.

This sense of wrongness with the outside we have already seen expressed by Tim Howller in "After King Kong Fell," but it is more typically expressed in stories built around some alien, controlling force at work in the universe, which often becomes a metaphoric expression of man's helplessness. We have seen this in *Feast,* where the Nine represent not only archaic drives in man but forces of evil and chaos endemic to the universe. In *Dare* a wise old horstel, describing his painting of one of the Arra, makes the symbolic pattern clear while presenting a more optimistic view of such forces:

You will notice the benignity on its great face; it also looks threatening, perhaps sinister. I have tried to portray the Arra as a symbol of the universe. This immense and nonhuman creature stands both for the physical, which works best with man if he is not vicious or arrogant, and also for that beyond the material face of things...[which is] powerful but kindly...likely to use means terrifying but seemingly hostile to men in order to teach them their lesson... The Arra stand for both the reality we know and the reality behind that (pp.35-36).

Since the Arra never appear, this faith in the kindliness of "the reality behind" is not shaken, and Jack Cage manages to reconcile himself to his universe; but more often that reality is either ambiguous or outright malevolent. In *Blown* (1969) and *The Other Log of Phileas Fogg* (1973) the forces involved are opposing groups of extraterrestrials using Earth as a battleground; in the latter, one of the groups is clearly good and the other evil, but in *Blown*, it is not so clear, and in "Toward the Beloved City" (1972) we do not know which force is really good or evil or whether the opposing force simply uses man, like the galactic movie company in "Heel" (1960), which staged the Trojan War, using its own actors for the gods' parts. Here men are as flies whom the gods kill for sport, a theme repeated with the Lords in the Wolff-Kickaha series and the Nine in the Grandrith-Caliban series. Sometimes they have strange designs upon man: in "How Deep the Grooves" (1963) it is discovered that someone has for some reason completely programmed all of man's actions and thoughts, including the discovery of the programming. Often these forces, like the Arra, are trying to teach us some sort of lesson, to make us better, but most often they are somehow botching the job, presuming too far, as do the Immortals of *Inside Outside* or the Ethicals of Riverworld. In "Down in the Black Gang" (1969) the universe is a ship on a voyage somewhere, propelled by "philiac thrust," the power of love, and held back by "phobiac drag"; the black gang, the ship's stokers, are creatures who manipulate human beings into extreme situations where great love can be generated but only at tremendous cost in human pain and suffering. Mecca Mike, a stoker we watch completing such a job, ends up rebelling against the system, like Ivan Karamazov's giving back his ticket declaring, "Somehow, there has to be a better way to run The Ship."[30]

The difficulty is both inner and outer: man is the victim of forces outside himself, but just as great a problem is man's intractability the fact that it takes such pain and suffering for some humans to learn how to love. This dilemma tends to be presented in terms of irreconcilable contradictions that inspire responses ranging from laughter to howls of pain. *Inside Outside* is full of such contradictions: physical, moral, and intellectual dilemmas that drive the characters around in pointless circles and literally leave them hanging in midair.

Most typically Farmer expresses this ambivalence by placing a flawed hero in a world which somehow functions as a prison, usually some sort of pocket universe, literally and symbolically; the outside situation inspires in the hero a Promethean response, some sort of attempt to find or depose the lord or master of the world, but the hero's quest seems always compromised by the suggestion that he is chasing his own shadow. And typically the quest is only partially achieved. Farmer seems to raise the action-adventure serial to a philosophic level, for the questions can never be answered, the possibility always emerges of a reality behind the one discovered, and every quest ends with a new quest emerging, with Chaos still breeding, setting up the inevitable sequel.

To put the problem in archetypal terms, there seems to be a fundamental conflict in Farmer between the myth of the hunter and the myth of the shaman, between the ideals of mastering the world by power and by sympathy. This is no more apparent than in the Riverworld series, especially *To Your Scattered Bodies Go* (1971), where Richard Burton is set over against Herman Goering. Burton is the perpetual hunter, traveller, quester, fighter, ever seeking knowledge, while Goering is the tortured, guilty man, ever fleeing from himself. At the end of the novel Goering seems finally to have found peace in the Church of the Second Chance, while Burton is still planning an assault on the Ethicals. John Collop tells Burton the difference between them. "While you, my friend, have been questing after some irrelevant grail outside you, he has found the Holy Grail inside himself."[31] But whether Goering has indeed found the truth or only a fool's paradise is something we may never know, even in sequels, since Farmer typically answers this sort of question ambiguously. The ways of power and of sympathy, though mutually contradictory, nevertheless seem to be responses which are both demanded by the universe and which tear human beings apart. Indeed, the only types who appear capable of containing such contradictory impulses are the god, the superhero, and Trickster. But whereas god and superhero reconcile contradictions by rising above them, Trickster stands in the human position, between god and animal, power and sympathy, hunter and shaman, expressing not the reconciliation of opposites but the tension, at once comic and tragic, of their grotesque conjunction in man. As Radin describes him, Trickster is "an archaic *spectrum mentis*," a mirror of the mind of man, "wherein is depicted man's struggle with himself and with a world into which he has been thrust without his volition and consent...the number, or the adumbration of an answer, to questions forced upon him, consciously or unconsciously, since his appearance on earth" (p.x.)

The trickster is thus revealed as a peculiarly illuminating symbol of Farmer's own endeavors as an artist, a mythological projection or reflection, an inside—out version of himself. The trickster image can thus help explain the contradictory qualities of Farmer as an artist.

The Trickster As Artist

Farmer's conception of himself and his function is especially revealed in those stories into which he projects something of his own person. There is usually an element of the playful in such figures, as in the image implied by the subtitle to *The Book of Farmer: or The Wares of Simple Simon's Custard Pie and Space Man* (1973). He plays with the idea of his own presence in the work in *The Other Log of Phileas Fogg,* which concludes with Farmer as editor commenting, "That Fogg's initials and your editor's are the same is, I assure you, only a coincidence"[32]; but the possibility is called to our attention and left open so that Gunnar Gällmo, in an afterward to the Swedish edition, "proves" that Fogg is in fact Farmer.[33]

There is also a more serious element in some of these figures insofar as Kickaha and Fogg are both saviors. Layard says the fundamental *raison d' être* of Trickster is "to achieve the status of savior" (p.110), a connection which is manifested in several cycles in which the trickster grows, loses his stupidity, and becomes a deity, even the creator god. Kickaha goes through such an evolution, functioning in *The Maker of Universes* (1965) as a kind of teasing spirit who manipulates circumstances so that Wolff can discover for himself who he is. In *A Private Cosmos* (1968) he is forced to become an active savior, to forego the delights of his universe as playground and to assume responsibility for it as well as for our own. He assumes that role, however, in a spirit of courageous recklessness and survives as much by luck as by boldness, retaining Trickster's flexibility and cunning as well as his temper. In *Behind the Walls of Terra* (1970), where he next appears, we see him in one of Trickster's comic fits of anger:

He jumped up and down and yelled his frustration and hit the palm of one hand with the fist of the other. He kicked at a small boulder and then went howling and hopping away with pain. He pulled his hair and slapped the side of his head and then turned his face toward the blind blue sky and deaf bright yellow sun and howled like a wolf whose tail was caught in a bear trap.[34]

More often Farmer presents his darker sides, but usually in a manner which suggests the frustrated and self-contradictory nature of Trickster. Tom Bonder in "Down in the Black Gang" is a projection of Farmer's five-year sojourn in Southern California as a technical writer trying to write fiction on the side. Descriptions of Bonder like the following reveal something of the personal source for the tensions apparent in Farmer's work:

...he was an atheist who had never been able to shake himself free of his desire to know a God, a hardheaded pragmatist who lusted for mysticism as an alcoholic lusts for the bottle he has renounced, a scoffer of religions whose eyes became teary whenever he watched the hoakiest, most putridly sentimental religious movies on TV with Bing Crosby, Barry Fitzgerald and Humphrey Bogart as priests (p.17).

Peter Jairus Frigate in *To Your Scattered Bodies Go* (1971) describes himself in similarly contradictory terms as an agnostic from the age of fourteen who died at ninety thinking about calling in a priest (p.61). Frigate also seems destined to mediate somehow between Burton and Goering, between the compulsive action of the hunter and the contemplative wisdom of the shaman. Another such character whom we saw earlier is Timothy Howller, a man like Farmer "always looking for codes...and when he found them, unable to decipher them."

Sometimes that darker self, like Trickster, is not only contradictory but destructive. Fiedler noticed and Farmer acknowledged in the *Luna* interview that Boygur in *Lord Tyger* "is a caricature of me as the mad scientist who tries to raise his own Tarzan and continually has to compromise with reality" (p.10). Moreover, as a creator god over the pocket universe of the African valley in which *Lord Tyger* is raised, Boygur suggests the connection between Farmer and all his godlike characters, his manipulators of mankind. This is a point reinforced by Leo Tincrowdor, the cynical, alcohol sf writer in *Stations of the Nightmare* (1974), who represents Farmer's own jaundiced view of man without the balancing view of man's capacity to understand himself and deal effectively with at least some of his problems. After Tincrowder summarizes his stories, *Osiris on Crutches* (which Farmer later wrote as a short story)[35] and *The Hole in the Coolth,* irrelevant retellings of the myths of Osiris and of Adam and Eve, his wife comments, "That's the man I have to live with! And when he's telling you about Osiris and God, he's telling you about himself!"[36]

Farmer sees this putting of thinly disguised versions of himself into his works as a way to "study various aspects of myself"; it is also "a sort of signature" and "a subtle method of control of the world," a way of playing "the man who knows no boundaries...the anonymous demiurge of the created world" (*Luna,* p.10); of playing, in short, Trickster. It is also a comical way of playing with perspective, by placing the artist in the work in such a way that he looks out at the reader looking at him, a trick with mirrors by means of which we are conned into seeing reflections of ourselves as well. Farmer, like so many of his god figures, is trying to teach us a lesson, but he is the first to admit he is part of the problem. The trickster figure becomes, therefore, a means of survival, an irrepressible source of vitality and a reminder of his and our own foolishness. Layard's final description of Trickster provides a remarkably accurate picture of the personality of the artist apparently behind the work of Farmer:

He swears and curses at the misfortunes which come to him, but he never masochises or remains downcast too long. His patience, which is equivalent to curiosity, is inexhaustible. He has the resilience of a child, which is the character also of a hero, always ready to take what comes, without prejudgment of what "should" be. He is a "philosopher" in the most popular sense, as well as that of the pragmatic scientist. He functions at all levels. And so these tales of his doings are fit to bring laughter to the unsophisticated who take them on their face value, and to the sophisticated who can see in them a humour of the most complex possible kind, embracing subtle psychic changes in an atmosphere of joint intellectual perception and high childish delight (p.111).

Where Farmer, as Trickster, will take us from here is hard to say, although suggestions may be found in the trickster myths. Many versions point to the trickster as symbolic of a stage in human development. In such myths, H.R. Hays tells us, Trickster finally becomes "a fully conscious man aware of social responsibilities. Thus his history becomes a kind of parable of the socializing of man, a fable in which the wildest drives of the unconscious are tamed by the necessities of group life" (p.442). A story which could be seen to reflect this kind of growing up is the recent "Fundamental Issue,"[37] a story about a Supreme Court chief justice grappling with a decision over whether or not to permit the construction of a complex of nuclear power plants. Issues of immediate social import are not, however, particularly new to Farmer, although they tend to be treated as broadly cultural problems, as in *Dare*, or to be slipped in sideways. In *The Image of the Beast*, for instance, Childe sees an old witch in what seems to him to be the act of conjuring up the worst smog attack in history, which holds Los Angeles in its grip throughout the novel; at the end he discovers that she was trying to conjure it *away*, that his symbol of choking corruption permeating the land is totally of human origin and has been bothering the monsters as much as the human beings, and torturing and killing far more people through respiratory afflictions than all the sadistic terrors of the Gothic imagination. Even "Fundamental Issue" drives its point home with typically tricksterish scatology, for the justice, afflicted with constipation, arrives at his decision as his bowels move in an airport restroom. Indeed, constipation becomes a symbol of mankind's attitude toward the future, and the trickster reminds us again, as he so often does, that man's highest dreams and ideals are indissolubly linked to those most basic animal functions of consumption, elimination, and generation.

Hays also points out how Trickster sometimes develops into the shaman and suggests interesting connections between the two:

The trickster, on the one hand, is a breaker of taboos, he represents the anarchistic individual protest against the inhibitions of good behavior and formalized sex expression which must exist in the simplest of social groupings. On the other hand, the shaman, too, is an outlaw who makes use of the dire power of mana to brave the supernatural world and make use of it. Selfish individualism and the individualism of the unusually gifted, the sensitive, epilepsoid, primitive intellectual here coincide, as indeed they have, to an extent, throughout history. The artist and visionary has always tapped the power of the unconscious and has always broken through the norm of conformity (p.530).

Indeed we have already seen Farmer suggesting this connection in several stories, but there is no clear pattern of movement in that direction or away from it.

There is no necessity, however, for there to be any fundamental change, since Trickster may be seen to serve a perennial purpose. As one commentator put it:

Disorder belongs to the totality of life, and the spirit of this disorder is the trickster. His function in an archaic society, or rather the function of his mythology, of the tales told about him, is to add disorder to order and so make a whole, to render possible within the fixed bounds of what is permitted, an experience of what is not permitted.[38]

Farmer demonstrates especially well in "Riders of the Purple Wage" that Trickster is as necessary to modern society as he was to archaic society, that the spirit of irrepressible comic defiance may be the major means of defense and source of creativity left in an increasingly homogenized and homogenizing society.

Trickster's peculiar gift to us is the paradoxical realization that imbalance is the way to balance, that contradiction is the way to understanding. Farmer bewilders and enriches because of his sense of what Layard calls "The 'trickster' mentality of two-way thinking, and the combination of wonder and exactitude which this mentality induces" (p.111). This is a tendency of all science fiction, insofar as it embodies the contradictory impulses of realism and romance, but Farmer imagines such contradictions with unique intensity, variety, and awareness. Perhaps the key contradiction is Farmer's capacity to present a vision of an ironic universe which evokes comic and tragic howls of pain and frustration but in which it is possible, through the energy of Trickster's vitality and resilience, to affirm the adventure of that continually running serial which is life.

David N. Samuelson

The Lost Canticles of Walter M. Miller, Jr.

Walter M. Miller, Jr., is an enigmatic figure in mid-century American science fiction. An engineer with World War Two flying experience, who wrote science fiction of a technophilic variety, he also studded his stories with allusions, clear and cloudy, to the Judeo-Christian tradition, generally bathed in a generous light. A commercial writer who boasted a million words in 1955, including scripts for television's *Captain Video,* he came to write progressively more complex, sophisticated, problematic stories until, having more or less perfected his art, he stopped writing at the pinnacle of his success, at age 36. A Southern Catholic, born in Florida in 1923, he wrote his best known work about a future order of monks founded in Arizona in the name of a Jewish engineer.

Miller restricted almost all of his writing to science fiction; in a short career, reaching from January 1951 through August 1957, forty-one stories appeared in the American science fiction magazines over Miller's by-line.[1] Three of them were later to comprise his award-winning novel, *A Canticle for Leibowitz* (1960). Three others were collected under the title of one of them, *Conditionally Human* (1962), and another nine were assembled two years later under the title, *The View from the Stars* (1964). Both collections are out of print, as are most of the anthologies in which at least seven other Miller stories have been reprinted (along with nine of the fifteen in the three books). A goodly number of these stories are worth looking into, either for some instrinsic value, or in connection with his best work; the themes and motifs of *A Canticle for Leibowitz* had a long period of incubation. And even Miller's

Although Samuelson originally wrote this article at my request for *Voices for the Future,* a version of it was published in *Science-Fiction Studies,* 3 (March 1976), 3-26. Permission to reprint has been granted by the author.

worst were often better than the many words that filled up to thirty magazines in 1952 and thirty anthologies in 1954.[2] Since 1957, however, Miller's name has been associated with no new science fiction, and very little writing for the public of any kind.[3] It may be that his novel obsessed him, draining his writing energy; it may be that it set him a standard he felt unable to maintain; perhaps it expressed so well the themes which concerned him that its completion left him with nothing to say. Even if other concerns entirely apart from writing took him away from science fiction, it must be inferred that his reasons involved what satisfaction he was or was not getting from writing.[4] In reviewing his career, then it is impossible to ignore *A Canticle for Leibowitz* as the culmination of a decade's work, but it would probably be unwise to assume that everything that preceded it was in some way directed toward that final achievement.

The biographical information available on Miller is sketchy indeed: an early autobiographical sketch accompanying "Dark Benediction" (1951) in *Fantastic Adventures*; a brief portrait in *Library Journal* (June 1, 1958); an entry in Donald H. Tuck's *A Handbook of Science Fiction and Fantasy* (1959); the dust jacket of *A Canticle for Leibowitz;* and headnotes both in the March 1957 issue of *Venture* and in anthologies edited by T.E. Dikty, Judith Merril, and William Nolan comprise the lot which I have been able to unearth. But his personal experience and the ambience of the decade in which he wrote are certainly discernible in his fiction. His Southern origins, his wartime flying, his engineering education, his reading of history and anthropology, and his personal vision of his religion are all reflected in some of his stories. How his more private life might be involved is conjectural, but the social environment of America in the years following World War II is eminently visible.[5] In that war, a technological elite had come to power, had defeated an evil enemy of seemingly archetypal proportions, and had emerged with a vision of unlimited energy and growth in peacetime. Today's harbingers of ecotastrophe are one ironic result of that blind faith in progress, but the destructive use of atomic power had already shown the negative side of technology, its potential to bring about a culture with a forcibly much lower level of technology, which implied a corresponding social regression. The disillusionment of the postwar decade was not long in coming either, with the Cold War turning hot in Korea, paranoia about national security (the Rosenberg trial, McCarthyism, the blacklist in show business), suburban sameness and an obsession with conformity. Conformity, security, overpopulation, hot and Cold wars all figure in Miller's stories, though the dominant themes, an interrelated pair, are socio-technological regression and its presumed antithesis, continued technological advance. All of these he treated with respect to their social implications, particularly for the United States, but perhaps more importantly, with regard to their effect on individual behavior, including that side of behavior which can only be termed religious.

Most science fiction writers and readers would probably accede to the dictum of Leslie A. Fiedler in *Love and Death in the American Novel* that science fiction "believes God is dead, but sees no reason for getting hysterical about it."[6] To be sure, an explicit role for religion is not uncommon in science fiction. Numerous writers have used the Church as a vehicle of government or a front for revolutionary activity, in other words, as a political entity. For others, religion represents a storehouse of tradition, imagery, allusions, and riddles which they have looted for its trinkets or ornaments. Occasionally, as in C.S. Lewis' trilogy, *Out of the Silent Planet, Perelandra,* and *That Hideous Strength,* the science fiction becomes the ornament in an unabashed exercise in popular Christianity, attacking the popular beliefs associated with materialistic science and technology. The assumption in general, however, is that serious science fiction and serious religion don't mix.[7]

This assumption also seems to have distorted critical discussions of Miller's *A Canticle for Leibowitz.* Marketed simply as "a novel," it has been read as if it had little or no connection with science fiction, as if the author sprang full-blown into the literary landscape in 1960, as an apologist for, or a would-be reformer of, medieval or modern Catholicism, before the winds of change which emanated from the Vatican Council convened by Pope John.[8] Most published critiques take little note of the novel's polyphonic structure, in which other viewpoints are given almost equal time and equal weight, with a special emphasis on the viewpoint associated with science and technology.[9] Few of them have recognized either Miller's long apprenticeship in the science fiction magazines, or the continuity between the novel and what preceded it. In these stories, and I think in the novel as well, Miller comes across as an unashamed technophile, as well as a Catholic believer, however incongruous that combination may seem to opponents of either or both positions. In addition, the author is shown as a commercial writer learning his trade, willing to play along with the conventions and categories of magazine science fiction, while honing his tools so as to convert a craft into an art.

Miller's development as an artist is not as easily demonstrated as is the thematic content of his stories. The book version of *Canticle* shows decided improvements in its three parts over their magazine versions, and the story, "Conditionally Human," (1952) has been revised upward for book publication, but other changes are less obvious. Since he uses the same themes more than once, some improvement in handling can be inferred, *if* the "improved" story was actually *written* after the "rougher" draft, something which it is impossible to know, given the vagaries of magazine publishing schedules, without direct information from the author himself. There is also a tremendous difference between the first and last science fiction stories Miller published, but the progress in between is very uneven, which may not be explained simply by the fact that dates of writing and publication do not coincide. In such a short career, the chronology of publication may be of limited value. The fact that his annual publication record from 1951 to 1957 was 7, 15, 5, 5, 1 and 4 stories, novelettes, and short novels does suggest one obvious break in terms of rate of production. Moreover, although his best work is spread across the decade, the first two years have more than their share of trivia, impossible to take seriously but utterly lacking in humor. By contrast, the last five years show an increase in serious subject matter and a higher value placed on humor. That he did not always write fast is evident in *Canticle*, which was at least five years in the making. But its richness is foreshadowed by the increasing complexity of his later stories, which were published after the first Leibowitz short novel. During these years there is evidence that Miller was learning how to illustrate a point more and to preach it less, learning how to avoid the most blatantly clichéd stereotypes and conventions, learning how to concentrate the reader's interest on a single character immersed in an action the meaning of which transcends the individual. In addition, the growth of Miller's ability to utilize humor more or less parallels the change in his writing to a more complex conception of the role of characters, and a more ambiguous and problematic approach to values, culminating in that work of utmost seriousness which is little short of a "comic" masterpiece. But this change, which I see as an improvement, is gradual and uneven, not a matter of simple chronology.

In examining Miller's thematic concerns, and his maturing as an artist, I have almost disregarded the order of publication of his stories. In the pages which follow, I will briefly survey most of his work under three thematic categories: technological collapse and social regression; "hard" technology and social advance; and "soft" or biological technology and social or psychological ambivalence. Building on these summaries, I will then survey the role of religion in Miller's fiction, and his growth as an artist, culminating in a more detailed examination of his best stories and a final estimate of his accomplishment.

The cyclical theme of technological progress and regress which is the foundation-stone on which *A Canticle for Leibowitz* is built is present in much of Miller's earlier writing, too. Two stories foretell complete collapse of our civilization or race, two concern political stalemates in which technological progress is at least slowed, and five more involve directly the theme of rebuilding society after the collapse of technology.

The collapse stories are negligible accomplishments. "The Little Creeps" (1951) desribes, from the viewpoint of a blustering General, how "energy creatures" from the future (tomorrow!) fail to get him to change several small actions within his control so as to avoid nuclear war and devastation of which they are a product. "The Song of Vorhu" (1951) is a grisly "love story" of a farther future in which a spaceship pilot tries to preserve some fragment of sanity and the human race from a nameless "plague." Seeking "another" resurrection of mankind, he is haunted by disembodied lines from the Bible (Abraham and Sarah, the Messiah, the Red Sea, "What is man that thou are mindful of him," "lower than angels," "to have dominion," "from the mud of Earth.").

The political satires are more considerable, as fictions, if not as science fiction. "Check and Checkmate" (1953) places some promising satirical ideas in a setting so far removed from reality as to rob them of some of their sting. Extrapolating Cold War barriers forward several generations, Miller gives us an American president, John Smith XVI, who is selected rather than elected; who wears the golden mask of tragedy; and who must circulate among dozens of identical "Stand-Ins" to insure his anonymity and bodily safety. After forty years of Big Silence, he re-opens contact with the East, in the person of Ivan Ivanovitch IX, who wears a red mask (of Lenin); who literally "faces" Smith down (without masks); and who invites him to an Antarctic summit. While Congress convenes to conduct a "witch hunt," bringing thousands to "justice" for breaches of security, both sides trade charges but continue negotiations. Planning to launch an attack on the day of their meeting, Smith shows up with an explosive device strapped to his chest, only to find out what Ivan had meant when he said a certain discovery had eliminated both the need for "atomics" and the existence of the proletariat: Ivan himself is a robot. Miller makes no attempt at realism, maintaining only the tiniest bit of suspense before the manifest ability of technology, even when it is suppressed, to transcend security precautions, conclusively reduces to the absurd that preoccupation of the Cold War era. "Vengeance for Nikolai" (1957) is only minimally science fiction, with no extrapolated technology, rather an implicit standstill. A tale of bizarre assassination, it concerns a Russian girl who carries poison in her breasts for the brilliant general of the American "Blue Shirt" invading forces. Marya is a creature of legend, Miller indicates, whose sheer intensity of purpose seems to get her through the lines without much damage. No didacticism, except for the warning against American fascism, detracts from the purity of her mission, vengeance for her dead baby channeled into an act of heroism on behalf of the Fatherland.

Miller's first attempt at the theme of regression, "The Soul-Empty Ones" (1951), is a confusing blood-and-thunder melodrama, the coincidences of the plot shattering a degree of credibility built up by the relatively sensitive handling of character and exposition. Primitive tribesmen on Earth are caving in to invaders from the sky, except for one, whose fortunes we follow, as he discovers his identity as an "android," and helps to rescue the "true men" from their Martian masters who have brought them back to resettle Earth. The rendering of primitive ritual and the determination of Falon to rise above submission to tradition are done reasonably well, but the distance to technological mastery is too great to be overcome with any believability.

In "The Reluctant Traitor," (1952) Miller's viewpoint character is an intruder in the primitive society, a human on Mars who rebels against a restrictive city-state which forbids fraternizing with the natives. In exile, he learns more about the "androons," who turn out to be humans whose forebears came as Martian captives, and manages to reverse their defensive posture and to overturn the city government. The conclusion seems to promise an open frontier society like the Old West, but with a higher level of technology and some brotherly love, or at least mutual tolerance. The action is terrifically fast-paced, including some sexual and sado-masochistic titillation, but the conversion of the primitive androons on their flying bats into conquerors of a high-technology city-state is just not convincing.

Miller's best variation on this theme is his shortest, "It Takes a Thief" (1952; reprinted as "Big Joe and the Nth Generation" in *The View from the Stars*).

Earth is no longer, and the remnants of Martian colonists have fallen back into scattered tribes which keep ancient knowledge fragmented by restricting it to ritualistic sayings "owned" one to a person. Asir has "stolen" the saying of others, and has put enough together in his mind to realize that a catastrophe threatens unless the people regain control over the technology governing their life-support system. At the story's beginning, he narrowly misses execution for his theft and, not having learned his lesson, takes off with his girl friend on a flying "huffen" (jet-propelled by means of bellows-like lungs) for the sacred vaults. Hotly pursued, he nevertheless deciphers the system by which to get past the ancient robot guard (Big Joe) which kills one of his pursuers. Having advanced from the paradigm of magic to that of science, however primitive, he can now use the robot (technology) to help bring his tribe up to the knowledge which will be needed within twelve Mars-years to save the world.

The same story is told still another way in "Please Me Plus

Three" (1952), which takes place on Earth, where the survivors of the catastrophe are primitives who worship Bel (the Bell communications satellite, whose pylons are cult centers). Another exiled hero, Ton, is befriended by outcasts, this time a band of wandering monks, who have kept alive some knowledge of the true nature of Bel and of the history of human society. He escapes from them, too, and after edging through an area irradiated by Bel's peace-keeping efforts and coming upon some misshapen mutants, manages to take control of a repair-robot who has been waiting over 500 years for equipment and orders to fix pylon G[eorge]—86. Returning home "riding on an ass's colt," Ton overpowers, with the help of George, the guardian of pylon G-80, and directly challenges Bel. The confrontation is partly electrical, partly mystical, as Ton and Bel seem to exchange personalities, so that Bel can be made to feel pain and, punished, explode. Restoration of human civilization apparently can proceed, but how we got to this point and through it is not at all clear.

Finally, in "The Yokel" (1953), Miller takes up a much less devastating and more localized case of regression. Technological haves and have-nots in the city and country, respectively, are at odds in a post-catastrophe low-grade kind of warfare. The hero's equivocal actions take him to both sides of the border on land and in the air (he's a frustrated veteran pilot), as a good sense of Northern Florida local color comes through. Although the hero's survival may be in doubt, through all of the melodramatic maneuverings, the city's victory never seems threatened. Its power supports a dilute utopian ideal of technological society without the problems posed by anti-technological inhabitants, who are kept outside. Undigested anthropology (Ruth Benedict) fails to supply a rationale for all of this action, but the hero's opportunism is fairly convincing; from the beginning, he longs for a world in which "things work" again.

In none of these stories is there any hint that technological progress itself is to blame for the past or coming cataclysm; rather some shadowy kind of mismanagement seems to be responsible. No credible character argues against progress, and the most positive characters are always involved in rebuilding or at least preserving some semblance of technological civilization. In another dozen or so stories, technological advance is extrapolated from our present situation and, if not slavishly approved, at least favorably treated. Five of these tales treat what is perhaps the favorite of all science fiction themes, man's getting into space. Six are concerned with contolling technology, which to some extent means being controlled by technology. In two stories, faith in technology is taken to almost mystical heights.

"No Moon for Me" (1952) is a shaggy-dog story, about a hoax that comes true. A voice from the moon has by its presence challenged mankind to get there, in order to confront the alien invaders. But the ship which is launched, amid prayers, last-minute instructions, and self-congratulations ("space opens tonight"), has one man on it who seems to desire its destruction. Colonel Denin, father of the American space program, was responsible for planting the voice's transmitter, and his martyrdom is narrowly averted by the pilot, Major Long. Denin's disgrace is also averted, however, because Long discovers alien footprints around the earlier rocket, and signs of another ship. As the third crew member, Dr. Gedrin, whimpers in his terror, "no moon for me," representing those who do not want space travel, Long mutters to him, the Colonel, and us: "You've got it, fellow. Like it or not."

"Cold Awakening" (1952) is a heavily melodramatic story of cops-and-robbers, plot-and-counterplot, on board a starship about to take off on a 500-year journey with its occupants in suspended animation. Enmities build, unfounded rumors fly, and the "number two fuse," the back-up man who would be awakened in case of trouble (and die, long before arrival), is killed. Joley, the "main fuse," whose story this is, engages in some clever detective work, but lucks into the solution. Morphine addicts (a pet peeve of editor John Campbell's) plan to wake up early and live it up, unable to face withdrawal on landing. Joley narrowly escapes a plot on his life and, thanks to a kind of shell game with the leads to the three fuses' cold lockers, the evil Dr. Fraylin is cooked instead. The bad guys punished, the ship can depart, with Joley "promoted" to the status of colonist, and new "fuses" installed. The whole thing is very silly, the technological situation seemingly invented in order to make an irrational plot vaguely plausible, and to justify a tirade against drugs.

A kind of prose poem, "The Big Hunger" (1952) more or less establishes a rationale for some of Miller's other stories of man's evolution. A lyrical flight of fancy about space exploration, ostensibly narrated by the "spirit of adventure," this story alternates florid rhetoric and sentimental vignettes to take us far into the future, through several pendulum swings of expansion and contraction, as waves of explorers leave this world and others, while those who are left behind make peace with the land. A Stapledonian chronicle in miniature, it is largely successful in evoking that longing which Germans call *Fernweh* and one of the characters calls "the star-craze," a hunger which has always echoed through science fiction and which no amount of details about real space travel can ever satisfy. Echoes of this story, or of the concept it tries to dramatize, can be heard in the regression stories, in stories of human evolution, and in two elegies for the loss by certain individuals of the "freedom" of space.

"Death of a Spaceman" (1954; reprinted as "Memento Homo")

is a corny farewell to a man whose decrepit body lies in bed while his mind and his yearnings remain in space. Old Donegal is rough-tongued and cantankerous, a renegade Catholic who knows he's dying but tries to humor his wife and the inevitable priest. Although he accepts reluctantly the administration of the last rites, his true farewell ritual is hearing one last blastoff from the not too distant spaceport, for which a party next door is quieted down, and after which a solitary trumpeter plays "Taps." Miller admits he "translated" into science fictional terms the story of an old railroad man of his acquaintance, but the tale's sentimentality is effective despite the transparent manipulations.[10]

A more ambitious version of the same theme is "The Hoofer" (1955). A more active character, Hogey Parker is also rambunctious and querulous, an unintentionally comic character on Earth, where he has come home one last time after squandering in a poker game and on alcohol his earnings as a touring entertainer (a tumbler or hoofer). Using Hogey's drunken condition as a vehicle, the story uses flashbacks to cram a lot of detail into a small space. Although he is disagreeable, he earns some sympathy because of his genuine hunger for what he has lost, because he is a fish out of water, and because in his drunken stupor he stumbles into wet cement which hardens during the night and denies him any chance of ever returning to space. This story is also a kind of "translation"—Hogey could be an Earthside entertainer—but the sense of future and advances, though on the periphery, is definitely present, counterpointed by the backward wasteland which is his home on Earth.

By contrast to the peripheral role played by technology in those two stories, "I Made You" (1954) is a pure "sorcerer's apprentice" sketch about a war machine on the moon which kills anyone who comes within its range, including one of its programmers, because its control circuits are damaged. The reactions and "feelings" of Grumbler are included from one of several viewpoints, but no one or thing seems to matter very much. A more conventional *Astounding* puzzle-story, with Campbellian disdain for anti-technology forces, is "Dumb Waiter" (1952), an early attempt at comedy. In a future when cities have become completely automated, but people have been driven out of them by a war their machines continue to fight even without ammunition, Mitch Laskell enters one city to try to restore sanity to the man-machine interface. Whereas the crowd wants to destroy the central computer, Mitch, with his engineering background and technophilic orientation, only wants to program it. To make the problem more urgent, Miller not only has the city threatening him, with its blind obedience to outmoded laws; he also introduces a young woman and child Mitch must try to rescue, while the crowd of Luddites are only one jump behind him. The behavior of this ingenue and of the villain seems to be turned on and off by a switch in the author's hand, Mitch's solution to the problem hardly requires "enlightened" celebration, and the whole piece is a thinly disguised lecture on the need for men to learn to understand machines so as to keep them in their place. A bit of slapstick action, in the simple-minded antics of the city and its robot cops, presumably is supposed to turn into gallows humor, but it is difficult to take anything here seriously enough for that.

Even more of a lecture, but one which seems to be heartfelt and is not compromised by much in the way of "story values," is "Way of a Rebel" (1954), with the same protagonist, published two years later. Now a Navy lieutenant aboard a one-man submarine, Mitch rejects orders to return to port when the autocratic American government issues an ultimatum to the Soviets. Unable to participate in the destruction of technological civilization (cf. "The Yokel"), he feels no compunction, however, about "destroying the destroyers," an oncoming fleet of Soviet submarines of which the American command is unaware, and sacrifices his own life in the process.

In three of his best stories, Miller sides with those who are to some extent victims of technological progress, in their coming to terms with the presumed advance of civilization. "Crucifixis Etiam" (1953) his best short piece, shows us a day laborer on Mars, whose lungs are being sacrificed to the dream of making Mars air breathable for colonists within a thousand years. This story will be examined later in more detail, as will "The Darfsteller" (1955), the Hugo-award-winning short novel about an ageing ham actor displaced by life-size mannequins in a mechanized theater of the future, and his attempt to beat the new technology at its own game. Not quite so successful is "The Lineman" (1957), Miller's last published story, a "day in the life" of a worker on the Moon. In contrast to the "tragedies" of Manue Nanti and Ryan Thornier in the stories above, Relke's experience is dark comedy, about the time a travelling whorehouse came from Earth and put the work force off schedule. Not everything is lighthearted—Relke is threatened and beaten up by labor goons, two men are killed (one in a well-executed scene of "black humor," when he takes a bottle of champagne from the whores' ship into airless space)—but the general tone is one of achievement, not just survival, in the midst of ever-present danger. Though the line crew of the Lunar Power Project get to take a brief vacation, they are reminded forcibly that Lunar interdependence cannot tolerate an Earthly margin of error or freedom. As one result of this venture in free enterprise, more women presumably will be allowed to come from Earth, but Relke personally learns something more fundamental from this series of mishaps. Besides educating him about sex and politics, this episode has taught him that "there was a God," whose creations of the universe and of human beings were on pretty equal footing.

This sense of faith is carried to extremes in two earlier stories. In "The Will" (1954) the impending death of a child is thwarted by his faith in the ability and the willingness of future time travellers to rescue and cure him after digging up his buried stamp collection. Although the premise is uncomfortably silly, the story is almost rescued by its mundane details: the parents' grief, the boy's addiction to the *Captain Chronos* television show, and the public relations use to which he is put by the program's star and producers (based presumably on Miller's own experiences with *Captain Video*). Technology veers into the supernatural, not just in the eyes of primitives, but in those of a computer scientist, in "Izzard and the Membrane." A Cold War melodrama, replete with brainwashing, counter-espionage, and the scientist's defection, this short novel is full of action, much of it vague, that ends when the hero saves the West almost single-handedly. Some of the vagueness may be excusable, since one of the characters, the spiritual part of an "electronic brain" (i.e. the "membrane" attached to "Izzard" or "Izzy"), turns out to be God, or a reasonable analog. Enabling the hero to win, it then transports his "transor" (soul), and those of his immediate family, into a parallel universe, with orders to "increase and multiply."

As some of these stories show, Miller is not always sure that the fruits of technology will be as delicious as the planners contend, but the drive to progress is not to be halted, as it was in the stories of regression. In all cases, however, the technology was "hard," based primarily on the physical sciences. The Church, which has pretty much given up most claims to insert morality into physical science, has a much greater stake in the futures mankind is offered by the biological sciences. Correspondingly, questions of biological "advance" Miller treats with more circumspection; "progress" is a much more ambivalent quality in his "biological" stories. Seven of these concern intelligent aliens, all dangerous to man, some of whch are clearly negative symbols of possible paths of man's biological progress. Two stories, one of them involving aliens, concern the temptation and threat of telepathy. Seven others focus on other questions of possible human evolution, whether natural or forced, a distinction that breaks down under analysis.

Aliens are featured in "The Song of Vorhu," "The Soul-Empty Ones," and "No Moon for Me," and the possibility of aliens, or at least Unidentified Flying Objects, is a significant motif in "The Lineman," but few details are given. Details are also a little sparse in some of the other stories, but the menace is plain enough. "The Space Witch" (1951) has hypnotic powers that disguise her true form from Kenneth Johnson, and allow her to masquerade as his estranged wife (who in fact has just drowned). Hunted by other aliens, she seeks refuge, endangering the Northeastern United States, but Ken, after a glimpse of her "true self" (with tentacles), hijacks her ship, condemning them to each other for good. Almost as jejune are three other alien stories. "The Triflin' Man" (1955; reprinted as "You Triflin' Skunk") is an alien father of an Earth child who is coming to claim his offspring, causing the child nightmares and severe headaches. The child's mother, however, a Southern country woman, drives away her one-time seducer with a shotgun.

"Six and Ten are Johnny" (1952) finds humans from the exploratory starship "Archangel" invading aliens. The planet "Nun" is inhabited by a world-girdling intelligent plant which ingests and learns to replicate humans. When it separates one of its progeny to make the trip back to Earth, it plans to take over that world from its unsuspecting hosts. Another alien who ultimately turns out to be dangerous, indirectly, is the "Martian" in "The Corpse in Your Bed Is Me" (1957; written in collaboration with Lincoln Boon). His sense of humor is so bizarre that a successful television comic feels compelled to make him laugh. Failing repeatedly, he declines and disappears, to return, dead, as the only sure way to produce a Martian laugh. The "Martian" does not make the story science fiction, however, and the overall air of unreality turns what might have been humorous into an insipid enigma.

"Secret of the Death Dome" (1951), Miller's first published story, is also insipid, a melodramatic shoot-out between invading Martians, whose dome floats harmlessly but impregnably above the Southwestern desert, and an Army sergeant seeking revenge for the castration-killing of his best friend, the husband of the girl he's always loved. If the story has any importance at all, it's because of the Martians' problems with reproduction; reversing the usual insect dependence on queens, they have only three ageing males left, one of which the hero kills, as he rescues the girl and drives the menace off-planet. Biological specialization is not limited to sex in the more promising "Let My People Go" (1952). An "ark" full of human colonists finds Epsilon Eridani II is inhabited, and a cavern on its moon offers evidence that human captives had once been brought from Earth. Three mismatched envoys accept an invitation to visit the planet where they discover the inhabitants have bred and trained other animals, including humans, to serve them as communication systems, organic building materials, even as food sources (including humans!). Rage, as in "Death Dome," enables one returning envoy to break a hypnotic block so as to provide the colonists with the key to their gaining a foothold on the planet. They release the "vermin" they carry aboard ship, and the overspecialized *Piszjil* are forced to deal with those who know how to control the pests.

Although telepathy may not be a case of overspecialization, as a potential human talent, it may be said to represent a projected step in human evolution. Aside from "Gravesong" (1952) and "Let My People Go," in which it is a simple communication convenience, telepathy figures in only three of Miller's stories. In "Bitter Victory" (1952), *psi* powers are possessed by aliens who use them to assume human form and to stalk each other on Earth. The story involves their becoming too attached to human forms, ways, and emotions, such that when the final conflict comes (one of mental powers but rendered in terms of physical effects), they find themselves both crippled—one blind, one lame—and they seem to accept each other, love, and human form. A recurrent phrase, "for the love of man," underlines the implication of man's moral superiority to these more "advanced" life forms. In "The Wolf Pack" (1953), dreams of an American airman turn out to be telepathic messages from a girl in the town of Perugia, Italy, over which he must fly another bombing raid. Religious allusions ("jovial Wotan," "through crucifixion came redemption," "o my people," and a more or less literal "for God's sake") stud Lt. Mark Kessel's wrestling with his conscience. His observation that the existence of his pack of fighter planes is "paradoxical proof that men by nature are cooperative beings" does not do much to salve his conscience when he gets the last message from the girl, dying amid flames and rubble: "If you had known...would all have been spared for the sake of one?" As in these stories, telepathic sharing seems to bring about more pain than good in "Command Performance," a slick satire in the *Galaxy* mode which will be discussed later.

If man is destined, as "The Big Hunger" claims, to expand outward from Earth in waves of exploration and conquest, human evolution may take some strange jumps. This is the subject of two stories of the far future. The slighter piece, "Gravesong," is an elegy for man as he was (i.e., is now), vaguely satirizing two possible paths he may take. Emilish, returning the ashes of his mother to ancient Earth, meets the grave-tender, Eva, whose *anima*-like beauty marks her as a throwback from the mud-creatures which men on Earth have become. Amid memories of the galactic corporate state from which he comes, and the contrast stressed by Eva that she is a creature of Earth and he is a creature of space, he ponders the warning of his mother that, given unlimited power, "Man is no longer man," and wonders what he is.

Two other paths are suggested in "The Ties that Bind" (1954), a puzzle-story of a sort which pits a pacifist Earth society, twenty thousand years from now, against the militarism of a fleet using the planet as a refueling station (its resources apparently not having been exhausted) *en route* to a battle somewhere else. Using the old ballad, "Edward," as a backdrop—five stanzas serve as epigraphs to the story's five sections—Miller develops these antithetical milieus and psychologies, emphasizing their mutual incomprehension and their ironic interrelations. Only the fleet's cultural Analyst, Meikl, seems to have a firm grasp of what's happening: he and the narrator call it *Kulturverlangerung*, the power of unconscious vestiges of man's culture. Like Cassandra, however, he is not understood in time. Desertions and rebellion by some crewmen become a problem before long. Then another piece of the puzzle is supplied when an Earthman picks up a sword which he does not intend to use and finds that it seems to "fit" his hand; his muscles, affected by *Kulturverlangerung*, seem to recognize an affinity for the weapon. The real problem is that the descendants of this Eden-like Earth carry within them an inner hell with which Earth once infected the galaxy. And even the now "innocent" Earthmen are potential killers, although that potential is not realized at this time; evolution has not changed the fact that Man is subject to this version of "original sin."

If these stories represent natural evolution, the same is not unequivocally true in "Blood Bank" (1952), in which Terrans play the role of the heavy. In this *Astounding* space opera, moral indignation runs high as one puzzle: what did Commander Roki do wrong? (he ordered the destruction of an Earth ship carrying "surgibank" supplies to a disaster-stricken planet, because the ship would not stand by for inspection) gives way to another: how will Commander Roki vindicate himself, so as not to have to commit suicide as the code of his world demands of his honor? Admirably controlling suspense as Roki gradually uncovers the clues, Miller keeps us from doing the same until we have learned the particulars of this milieu and have accepted to some extent a degree of cultural relativism which most of the characters in the story do not have. Each cultural idiosyncrasy is embodied in a person and rooted in some physical, biological, or cultural peculiarity of his or her world. Although the heart of the adventure is conquest of the "Solarians," a predatory race evolved on Earth which uses standard humans as medical supplies to trade for nuclear fuel and a fascist renaissance, the story's center of interest is not in Earth, its legendary past or aborted future. Nor is it in the comic confrontation between Roki and the female pilot from a frontier world whose rickety cargo ship transports him to the Sol planetary system. The primary concern is the solving of puzzles, from the technological (faster-than-light drive, reaction engine limits, ship-to-ship grapples) to the anthropological (humanity's alleged origin on Earth, the amount of space an empire can govern, how much diversity a widespread civilization can and must tolerate). These cross at the point of conflict between non-Earth humans and Solarians; not being human, the latter threaten humanity, an implicit act of war which tolerance for local customs and local biological variation cannot encompass. Common romantic and melodramatic motifs are employed for surface excitement, but the real interest is more of a cerebral nature, with the moral concern for intraspecies savagery almost a side-issue.

Although the evolution in that story may have occurred naturally, the evolved Solarians ensured their "superiority" by means of brute strength, greying the distinction between natural and forced evolution. Two other examples of forced evolution, which may not be against nature, but which important characters see as unnatural, are a pair of poor stories about cyborg spaceships, employing the brains of human "children." Whereas other writers have seen this process as a means by which cripples might live useful lives, Miller emphasizes the inhumanity of their existence by emphasizing the children's innocence and the despair of ostensibly sympathetic mother figures. The condemnation of the practice of using human brains to complement computer logic in piloting spaceships seems to come from an irrational base which is at least peripherally doctrinal. In "A Family Matter" (1952), the woman is a stowaway (of all things) who claims to be his mother, lamenting her loss of *twenty years* ago, and raging at him, threatening his "fleshorgan." In self-defense, he accelerates too fast, killing both her and his human part, and, having lost all sense of identity and responsibility, heads out to nowhere, instead of returning to base from this "test" of his abilities which has also turned into a test of his "humanity." In "I, Dreamer" (1953), the early training of a child to distinguish between self, semi-self, and non-self, though effective, seems grafted on. The story proper, again told by the cyborg, is a ridiculous mish-mash of revolutionary politics and melodramatic seduction, with a little sadism mixed in. It is ended by the narrator's empathy for the girl's pain and his longing to be a "Two-Legs" forever, which for some odd reason causes him to plummet into the palace of the dictator, even as the secret police are rounding up all the revolutionary conspirators. Inherent in the basic situation is only a little pathos; Miller, in trying to exploit the "horror" of this man-machine interface, was forced to introduce melodramatic conflicts which make both stories ludicrous. Yet he thought the idea worth two stories, and even reprinted one of them in his collection of short fiction, suggesting that the idea, at least, of forced evolution presented in them was of some importance to him.

In two other, longer tales, which will be examined in more detail later, Miller is more successful in raising hard "religious" questions about "forced" evolution, while telling convincing stories in an effective symbolic manner. "Conditionally Human" questions man's right to play God with life and death and the fate of "lower" animals. "Dark Benediction" asks how humanity would respond to a gift from the skies promising great powers, if it also demanded a physical change of the color and texture of the skin.

Both stories explicitly involve religious questions and symbolism, and feature Catholic priests in advisory, but fallible, roles. Miller's other Catholic priests are characters in "No Moon for Me," "Crucifuxus Etiam," and "Please Me Plus Three." Primitive priests are negative figures in the last-named, and in "It Takes a Thief" and "The Reluctant Traitor," where they represent stagnant tradition in the way of progress. Prayer is explicit in "No Moon for Me," "Death of a Spaceman," "The Triflin' Man," "The Lineman," and "The Wolf Pack," and implicit in "The Will" and in "Izzard and the Membrane" which features God as or in a computer. Scriptural tags are employed in "Izzard," "The Song of Vorhu," "Crucifixus Etiam," "The Lineman," "The Wolf Pack," and "Let My People Go." Religious titles and imagery are apparent in "Six and Ten are Johnny," "Grave Song," "Crucifixus Etiam," "Momento Mori" ("Death of a Spaceman"), "No Moon for Me," "The Song of Vorhu," "Izzard and the Membrane," "The Soul-Empty Ones," "The Reluctant Traitor," "It Takes a Thief," "Please Plus Three," and "The Ties that Bind." And Christian doctrine may be instrumental in "A Family Matter," "I, Dreamer," and "Blood Bank" as well as in the "original sin" stories, "Grave Song," "The Ties that Bind," "Conditionally Human," and "Dark Benediction."

Hardly an obligatory convention, like the boy-girl romances and repulsive villains Miller brings in occasionally, religion (especially the Roman Catholic version of Christianity) usually has a negative connotation in science fiction. Miller's primitive priests are conventional in that way. But the priest in "Death of a Spaceman" is a sympathetic figure, as are those in "Conditionally Human" and "Dark Benediction," while the clergy in "No Moon for Me" and "Crucifixus Etiam" are neutral tones in the moral landscape. Christian doctrine does suggest a bass tone of conviction as a contrast to the uncertainty of modern man, a role it plays convincingly in *A Canticle for Leibowitz.* But the doctrine or its exponent, as in Miller's novel, may be naive, lacking in understanding of the whole picture, or otherwise irrelevant. The exponent need not be nominally religious, either: although the psychiatrist in "Command Performance" cannot play this role because his advocacy of conformity is so much a part of the conventional milieu of the Fifties, the Analyst in "The Ties that Bind" *is* a reasonable facsimile of a priestly *raisonneur* because of the antiquity of his anthropological teachings, which predate in a sense the secular humanism of that story's Eden-like Earth.

For the technophilic Miller, unlike the technophobic C. S. Lewis, the direct opposition of science and religion won't do, at least not if it means the downgrading of science and technology. They represent for him the best that we can do today and in the foreseeable future, when it comes to knowledge and concrete achievement. As in *A Canticle for Leibowitz*, however, religion suggests a kind of wisdom, traditional, irrational, humane, which knowledge alone cannot reach, but a kind of wisdom which, divorced from social and technological, and even aesthetic reality, is also inadequate as a guide for conduct. It complements the engineering question, How, with the age-old poetico-religious question, Why, even if it does not reveal *the* Answer. At the least, its presence in a Miller story indicates continuity with the present, and by implication, a universal need of mankind. At best, the religious connotation of the parable—and most of Miller's stories are parabolic in their didacticism—underlines the moral ambiguity of a situation, its need for a moral resolution. When the mass of American and British science fiction magazines were topheavy with laboratories, machines, and the "social" effects of science and technology (i.e. the effects of hypothetical inventions and discoveries on "masses" of people), Miller was one of a handful of writers concerned with effects on individuals, who stand alone, lacking the kind of certainty that only dogma can provide, and aware of both the lack and the inadequacy of the outmoded dogma.

Philosophy, or sententious content, does not by itself make a story or a writer, of course. On other counts, Miller was neither consistent nor outstanding. Writing for science fiction magazines, he had to keep in mind the prejudices of their editors and readers if he were going to sell his stories even at their low rates of pay. One thing he had to do was to keep the story moving, often at the expense of character, structure, or even logical coherence, and many if not most of his stories suffer from that requirement. The melodrama has not worn well. His best, however, seem to have incorporated that principle of efficient story-telling without harm to their integrity.

If he were writing for *Astounding* or *Galaxy*, the highest-paying markets, he had to try to please their editors. John Campbell's technophilia was congenial, and his predilection for the puzzle-story could have dictated the writing of "Blood Bank." Other Campbell buttons probably were pushed by "No Moon for Me" (space at any cost), "Izzard and the Membrane" (Cold War hostilities, brainwashing, and defecting scientists), and "Cold Awakening" (the horror of drugs). The man-machine interface dominates "Dumb Waiter," "I Made You," and "The Darfsteller," which Campbell bought along with the mood-pieces, "Crucifixus Etiam" and "The Big Hunger." Mood may also have caught Campbell's eye in "The Soul-Empty Ones," which is otherwise a good example of Miller's bad handling of melodrama, something that stands out in most of the stories published before 1954.

Horace Gold at *Galaxy* preferred satire, which "Conditionally Human" and "Command Performance" powerfully exhibit, as Miller's only sales to that magazine. Other attempts at satire, possibly written for *Galaxy* but published elsewhere, were less successful: "Check and Checkmate," "Bitter Victory," "The Triflin' Man," "The Hoofer," and "The Corpse in Your Bed Is Me."

The predilection of Anthony Boucher and his successors at *The Magazine of Fantasy and Science Fiction* and its short-lived sister publication, *Venture,* were for careful writing and characterization, when they could get them. The three parts of *Canticle* were published in *The Magazine of Fantasy and Science Fiction,* as was "The Lineman"; *Venture* printed "Vengeance for Nikolai" and "The Corpse in Your Bed Is Me," both of which are only borderline science fiction, but enigmatic character-studies and a bit shocking for the Fifties (*Venture's* editorial policy favored material which was "strong" for the times). That six of Miller's last nine publications were with Mercury Press is indicative of the turn his writing had taken toward "human" stories, less crowded with incident, more concerned with values.

Melodrama was dominant in his 1951 stories, except for "Dark Benediction." "The Secret of the Death Dome" is a traditional Western with a Gothic twist, and incompletely visualized action, a problem which beset several of Miller's early stories. The world was saved in four of those first seven tales, by implausible means, implausibly and humorlessly described. Overplotting and cardboard stereotypes ruined "The Reluctant Traitor," "Cold Awakening," "Dumb Waiter," and "Let My People Go" in 1952, though the last-named has its moments and is almost long enough not to buckle under the weight of events. Sentimentality is another risk he took frequently, especially with irrelevant love-interests, but also with whole stories, such as "The Song of Vorhu," "Bitter Victory," "Grave Song," the cyborg stories, "The Wolf Pack," and "The Will," using it to good advantage only in "The Big Hunger," "Death of a Spaceman," and "Conditionally Human." From the humorlessness of his earliest travesties, Miller proceeded to satire as early as 1952, but a more feeling kind of humor does not show up until "Death of a Spaceman" in 1954, after which it is featured in more of his stories than it is not. He was always concerned with values, and even found successful aesthetic vehicles to express them as early as 1951 ("Dark Benediction," and, published just after the turn of the year, "Conditionally Human"), but not with the richness and ambiguity only humor can supply.

In his best stories, Miller managed to combine thought and action, to make ideas personal and involving, by approaching a universal ("truth" or problem) by means of strong identification with an individual, who must demonstrate an important decision by means of an action, the significance of which is underscored by the fact that there is not a lot of action for action's sake cluttering up the pages. One exception is "The Big Hunger," in which mankind as a whole is the protagonist, but the role holds for the sentimental or near sentimental "Death of a Spaceman" and "The Hoofer," for the melodramatic "It Takes a Thief" and "Blood Bank," for the "Lineman" and "The Ties That Bind," which just miss being in the first rank. And it definitely holds for those stories which are in the first rank.

"Command Performance" is a very human story of suburban loneliness and conformity, and the conviction of Lisa (Miller's only female protagonist except for Marya in "Vengeance for Nikolai") that she is rightfully different from the conventional image to which her husband and her analyst want her to conform. Telepathic communication with another, which should convince her that she is right, instead upsets her terribly; she is to some extent attached to that conventional image she wishes to reject. She can only accept her talent after she has used it to fend off the "attacker" who wants to mate with her to perpetuate a super-race. The scenes of her communication with him are rendered well, from his discovery of her, dancing naked in the rain in her backyard; to his prevention of her calling the police, by means of illusion, causing her to see things that are not there; to her own switch from passive reception to active sending, as she stops his physical progress toward her by means of imaginary cars in the street. He pushes on, disregarding them, only to be killed by a real automobile, leaving her safe but empty again, and this time knowing why. Lisa wastes no time on remorse; she begins, as her would-be ravisher presumably once did, tentatively questing in the telepathic "communication band" for someone else like her. Her prospective mate and his plans for a race of supermen are melodramatic, but Lisa's character and situation are real enough and realistically presented, with the kind of satire of contemporary mores (conformity and all that) for which *Galaxy* was noted.

In "Conditionally Human," Terry Norris, a veterinarian, cares for animals whose intelligence has been increased to put them midway between pets and children (children are rare, because of restrictive population laws), and his occupation upsets his newlywed wife whose maternal reflexes are strong. Terry's crisis point is an order to destroy certain "units," in this case "neutroids" (apes transmuted into baby girls with tails), which exceed the allowable intelligence limits. After Terry has located one of these units, named Peony, and taken it away from its "Daddy," a petshop owner, he is visited by Father Paulson (Father Mulreany in the book version) on behalf of his bereft parishioner. The priest acts reluctantly as a moral guide for the unreligious Terry, who uses him in turn as a sounding board, then goes to excesses not sanctioned by the priest. He not only hides the illegal "deviant,"he also kills by a carefully planned "accident" his supervisor who has come to see that the order and the "neutroid" are executed. Then he decides to take a new job with the company that produces "newts," to carry on the work of the fired employee who made the newts not only too intelligent, but also functionally, biologically human.

In a society forced by population pressures to restrict the freedom to breed, there are many malcontents, from Terry's wife and the priest, to pet owners who identify themselves as parents, to the kind of technician who "humanized" the newts. In this situation, Terry finds himself "adapting to an era," at first to the status quo, but then to the possible future that an artificially created race might bring about. Either choice requires a kind of moral toughness and seems to demand that he kill, if not Peony then supervisor Franklin. By contrast, the priest could never sanction murder, though he may be an indirect cause of one; he finds the creation of the neutroids an abomination but their destruction possibly even more so. Peony has an edge on Man, since she "hasn't picked an apple yet," in the words of the priest; i.e. she is not tainted by original sin (compare the reading of a play fragment in Part Two and the consecration of Rachel in Part Three of *A Canticle for Leibowitz*). But Miller seems determined to stretch the Church's teachings to the limit; what if you *have* to choose between murders? Terry and Anne both make that choice—*she* threatens to kill *him*— on behalf of the freedom to breed or "create," but the reader, having been taken only part way down that path of argumentation, is left with a moral ambiguity. The satire *(Galaxy* again) cuts both ways, but seems aimed at the kind of society which makes such choices necessary.

Heavy with implications, the story is not weighty in a ponderous sense; things happen too fast for that. Miller sets the stage with a honeymoon quarrel, sends Terry off on a collecting mission, and intersperses social background and lampoons of oversensitive "mothers" before we even find out what a neutroid is. Before the first, "unimproved" batch die, Anne risks too much attachment to them by feeding them *apples*; she also declares her intention to risk an illegal baby of her own. Scenes flash by, such as Terry's conversations with the police chief, with Anne, with "Doggy" O'Reilly (Peony's "Daddy"). Tension builds, Peony is shown to be adorable, and the die is cast. Though the moralizing increases, the pace never flags. The end finds the Norrises waiting it out, aware that they are pitting themselves against society. Quixotically they pursue a goal they are unlikely to achieve, recognizing that they have elected—as has the whole society, unconsciously, and in an opposite manner—to play God to a "new people."

"Dark Benediction" raises other interesting questions about man's fate, positing a biological transformation of the human race into a new "improved" model, a transformation which is resisted by almost all before it takes place. Sharing the senses of Paul Oberlin, we share his repugnance to the "dermies" whose skin has turned scaly and gray, and whose desire to touch others and spread the contagion is little short of obscene. Overtones of racial prejudice, (the locale is the South), leprosy, violation of the integrity of the individual, fear of the unknown in general, and the known transition period of often fatal fever make it clear that a considerable trade-off is required. For those who are not dermies, who do not know or believe that there are benefits involved, it is less a trade-off than a betrayal of all that's human, a conversion of men into monsters. Rather than chronicled, this background is given to us through flashbacks and conversations, as we follow Paul, alone on the road. In Houston, he is impressed into the service of a paramilitary local government concerned with maintaining racial purity, a safe from contagion, and anxious to have him, as a trained technician. He makes his escape in a truck, one of the few vehicles that runs and has gas in this age of chaos, but on impulse he rescues a girl, Willy, whose incubation has started and who is about to be executed for it. Making her ride in the open back of the truck, Paul heads for Galveston Island, which he hopes will be a haven. His hope is doubly ironic, given the contemporary reputation of Galveston as a "sin city," and the coming twist of the plot.

Having rescued Willy from the moral equivalent of a Nazi concentration camp, Paul is now obligated by decency to get her to safety, provided that she doesn't try to touch him. The island, however, is a colony of "hypers," their term for dermie. Only in the hospital, run by priests, where he takes her for help, can Paul find any security, and that in a sterile room, avoided by hospital personnel, who wear noseplugs to maintain their self-control in his presence. He lingers on, partly because Willy is responding poorly—fearful that she might have touched him, she attempts suicide—partly because he has been promised a boat in which to escape. While he is waiting, he learns from a Dr. Seevers what truth he has managed to extract from his research into the transformation and its cause. One night, however, Paul wakes up terrified, with memories of being caressed; over the first fright, he realizes it was Willy, and discovers that she has run away. He chases after her to the sea, and accepts the inevitable, his transformation and her love.

As in all Miller's best stories, the science fiction rationalization is clear, the behavior believable, the focus not on the science fiction itself but on the situation of one troubled person. Unlike in others, however, the biological transformation in this one is a positive one, with utopian overtones. Although the repellent characteristics are given their due, the parasite which Dr. Seevers explains is responsible for them is also responsible for an increase in sensory perception and, apparently, cooperative behavior. At least the islanders are better behaved than the mainland totalitarians; this may be partly due to the influence of the priests, but where else is their wisdom respected? And islands are traditional utopian locales. The real reason why this metamorphosis is more acceptable may be its resemblance to a divine blessing. The parasite is a gift from the sky, having arrived in meteorites launched by some alien civilization; though labelled with warnings, the pods were first opened by the ignorant, unable to read the signs and driven by their "monkey-like" curiosity. As from Pandora's Box or the apple of Genesis, but perhaps in reverse, as a distribution of good, the contents spread everywhere, making it likely that everyone, eventually, will have to give in to this "dark benediction." Reception of the parasite is a passive act, moreover, requiring acceptance only of the "laying on of hands." Believing it is beneficial, that the scientist's findings are accurate, requires, as does believing the disease is harmful, an act of faith (parasites in "Let My People Go," clearly in the service of overspecialized aliens, were regarded with fear and loathing). Paul and the reader can only decide on the basis of others' behavior; the paranoia of the mainlanders can hardly be preferable to the love and respect shown by Willy and the priestly medicine men.

An act of faith is also crucial in "Crucifixus Etiam," Miller's best short story, but the faith is not sustained by the protagonist's Catholic religion. An elegiac, near-future projection, this story makes of technophilia a secular religious faith. Although the passage of two decades has brought into question some of the details (the limited amount of social change in a century, the stated "high" rate of pay of five dollars an hour, the use of English rather than metric measures), the basics of the story are universal, as the title suggests. Roughly translated, it means "crucified still or again." This is the story of a man who takes great risks to his health for the chance of high rewards; as his health begins to fail, and the rewards come to seem unobtainable, he wonders what the justification of his work is, then comes to identify with the goal he serves but will never attain.

The man is Manue Tanti, a Peruvian laborer at work on Mars, his health endangered by implanted oxygenation equipment which encourages atrophy of the lungs. The justification is "faith in the destiny of the race of man." The science fictional trappings are necessary, since no job on Earth offers quite this kind of risk, and certainly none is so dependent upon future realization. The project of making a breathable atmosphere for Mars is already almost a century old, with eight centuries yet to go. But the handling is in no way impersonal. Our concern is not with the project, but with the suffering of one man, representative of many. We start with the basics of his situation, his longing to travel, his pain from the oxygenator, his struggle to maintain his lungs so he can indeed realize his ambition. We hear that the engineers have life much easier than the laborers, we hear that Mars is growing her own labor force, we hear that the object of the drilling job is to tap a well of tritium oxide, and we know no more than he does which is fact and which is rumor. We see his estrangement from his fellow-workers and how they and the elements seem to conspire to make him give in, to breathe less, to let the oxygenator work more. In the hospital, we dream with him of falling and wake with him in the death-fear this inspires, only to discover to his horror that he has not been doing any breathing at all on his own. Facing his being trapped on Mars, we ask with him the purpose of all this, whose ends he is serving, and we see the inadequacy of the faith proffered by the itinerant clergy who come to offer comfort. As he gradually gives in to the pain and its easement, we follow Manue in his quest for understanding: a repairman tells him Mars is a dumping ground for Earth's surplus, tritium suggests to him hydrogen fusion as an energy source, the "quiet secrecy" implies that the men are not to be trusted with the knowledge of what in fact they are doing.

As the work goes on and he becomes an oxygen "addict," we follow the curve of his emotions to cynicism and despair, to a controlled cursing in lieu of prayer. On the day a controlled chain reaction is started deep beneath the Martian crust, the men are finally informed of the significance of their job, laboring so that others may breathe, far in the future. Pent-up resentment and a momentary fear that the reaction might not be controlled almost lead to a riot. Quite unexpectedly, Manue knocks out the ringleader, and his frenzied threat to pull out the rioters' air hoses quells the rebellion. He finds the answer bitter—Miller calls it Manue's "Gethsemane"—but also glorious. One man asks "What man ever made his own salvation?" Another says "Some sow, some reap," and asks Manue which he would rather do. Manue himself picks up a handful of soil and thinks "Here was Mars. His planet now."

The roughly 8000 words that comprise this story are very efficiently employed. Miller uses vignettes, rather than long scenes, and avoids the sentimentality that technique seems to lead to in other short stories. Bits of action and dialogue, nothing extended, break up what is mainly narrative. The characters, bit players except for Manue, are solid individuals: the Tibetan, Gee, Manue's digging partner with whom he has nothing in common; the foreman, Vogeli, who is quick-tempered and efficient, trying to maintain his men like tools; Sam Donnell, the "troffie" (atrophied) repairman, who is a mine of misinformation; even the riot leader, Handell, and the supervisor, Kinley, though little more than roles with names, seem right in their parts. The local color and slang, brought in as if in passing, make Mars feel lived in. And the third person narration, limited to the consciousness of Manue, is particularly effective in that it restricts our senses almost claustrophobically to those of the perfect observer for this story: a Peruvian, used to thin air and small social horizons, ignorant of much but proud of his ancient heritage and comfortable in his ambition, Catholic in upbringing but able to recognize how ill-fitted his religion is to this alien world.

On a larger scale, Miller managed a similar triumph in the short novel, "The Darfsteller." This, too, is limited to the consciousness of one person, for whom technological advance is no unmixed blessing. Ryan Thornier, an ageing former matinee idol in the days before the stage was automated, has consistently refused to make a "tape" of his acting personality, or to work in the production or sales ends of the autodrama business. Steeped in theatrical tradition, proud of his art and even of the poverty to which his pride has brought him, Thornier is reduced to janitorial duties in an autodrama theater, his chief joy in life being the rare chance to see a third-rate live touring company play to a sparse audience. Denied that opportunity, he is given two weeks' notice before he is replaced in this job, too, by an automaton. Since this is on the eve of a mechanical stage run of a play he once starred in, the actor conceives and executes a plan to make one last performance the culmination of his career and simultaneously an act of revenge against his boss, his profession, and the world. "The Darfsteller" is the story of what he accomplishes, and how.

On one level this is a personal story, a near-tragedy. Learning quickly enough how the technology of the autodrama operates, Thornier sabotages the tape of an actor intended for a role he once played. Then, since there is not enough time to get a new tape before opening night, he offers himself as a replacement. Against the better judgment of everyone involved, his offer is accepted, and he puts a real bullet into the gun with which the mannequin playing his enemy is supposed to shoot him. In the actual performance, however, in which he competes against the "Maestro," the mechanical director that operates the tapes and mannequins, adjusting them to each other and to audience reactions, Thornier is reinvigorated. He dodges the bullet and catches it in his belly.

Allegorically, this is a fable of technological displacement. In case anyone missed the point, Rick, the projectionist, runs it through again in the coda. Explaining that a human specialist will inevitably lose to a specialized tool, a machine, Rick defines the function of Man as "creating new specialties." But the technology is more than a symbol; the autodrama, throughout the story, is continually vying with Thorny for center stage. To compete with it, he has to learn to understand it, which he has never tried to do before. Learning what he can from Rick, he becomes fascinated with it, to his dismay and the reader's edification. Seeing the Maestro at work, with Thornier in its system, is most instructive, and enough details are developed to make the automation of the theater, presumably the last bastion of personalized professions, seem believable.

The creation of this illusion is assisted, moreover, by the appearance of former actors and stage people associated with the autodrama who come into town in connection with the opening. Like any technology, this one requires preparation and tending, and they have been reduced to servants of the machine in Thornier's estimation, and to some extent in their own. It is, of course, the only game in town, and it even offers a kind of "immortality" to actors in their prime, he recognizes, comparing Mela, his one-time co-star and lover, with her unageing tapes and mannequins. The heart of the story, however, lies in Thorny's love affair with the theater, with its icons and superstitions, the image it gives him of himself (on our level of perception he is a querulous, vain popinjay), and the recaptured thrill of performance, even a mediocre performance on a stage full of mannequins and of threatening electrical equipment. As he thinks to himself, seeing the Maestro in human terms, the director—with his eyes on the whole play and on the reaction of the audience—is always in opposition to the *Darfsteller* (the true actor-artist), and prefers the mere *Schauspieler* (the crowd-pleasing entertainer). An excellent fictional creation, Ryan Thornier is always an actor, even in the role of himself with an audience of one, and the theater as microcosm is ideal for this "morality play" of man vs. machine. Though the reader may find himself in intellectual agreement with Rick, in his analysis of the situation, the rational conclusion is clearly at odds with the emotional identification with the quixotic Thornier, whose irrationality is more appealing.

The narrator in this short novel has the same distant, gently ironic detachment as in *A Canticle of Leibowitz*, with the same fondness for slapstick if not for puns as leavening in a serious tale. The construction is effective, alternating action and dialogue, narration and internal monologue, parallels and antitheses. The characters, aside from Thornier, are personalized functions, though only the theater owner, Thornier's boss, is an obvious stereotype, and even that may be excusable since he is a tormentor as seen through Thornier's eyes. And the didacticism, though clearly overt, is cleanly balanced by the felt reality of Thornier's lament. Perhaps the only thing the novel does not have, and does not need, which may be surprising in view of Miller's usual propensities, is any religious props or even a sense of religion, unless we assume that for the actor, the stage is his Church. The effect of the whole, however, is that of a minor masterpiece, as the 13th World Science Fiction Convention recognized by awarding it a "Hugo" as the best "novelette" of 1955.

The medium lengths—novelette, novella, short novel—were where Miller's strengths lay, where he could combine character, action, and import. Of his forty-one magazine publications, twenty-four were of middle length, including "Blood Bank," "The Ties that Bind," "The Lineman," four of the five we have just reviewed, and the three more or less independent parts of *A Canticle for Leibowitz*. Only "Crucifixus Etiam" really stands out among the shorter works, followed by "The Big Hunger," "It Takes a Thief," "Death of a Spaceman," "The Hoofer," and "Vengeance for Nikolai," most of which come dangerously close to sentimentality (melodrama in "It Takes a Thief"), and each of which relies heavily on a gimmick, the bane of so many short stories. Whether the sustained continuity of a more conventional novel was beyond him, we cannot know for certain, but it seems certain that part of the success of *A Canticle for Leibowitz* is due to its tripartite form, each third crisply etched in short novel size, with counterpoint, motifs, and allusions making up for the lack of more ordinary means of continuity. This, too, he learned in his apprenticeship in the science fiction magazines.

Five outstanding stories out of thirty-eight is not disastrous, but it would hardly have caused Miller to be remembered if he had not written *A Canticle for Leibowitz*. Against that standard, not very many science fiction stories or novels can measure up. Leading up to it, and to the enigma of Miller's abandoning writing afterwards, the whole canon has some extrinsic interest, chronicling as it does his development from a commercial writer to an artist, one who may have quit while he was ahead, rather than have everything thereafter compared to one book and found wanting.

H. Bruce Franklin

What Are We to Make of J. G. Ballard's Apocalypse?

More than any other writer, J. G. Ballard incarnates the apocalyptic imagination running riot in Anglo-American culture today. Ballard began projecting multiform visions of the end of the world in the late 1950s, even before these became the rage, and he has been consistently, in fact obsessively, at it every since. Along with other British and, somewhat later, American purveyors of literary gloomanddoom, Ballard has been a symbol of the ascendancy of the "New Wave" in science fiction. And the "New Wave" has been a leading force in the broad and deep expansion of a doomsday mentality in our culture.

From the beginning of the twentieth century until shortly before World War Two, there was a widespread belief, especially in England, the United States, and Germany, that explosive technological advances were about to cause a tremendous leap in progress for mankind, and the scientific-technical elite were the living embodiment of this creative potential. Obviously the one and only form of literary art congenial to such a vision was science fiction. Hence the creation of the mode of science fiction dominant in the first half of our century, personified by H. G. Wells in his "optimist" period (from *The Food of the Gods* in 1904 and *A Modern Utopia* in 1905 through *The Shape of Things to Come* in 1934[1]); Hugo Gernsback and his creation of technocratic science fiction as an autonomous, self-conscious genre; and German science fiction, with its theories of scientific genius, racial supermen, genetic purification, technological marvels, super-weapons, and world empire, all central to the emerging Nazi ideology.[2] Today—that is, roughly since the devastation of the European empires by the post-World War Two national liberation movements in Asia, Africa, and Latin America—there is an increasingly widespread belief, pulsating outward from England, that disintegrating homeland of a collapsed global empire, that the world is coming to an end—through overpopulation, pollution, plague, thermonuclear holocaust, alien invasion, universal madness, computers or insects running amok, the cooling or overheating of the planet, cosmic winds or radiation, a shriveling or exploding sun, and so on. Obviously the one and only form of literary art congenial to such fears is science fiction. Hence the "New Wave" and its leading role in the science fiction of the 1960s and 1970s.

We must be clear about one thing: although science fiction does have a cultural *influence*, it is primarily a cultural *expression*. Doomsday visions have been around for many centuries, if not millenia, but they become ascendant only during certain historical epochs and for specific historical reasons. J. G. Ballard and the other creators of an apocalyptic science fiction thrive because of certain conditions of the present era. One main goal of this essay is to investigate these conditions.

From the outset, we must understand the enormous significance of science fiction in the most developed capitalist nations. Science fiction has attained a modicum of academic respectability in the last decade, but those of us who teach it still find ourselves constantly on the defensive (with our colleagues in the humanities, not, of course, with those in the sciences, much less with our students). A course in science fiction, I have been told, is merely a luxury (though perhaps an attractive one) in the English department, to be sacrificed if the crisis in funds for public education continues. Well, the simple fact is that science fiction is the major non-realistic literary form of the twentieth century, intricately related to all areas of social, historical, and scientific thought. Another object of this essay is to show that a single science fiction writer, in this case J. G. Ballard, reveals to us—whether deliberately or not remains to be seen insights essential to our well-being if not our survival. For Ballard is not some oddity or aberration, but a representative Anglo-American intellectual who has chosen to write science fiction because it is the most suitable vehicle for the expression of ideas he holds in common with many other Anglo-American intellectuals.

Ballard makes little pretense that his fantasies of the death of the world or the human species are scientific, plausible, or even possible. The forms of his catastrophes are, in fact, mutually contradictory. There may be too many people, as in "Billenium" (1961), or too few people, as in "The Impossible Man" (1966). The world may get too dry ("Deep End," 1961; *The Drought*, 1964, 1965)[3] or too wet (*The Drowned World*, 1962). The environment may suddenly and inexplicably begin to move too fast (*The Wind from Nowhere, 1962)* or almost as suddenly and just as inexplicably begin to congeal (*The Crystal World*, 1966). The end may come about through hydrogen bombs, solipsism, suicide, ceaseless urbanization, or in a world-wide "autogeddon" of car crashes. Even within a single work there is often no consistent explanation of why the cataclysm is occurring other than some vague pseudo-scientific theory, presented like a magician's patter and perhaps offered to satisfy the conventional expectations of the readers of science fiction.

In *The Wind from Nowhere* there is one small paragraph of pseudo-scientifc mumbo-jumbo about "cosmic radiation" and the "gravitational drag" of "electromagnetic wave forms" to explain an utterly impossible meteorological phenomenon, a wind from the east blowing around the entire planet at a speed constantly increasing five miles per hour per day until it reaches 500 miles per hour and then suddenly begins to die out. The next paragraph offers an alternative suggestion: "Or again, maybe it's the deliberate act of an outraged Providence, determined to sweep man and his pestilence from the surface of this once green earth."[4] This actually seems the more plausible explanation, especially since the wind, after steadily increasing for months, begins to die down within minutes of the destruction of a heaven-defying pyramid, symbolic of the will and pride of an archetypal capitalist and would-be superman. In *The Drowned World,* solar flares melt the icecaps. In *The Crystal World,* "the creation of anti-galaxies" may have caused "the depletion of the time-store available to the materials of our own solar system."[5] *The Drought* contains one passage of explanation for the disappearance of rain, and this utilizes the theme of ecological disaster through pollution. "Millions of tons of highly reactive industrial wastes," "mingled with the wastes of atomic power stations and sewage schemes," have made a "brew" out of which "the sea had constructed a skin...a thin but resilient monomolecular film formed from a complex of saturated longchain polymers."[6] This prevents evaporation; hence all rain ceases; hence the land becomes a burning desert, devoid of rivers, lakes, even well water. *The Drought* baldly shows that even this early Ballard is not taking his fantasies of disaster seriously on the level of physical event. For not only do all the bodies of fresh water disappear, but the sea itself rapidly and continually recedes. Nowhere does Ballard bother to explain why the sea would diminish, rather than expand, when all fresh water had disappeared into it and no evaporation is taking place from it. Apparently he simply wants to express his vision in the form of a desert world, and the mechanism for creating this desert is, literally, immaterial. (In "Deep End" the oceans have been destroyed by having their oxygen "mined" in order to export an atmosphere for human settlements on other planets; in the loosely connected stories which make up *Vermilion Sands* [1973] there is no explicit reason why sands have come to substitute for oceans.)

Of course in these early novels there is usually at least one passage, and often a constantly reiterated reminder, indicating that the external landscapes are merely projections of an inner landscape. In the later novels, such as *The Atrocity Exhibition* (1970; published in America in 1972 as *Love and Napalm: Export U.S.A.*[7]), *Crash* (1973), *Concrete Island* (1973), and *High Rise* (1975), even the pretense of science fiction is gradually replaced by an awareness that the bizarre external environment is essentially a projection of a psychological state or a way of perceiving reality.

J G. Ballard, certainly a writer who wants to be taken very seriously (and is so by the British literary establishment), offers to us an endless series of doomsday fantasies as improbable and self-contradictory as oceans that dry up because no water is evaporating from them. At the exact same historical moment, large numbers of scientists and futurologists in England and America are arguing, with the utmost seriousness, that the world really is doomed, quite likely by the millenial year 2000, because there is a population "explosion" or "bomb," because it is too late to stop "ecocide," because computers prove that full-scale thermonuclear war is inevitable, because it is a mathematical certainty that worldwide plague and/or famine will begin in the next few decades, because the earth is about to become catastrophically overheated due to the second law of thermodynamics, because we are on the threshold of a new ice age, because we are about to use up all available sources of energy, because insects are about to become uncontrollable, because the increase of non-white people is causing the human race to become genetically inferior, because it is becoming impossible profitably to extract raw materials from many parts of the world, and so on.

Most of the readers of this essay probably accept some of these beliefs, particularly the notion of "overpopulation," so deeply that it will be difficult for me to communicate some of the fundamental ideas of this essay. I know from experience that the question of population is one that is now hard to discuss rationally in England or the United States. In the university, the blandest class becomes enraged at any argument that the world is not now, and is in no foreseeable danger of becoming, overpopulated. Nevertheless, such is the overwhelming consensus of population experts in most of the world, who view the Anglo-American orthodoxy as an archaic neo-Malthusian aberration. I shall not attempt to prove these assertions here. All I ask from readers is that they (1) recognize that the population question is extremely controversial; (2) agree that there are many reasonably intelligent, sane, well-informed people around the world, who, like myself, accept the Marxist rather than the Malthusian view of the population question (i.e., that the world's ability to support the standard of living for each human being is rapidly increasing, rather than decreasing, and will continue to do so into the foreseeable future); (3) allow that apparently selfconsistent and plausible arguments can be advanced on both sides of the population question; (4) open their minds to the possibility that one's views on population, as on many other questions, may possibly be determined by something other than the objective truth or falsity of a belief, and that this "something" may include official propaganda, a body of assumptions common to a culture, the outlook of a social class dominating the means of communication, or the point of view of one's own social class. I use the question of population because it is the key to all other questions of global catastrophe. To all readers who are prepared to go this far I say: Let us now consider the possibility that J.G. Ballard's implausible pseudo-scientific fantasies and the "scientific" apocalypses of Paul Ehrlich and the Club of Rome spring from the same sources. This has nothing to do with possible influences from science fiction to science or vice versa. Certainly Ballard is not just some kind of literary mouthpiece for certain scientific theories, as the self-contradictory nature of his fantasies proves. And certainly I am not arguing that *The Population Bomb* was published in 1968 because Paul Ehrlich had been reading too much Ballard and other Anglo-American science fiction of global disaster. My underlying theory is that Anglo-American science fiction and predictive Anglo-American scientific thought are both conditioned and determined by the socio-economic ambience of a collapsed British empire and a disintegrating American empire.[8] I shall try to test this theory in the particular case of the most eloquent and imaginative of the prophets of doom, J.G. Ballard.

To avoid another misunderstanding which usually takes place when a Marxist addresses an audience profoundly miseducated about Marxist criticism when I use the word "determined" I do so in the Marxist, not the positivist, sense. That is, social reality and one's class situation *determine* all forms of consciousness, including artistic and scientific, in the sense of constituting the range and limitations of what one finds conceivable and congenial. This *determination* (i.e., what shapes and forms something) is not in any sense part of a philosophic *determinism*. Though we all have ideas and feelings, fears and desires, plans and fantasies shaped and formed by our physical and social environments, each of us, including J.G. Ballard, I the writer, and you the reader, is free, within historical limitations, to choose among many conflicting patterns of thinking. Ballard might persuade me that the apocalypse is at hand and that it will take the form of a psychological autogeddon. I might persuade you that such a vision is a fantasy alien to the experience of the vast majority of human beings on the planet. But none of us is capable of viewing the world from the perspective of a pre-Columbian Aztec priest, the wife of a seventeenth-century New England Puritan minister, or any human being living in the year 2100, to use extreme examples.

Let me try to penetrate at once to the heart of Ballard's imaginative creation. His novels seem to me to fall rather neatly into two groupings: the early novels of world-wide physical catastrophe (*The Wind from Nowhere,The Drowned World, The Drought, The Crystal World)* and the later novels of psychological destruction *(The Atrocity Exhibition, Crash, Concrete Island, High Rise).* Of course there is plenty of psychological havoc in the early novels and physical mayhem in the later. Unifying all these novels, however, is the theme of the global catastrophe as an external projection of a deranged inner landscape. Prior to any of these novels, Ballard was publishing short stories, and in one of the earliest, "The Overloaded Man" (1960), he prefigures the most recent forms of his imaginings and provides us with a precis for the underlying content of them all. In this story he shows quite explicitly that the source, or at least one crucial source, of the central problem of all his fiction is the historical dichotomy between subject and object, a dichotomy which he perceives as becoming catastrophic as bourgeois society itself disintegrates. In "The Overloaded Man" it is explicitly the lone petty bourgeois intellectual who destroys the entire world not by bombing it with nuclear weapons or too many people but by withdrawing himself from it. The protagonist's solipsism is equated with suicide, murder, and global catastrophe. In short, "The Overloaded Man" is a paradigm for Ballard's artistic opus.

The story is set in the near future, subtly indicatd by the slight increase in automatic domestic appliances, a slight exaggeration of late 1950s suburban plastic architectural trends, a somewhat more leisured existence for the technocratic social class, and a small deterioration of social relationships within that class. The first sentence summarizes the story of the title character: "Faulkner was slowly going insane."[9] Two months have passed since he resigned from his job as "a lecturer at the Business School," and he has been lying around the house, pretending to his wife that he is "still on creative reflection." As soon as his wife, dressed in "the standard executive...brisk black suit and white blouse," leaves for her job, Faulkner is free "to begin his serious work" (pp.72,73).

This consists of turning all of objective reality into meaningless abstractions, "systematically obliterating all traces of meaning from the world around him, reducing everything to its formal visual values" (p.78). He finds it "pleasant to see the world afresh again, to wallow in an endless panorama of brilliantly coloured images. What did it matter if there was form but no content?" (p.76) His method is the same as that used by the main character in *The Atrocity Exhibition (Love and Napalm)*; Faulkner is able to convert houses, trees, people, whatever, into "geometric units," pieces of a gigantic "cubist landscape." In this early story, Ballard takes us step by step, in simple narrative, through the whole process. Faulkner has his first success with consumer goods, for reasons explicitly related to the essence of capitalism, which converts all good things into "goods"; that is, commodities: "Stripped of their accretions of sales slogans and status imperatives, their real claim to reality was so tenuous that it needed little mental effort to obliterate them altogether" (p.75). After he has then "obliterated the Village and the garden," he begins "to demolish the house." He sinks "deeper and deeper into his private reverie, into the demolished world of form and colour which hung motionlessly around him." Soon he has "obliterated not only the world around him, but his own body, and his limbs and trunk seemed an extension of his mind, disembodied forms whose physical dimensions pressed upon it like a dream's awareness of its own identity" (p.82)

In other words, he has achieved solipsism, reducing all objective reality to an appearance of his own mind. Solipsism is a danger inherent in bourgeois ideology right from the start, in its Cartesian assertion that *I* exist because *I* think. Faulkner's neighbor, also a lecturer at the Business School, had warned him of this danger: "'The subject-object relationship is not as polar as Descartes' *Cogito ergo sum* suggests. By any degree to which you devalue the external world so you devalue yourself.'" But Faulkner plunges down his chosen path to annihilation, converting his wife into "a softly squeaking lump of spongy rubber" as he murders her, and drowning himself in order to become, in the very last word of the story, "free."

The tendency toward solipsism in bourgeois ideology is held in check as long as the bourgeoisie is rising or ruling as a social class, extending or maintaining its "freedom." During these periods, the bourgeois split between subject and object manifests itself in what Ballard aptly calls Crusoeism: the individual man of action, relying on his own wits and ingenuity, and sometimes aided by inferior beings, conquers the natural and social environment. Ballard displays collapsing bourgeois society turning the Crusoeism of the rising bourgeoisie inside out. The hero of "Deep End" is "a Robinson Crusoe in reverse,"[10] trying to restore the last technological remnants on an abandoned earth. The hero of *The Drowned World* shows "inverted Crusoeism" in "the deliberate marooning of himself."[11] The protagonist of *Concrete Island*, an elaborate parody of *Robinson Crusoe*, expends his life attempting to "dominate" and to "escape from" an island of weeds and old cars which he could leave any time he chooses to walk away. Ballard is now showing us the bourgeois ideal of the "free" individual as a prisoner in the smallest of cells, his own ego.

In his early works, Ballard sometimes offers a wishful alternative to alienation and solipsism. It is a vision of cosmic unity with intelligent beings throughout the macrohistory of the universe. This vision, reminiscent of Olaf Stapledon and carried forward in different ways, in the works of Arthur C. Clarke and Ursula Le Guin, is expressed as a revelation in "The Waiting Grounds" (1959): 'Meanwhile we wait here, at the threshold of time and space, celebrating the identity and kinship of the particles within our bodies with those of the sun and the stars, of our brief private times with the vast periods of the galaxies, with the total unifying time of the cosmos..."[12] Before long, this unity between the microcosm and the macrocosm will be lost for Ballard and it will become the object of an endless quest, always reducing itself to the jungles and deserts of the entrapped and tormented individual psyche.

In "Build-Up" (1960), another of these revealing early stories, Ballard projects an endless three-dimensional city whose economy is based on the final commodity: space, which sells for about one dollar a cubic foot. The protagonist, trying to located what he calls 'free space' ("in both senses") discovers that time itself has become nullified by this ultimate form of capitalist super-development. His odyssey toward some limit of the boundless city leaves him right back where he started, defined with utmost precision in the final words of the story: "$$\$SHELL \times 10n.$$"

Brian Aldiss has called *The Wind from Nowhere,* the first of Ballard's novels, a pot-boiler.[13] It is true that the narrative method is straightforward, several adventure stories are interwoven into the apocalypse, and there is a not unhappy ending in which a few of the less unsympathetic characters survive. But in this novel Ballard for the first time develops at full length many of his characteristic themes, and certainly this is a book with a serious message.

Although London is explicitly called "a city of hell" (p.54) only after the wind has begun its havoc, nature's desolation is clearly revealing rather than creating a dry, sterile human wasteland. The main point-of-view character, Donald Maitland, is at the very opening in the act of deserting his wife, the spoiled, hedonistic only child of a wealthy shipping magnate. Like the prinicipal character in many of Ballard's tales, Maitland is in a branch of medicine or biology. His field is "research into virus genetics—the basic mechanisms of life itself," which, unlike "research on petroleum distillates or a new insecticide," merits little financial support in this profit-oriented society (p.9). So he is bought and kept by a rich wife. The world they both inhabit is barren and exploitative, and its rulers already maintain vast armed forces to preserve their own wealth, power, and comfort. Both "people in the War Office" and "the politicians" are merely carrying out their normal jobs in abnormal conditions when they decide to provide shelter only for the privileged: "As long as one-tenth of one percent of the population are catered for, everybody's happy," Maitland's friend in the Air Ministry tells him, "But God help the other 99.9" (p.21). Meanwhile in America the likely Democratic presidential nominee is General Van Damm, NATO Supreme Commander, whose death in a car crash in Spain while on a secret visit to Generalissimo Franco is being "hushed up for political reasons" (p.34). The dry and dusty inferno created by the wind, punctuated by "the sounds of falling masonry," is a symbolic representation of the state of capitalist society.

The main symbolic figure in *The Wind from Nowhere* is the multimillionaire Hardoon, who owns "vast construction interests" and is also, like Maitland's father-in-law, a shipping magnate. (One suggestion for his identity is the name of the one merchant ship mentioned—the *Onassis Flyer.*) Hardoon is an early avatar of a figure who will appear in various forms throughout the rest of Ballard's novels: the man of action and power who seeks to master nature, to subject the natural and human worlds to his own will and pride. This figure is the hero of much pro-capitalist science fiction of the 1930s in Germany, England, America, and among Russian emigres such as Ayn Rand. Hardoon is a caricature of this early science-fiction hero.

In the midst of the natural cataclysm, Hardoon constructs the only building supposedly capable of withstanding the storm, a gigantic pyramid which reminds someone of Cheops. He recruits a private fascist army, complete with black uniforms, black leather boots, and the emblematic white seal of his pyramid, obviously an ensign of death. When Maitland meets Hardoon, the man of power sneers at the intellectual as part of "the weak" incapable of understanding "the strong." Then he explains himself, in a passage which could come right out of Ayn Rand or any number of the positivists and technocrats dominant in science fiction until the mid-1950s:

As the wind has risen so everyone on the globe has built downward, trying to escape it... With one exception—myself. I alone have built upward, have dared to challenge the wind, asserting Man's courage and determination to master nature... Only I, in the face of the greatest holocaust ever to strike the earth, have had the moral courage to attempt to outstare nature. That is my sole reason for building this tower. Here on the surface of the globe I meet nature on her own terms, in the arena of her choice. If I fail, Man has no right to assert his innate superiority over the unreason of the natural world (p.142).

Needless to say, the destructive forces of nature win, and "the millionaire" is left "staring upward into the sky like some Wagnerian super-hero in a besieged Valhalla" (p.156). So ends the lone bourgeois hero. The nemesis of this superman does not appear in this novel, though he is prefigured somewhat by Maitland. This is a quietistic introvert, a biologist or doctor, who subordinates his own identity in nature. He is the principal figure of the subsequent three novels.

The Drowned World presents the characteristic structural conception of Ballard's fiction. Just as the drowned planet projects an inner landscape, so the body and psyche of the protagonist recapitulate in microcosm the world of nature. The sun, almost as a conscious power, is burning off the ionosphere and reclaiming the planet for itself. The Earth is becoming a steaming sea mingled with swamp and jungle, the artifacts of civilization are being inundated by water and taken over by reptiles, and the most sensitive human beings find their own minds booming to rhythms of the sun as they drift back into a primeval and preconscious world. Ballard presents as the highest reality produced by our own century paintings by Delvaux and Ernst, which prefigure scenes to be enacted out quite literally as the minds of the human race sink into the seas of the unconscious:

Over the mantelpiece was a huge painting by the early 20th-century surrealist Delvaux, in which ashen-faced women danced naked to the waist with dandified skeletons in tuxedos against a spectral bone-like landscape. On another wall one of Max Ernst's selfdevouring phantasmagoric jungles screamed silently to itself, like the sump of some insane unconscious (p.27).

Later these nightmare paintings, the external jungle, and the shared nightmares of the main characters merge into each other: the painting by Ernst and the jungle "more and more...were coming to resemble each other, and in turn the third nightscape each of them carried within his mind. They never discussed the dreams, the common zone of twilight where they moved at night like the phantoms in the Delvaux painting" (pp.73-74).

The embodiment of death, as painted by Delvaux, appears in the person of Strangman, a man as white as bones, dressed in white, and considered a dead man by his crew of Black pirates. Strangman is, like Hardoon, an avatar of the man of power, pride, will, and egoism who seeks to conquer nature. He appears, with machinery and a flotilla of half-trained alligators, to reverse the course of nature's reclamation. When he succeeds in pumping out the city of London, "the once translucent threshold of the womb had vanished, its place taken by the gateway to a sewer," and London again resembles "some imaginary city of hell" (p.121).

Strangman's nemesis is Dr. Robert Kerans, the protagonist, a biologist, isolated, quietistic, impotent, "too passive and introverted, too self-centered" (p.74) to take command of the situation. Kerans seeks to swim back into his own "drowned world of my uterine childhood" (p.26), to recapture "the amnionic paradise" (p.64), to merge with both sea and sun, to become the new Adam. He does succeeed in destroying Strangman's work, in flooding London once again, but then he leaves his symbolic Beatrice behind to lose himself in an endless self-destructive lone odyssey "through the increasing rain and heat, attacked by alligators and giant bats, a second Adam, searching for the forgotten paradises of the reborn sun" (p.158).

The Drowned World formulates the trap in which Ballard has been thrashing around ever since. To comprehend the larger relevance of this predicament, let us look at some difficulties posed by his symbols and characters. First we must recognize that Kerans' quest is, at bottom, destructive of all human relationships and ultimately suicidal. In seeking to merge with the sun and the sea, he renounces his humanity, in all senses. His quest for the sources of life is, in the last analysis, a search for death. On the other hand, Strangman, the symbol of death-in-life, is actually working, whatever his piratical intentions, to reclaim part of the planet for humanity from the alien forces of nature. So Kerans and Strangman are yoked, as opposites in a larger unity of life and death, which I think Ballard wishes us to perceive as a yin-yang. On the literal level, this involves a psychological doubling. Kerans descends in a diving suit into the drowned London planetarium, sees himself in a mirror, and "involuntarily" shouts "Strangman!" at his own reflection. Strangman understands Kerans' quest so deeply that he turns it into a sardonic joke:

At times he would subtly mimic Kerans, earnestly taking his arm during one of their dialogues and saying in a pious voice: "You know, Kerans, leaving the sea two hundred million years ago may have been a deep trauma from which we've never recovered"...(p.87).

Or, looking at Kerans in the diving suit, Strangman responds, parodying the author as well as his projected character:

It suits you, Kerans, you look like the man from inner space. The rictus of a smile twisted his face. "But don't try to reach the Unconscious, Kerans, remember it isn't equipped to go down that far!" (p.94).

When he does dive, Kerans subconsciously tries to lose his identity in the water and the drowned image of the heavens in the planetarium by killing himself. He blames his brush with death on Strangman, but it is actually Strangman's men who save him from himself, only to attempt to kill him ritually later on, as they crucify him as an embodiment of Neptune.

The fundamental paradox here is that Ballard's quietistic, suicidal, nature-loving hero is actually another avatar of his "Wagnerian super-hero." In fact his mission is even more cosmic, his hubris more presumptive, than that of a Hardoon or Strangman. One might compare this relationship at length to that between Ishmael, the would-be suicide who seeks to lose himself in the ocean, and Ahab, who defies and seeks to master nature. But there is a profound difference between Melville's art and Ballard's that has to do with basic values. Despite all the carnage and death in *Moby Dick,* that book affirms life and the ties of loyalty and trust which bind human beings together and which it is madness to sever. Despite all the yearning for life in Ballard's fiction, it is ultimately a literature of despair, negation, and death. Kerans' impulses, however cloaked in fantasies of embodying the sun and the sea, are merely another form of the madness incarnated by Faulkner in "The Overloaded Man." Kerans, and through him his author, is expressing a dying society.

Ballard of course knows this. What he means by the "surreal" or "super-real" is the psychological condition which he himself partly incarnates. The symbols of our age are for him its most horrifying historical events, and the progress of his fiction is largely into a deepening exploration of the psychological content of these events. The nuclear bombs of *Love and Napalm* were already the annihilating symbols of "The Terminal Beach" (1964); the auto crashes of *Crash* and *Concrete Island* were just as universally final in "The Impossible Man." In *The Drowned World* he explicitly states his unifying conception of historical and psychological events:

Just as the distinction between the latent and manifest contents of the dream had ceased to be valid, so had any division between the real and the super-real in the external world. Phantoms slid imperceptibly from nightmare to reality and back again, the terrestrial and psychic landscapes were now indistinguishable, as they had been at Hiroshima and Auschwitz, Golgotha and Gomorrah (p.67).

My criticism is that Ballard does not generally go down far enough below the unconscious to the sources of the alienation, self-destruction, and mass slaughter of our age. He therefore remains incapable of understanding the alternative to these death forces, the global movement toward human liberation which constitutes the main distinguishing characteristic of our epoch. The real nemesis of militarism, exploitation, and the rape of the environment is not the insane overloaded man who is seeking to be "free" by oblitering the entire world, nor the suicidal quietist, such as Dr. Robert Kerans in *The Drowned World,* Dr. Charles Ransom in *The Drought,* or Dr. Edward Sanders in *The Crystal World.* Nor is it the main figure of *Love and Napalm,* a doctor trying to cure the world by rearranging its pieces; nor Robert Maitland, the architect in *Concrete Island,* who maroons himself amidst British freeways; nor James Ballard, the revealingly-named narrator and protagonist of *Crash* (the only novel narrated in the first person), whose greatest pleasures are (1) looking in the rear-view mirror to see the man of power, Vaughan the "hoodlum scientist," copulating with Ballard's wife and then beating her; (2) having anal intercourse with Vaughan; and (3) finally arranging to follow Vaughan's leadership by killing himself, together with at least one attractive woman, in a car crash. Beyond the scope of Ballard's death-worshipping imagination are the people rescuing the world from the state of being that determined that imagination.

Of all Ballard's works, the one in which he comes closest to perceiving the rising forces of our epoch is a short story, "The Killing Ground," written in 1966 during the American invasion of Vietnam and clearly intended in part as propaganda against it. But even in this story he ends by turning away from his own best insights. The time is "thirty years after the original conflict in south-east Asia," and "the globe was now a huge insurrectionary torch, a world Viet Nam."[14] The scene is the Kennedy Memorial at Runnymede on the banks of the Thames, and the point-of-view is that of Major Pearson, leader of a scraggly band of "rebel" guerrillas harassing the technologically superior American invasion forces. In one striking passage, Ballard briefly imagines the masses of people creating a better future out of this holocaust: "...the war had turned the entire population of Europe into an armed peasantry, the first intelligent agrarian community since the 18th Century. *That* peasantry had produced the Industrial Revolution. This one, literally burrowing like some advanced species of termite into the sub-soil of the 20th century, might in time produce something greater" (p.144). But that seems a shadowy hope, and certainly Ballard is unable to imagine not only that future but the present society of his insurrectionary peasantry. They, like the impotent Major Pearson and his ragged soldiers, are dominated by the "immense technology" of the American invaders, who seem like "some archangelic legion on the day of Armageddon" (p.140). The Americans had won in Vietnam, had then "occupied the world," and at the end of the story they have killed Major Pearson and destroyed his unit. We must remind ourselves who did win in Vietnam. American technology was not invincible; the Tet offensive took place a little over a year after this story was published; within five years the vaunted American military machine was a shambles; and in less than a decade a socialist society.

We can grasp the ironies of Ballard's misunderstanding of history if we take a close look at two interrelated works prior to "The Killing Ground"—"The Garden of Time" (1962) and *The Crystal World*. "The Garden of Time" is almost pure allegory, a rarity for Ballard. It shows the last stand of feudalism, incarnated by Count Axel, a figure apparently derived both from *Axel*, the symbolist closet drama by Villiers de l'Isle Adam and from Edmund Wilson's interpretation of the play in *Axel's Castle*. In "The Garden of Time" Axel's castle, garden, and exquisite life with his flawless wife are besieged by "an immense rabble" appearing on the horizon and ineluctably advancing upon him across the plains and hills. Variously described as "the mob," a "horde," and "a vast concourse of laboring humanity," this army of "limitless extent" obviously represents the revolutionary masses storming the final symbolic bastion of feudal privilege, grace, and beauty. Axel's only defense is the crystal flowers of time in his garden. While growing, each crystal flower seems "to drain the air of its light and motion." When picked, each flower begins "to sparkle and deliquesce," causing an abrupt "reversal of time." As this happens, the entire revolutionary concourse is "flung back" away from the castle. Time, in the form of the crystal flowers, of course runs out for the Count, and he and his wife are left to stand as stone statues surrounded by the vulgar mob that overwhelms his ruined estate.

Those who have read *The Crystal World* will immediately recognize the cosmological symbolism of the crystallized plants, which represent a congealing of time and an alternative to the world of human activity. But the historical symbolism may seem irrelevant to the novel. I don't think so.

In *The Crystal World*, the force inevitably advancing is not the mass of oppressed people but some mysterious process that transmutes all organic matter into crystals. These crystals, like those in "The Garden of Time," drain light and motion, congeal time, and "deliquesce" in sparkling beauty when removed from their sustaining jungle environment. They are on their way to taking over and transforming the planet; no force will be able to stop them. The protagonist, Dr. Edward Sanders, leaves his position as head of a leprosarium, representing an apparently selfless dedication to help follow human beings, to become eventually a devotee of the crystal world and what it represents. As he writes during the process of his conversion:

...there is an immense reward to be found in that frozen forest. There the transfiguration of all living and inanimate forms occurs before our eyes, the gift of immortality a direct consequence of the surrender by each of us of our own physical and temporal identities. However apostate we may be in this world, there perforce we become apostles of the prismatic sun (p.154).

All this may seem exactly the opposite of the historical movement of "The Garden of Time." But then we need to take a close look at the historical and geographical setting for *The Crystal World*.

The story is set very neatly on the equator and at the vernal equinox. This place and time obviously have large symbolic significance in Ballard's cosmological yearnings. But more specifically the place is Africa, and the time is during the rising tide of the wars of national liberation sweeping across the continent. At the end of World War II the vast lands of Africa were still almost entirely owned by a handful of tiny European countries—England, France, Belgium, Spain, and Portugal. England and France together possessed over two-thirds of the continent. By the time *The Crystal World* was published in 1966, most of the countries of Africa had attained their independence, and liberation struggles were spreading rapidly in the others. The empire of Ballard's own nation was crumbling almost week by week. In the nine years preceding the book, thirteen of Britain's African possessions (Gold Coast, British Togoland, British Somaliland, British Southern Cameroons, Nigeria, Sierra Leone, Uganda, Tanganyika, Zanzibar, Kenya, Nyassaland, Northern Rhodesia, Gambia) broke loose from the empire. Although Britain purported to be "giving" these lands their freedom voluntarily, clearly it was bowing to the rising rebellions of the African peoples themselves, spearheaded by the armed struggle of the Mau Mau in Kenya and inspired by the Pan-African socialist ideology of leaders such as Kwame Nkrumah and Julius Nyerere. By 1966 several of these newly independent nations, including Nigeria, Ghana, and Tanzania, were helping to provide world-wide leadership for the emerging non-aligned African-Asian-Latin American bloc in their accelerating attacks against British, European, and U.S. imperialism. These facts are hardly irrelevant to Ballard's story or its symbolic content, since he himself introduces into *The Crystal World* the subjects of imperialism in Africa, including the role of European mining companies and the rebellions against the European empires.

The Crystal World is set explicitly in the Cameroon Republic, though Ballard has changed the country to suit his symbolism. Dr. Sanders is arriving in the fictional Port Matarre on a steamer from Libreville (capital of Gabon), but it is Gabon, not the Cameroons, that sits astride the equator (and, interestingly enough, the Crystal Mountains are also in Gabon, just upriver from Libreville). Ballard's fictional Cameroon Republic is still under French military control, though in actuality the country had become politically independent in 1960. (The date of the action is established as later than 1960 by an orbiting Echo satellite and retrospective narration about the Katanga revolt of 1960-1962.) The main industry is diamond mining, under the control of European corporations, though the Cameroon Republic has, in fact, virtually no mining for jewels.

Certainly the diamond mining has something to do with Ballard's main theme and main symbols. There are "the French owned mining settlements, with their over zealous security men" (p.17) and their "warehouses bearing the names of the mining companies" (p.55). "...the diamond companies don't intend to let anything get in their way" (p.81). When the rain forests begin to crystallize, huge jewels are smuggled out, causing the mining companies' "share prices on the Paris Bourse" to soar "to fantastic heights" (p.58). When a man is sent to investigate, the "vested interests" see to it that he ends up in the river (p.59). The "natives" smuggle out fantastically jewelled leaves and branches and sell them as commodities in the town marketplace. Two explicit themes are the self-destroying search for El Dorado and the myth of Midas. In the face of man's frantic efforts to rip up the earth in the search for wealth in the form of crystals, nature seems to respond by crystallizing all of itself, including man. It is "time with the Midas touch" now (p.75). And people at first respond by converting the products of this fabulous process into commodites and cash as they do ordinarily with gems.

Ballard relates this set of symbols directly to the African liberation movements—in opposition to them. The crystal plants in *The Crystal World* have a function very close to those in "The Garden of Time." Dr. Sanders' new-found lover, a Frenchwoman, darkly tells him "of some kind of humiliation" she had experienced in the Congo "during the revolt against the central government after independence, when she and several other journalists had been caught in the rebel province of Katanga by mutinous *gendarmerie*" (p.36). The Katanga revolt was of course financed by the European mining companies and the C.I.A.; that same "mutinous *gendarmerie*" were to become an anti-imperialist force, fighting in Angola, first against Portugal and then against the C.I.A.-supported invaders from Zaire and South Africa, returning later to Zaire as revolutionary socialists.

In Ballard's imagination these revolutionaries exist only as some dark, sinister force committing unmentionable acts on lone white women. The anti-imperialist forces in Ballard's semi-imaginary Cameroons may actually, and at least symbolically, have triggered the crystallization process that freezes time and history. That process had begun upriver, at the emerald and diamond mines around the symbolically named settlement of Mont Royal. Shortly before, the rebel forces had occupied precisely these locations. When Sanders arrives, he finds "this isolated corner of the Cameroon Republic was still recovering from an abortive coup ten years earlier, when a handful of rebels had seized the emerald and diamond mines at Mont Royal, fifty miles up the Matarre River" (p.10).

So this "inner landscape" is a projection of historical, as well as psychological, events. This is "a landscape without time" (p.14), the fond hope of Count Axel and all others seeking to freeze history. At first when Count Axel plucks his crystal flowers from his garden of time, he is able to make the "concourse of laboring humanity," that advancing vulgar "mob" and "rabble," actually disappear. As Dr. Sanders, the agent of Ballard's own odyssey, succeeds in losing himself in the crystal forest of a mythical Africa, Ballard is able to make the liberation movements of the 20th century, fitly represented by the African anti-colonial forces, actually disappear at least in his fiction. Sanders wants to stop time, so he plunges into the time-congealed crystal world. As Ballard shows us in "The Garden of Time" the inner meaning of the desire to stop time is to stop history. He also shows us in that story that the inner meaning of the desire to stop history is to stop revolution in order to preserve archaic privilege and order.

All this so far is on a rather general, highly symbolic level. But Ballard also directly presents to us his own images of the people in revolt in our century, the people dismembering his empire and leaving many British intellectuals, including himself, with the deepest convictions that the apocalypse has come and the whole world is dying. And these images are so disgustingly racist that they might embellish a Ku Klux Klan rally. Just as Count Axel is horrified by the thought of the unleashing of the laboring masses, J.G. Ballard seems terrified by the image of the unleashing of the non-white masses.

In the chapter "Mulatto on the catwalks," immediately after we are told of the unspeakable outrages of the Katangan *gendarmerie*, Dr. Sanders is for the first time attacked by a murderous mulatto, who moves "with the speed of a snake" (p.41). This "giant mulatto" (p.83) reappears with another assassin, a knife-wielding "Negro" with a "bony pointed face," to ambush Sanders in a maze of images reflected in the mirrors of an elegant European mansion out in the crystallized rain forest. Still later, in the chapter entitled "Duel with a crocodile," a crystallizing crocodile sidles clumsily toward Sanders. "Feeling a remote sympathy for this monster in its armor of light, unable to understand its own transfiguration," Sanders almost fails to note the gun barrel between the jewelled teeth. The bejewelled crocodile is merely the latest disguise for the treacherous mulatto hidden inside. Sanders kills him, and pauses briefly over the body with its glistening "black skin" (p.143). The only apparently civilized Black person in *The Crystal World* turns out to be one of the treacherous accomplices in this attack on Sanders, and he too must be disposed of by a shot from a white man.

In *The Drowned World*, the would-be assassins of Dr. Robert Kerans are the horde of "savage" Blacks ruled by Strangman. They speak in a Negro minstrel dialect and are constantly motivated by a primitive superstitious "fear and hatred of the sea" (p.124); and they therefore try to torture Kerans to death to the tune of "The Ballad of Mistah Bones" hammered out on bongos and a skull with a "rattle of femur and tibia, radius and ulna" (p.125). Chief among them is "Big Caesar," exact counterpart of the "giant mulatto" of *The Crystal World*, though instead of appearing like a snake and a crocodile, Caesar is "like an immense ape" (p.128) with a "huge knobbed face like an inflamed hippo's" (p.124).

In the four novels Ballard published in the 1960s, it is ostensibly some component of nature that goes berserk, though this is always at least an expression, if not an outright product, of human affairs. In the four novels published so far in the 1970s the apocalypse is man-made. In the first four novels, it is nature that obliterates twentieth-century urban civilization, with its machines and technology. In the last four novels, all located in one superurban environment (London), nature has disappeared and it is twentieth-century civilization that is self-destructing through its machines and technology and resulting psychological aberrations. In *Concrete Island*, for example, all that remains of the natural world is a small triangular plot of deep grass and weeds formed by the intersection of freeways, and in *High Rise* the fictional world is a self-contained apartment complex, something like a chunk of the unending urban hell of "Build-Up."

The unifying quest of the recent novels is no longer for a merging with nature, in the form of the ocean, sun, or forest, but with the machine itself. This quest characteristically takes the form of a bizarre attempt to achieve "a new sexuality born from a perverse technology."[15] *Love and Napalm:Export U.S.A.* sets forth this "new sexuality"[16] as the equation of human sex and "love" with car crashes, assassinations, napalm, B-52 raids, thermonuclear weapons, disembodied fragments of the human body, and the lines and angles of freeways, machines, wounds, and buildings (the sexiest structure is a multi-level parking garage that suggests both rape and death). The central symbol of this quest is the automobile.

Back in the short story "The Subliminal Man" (1963), Ballard had projected the automobile and the concrete milieu we construct for it as the basic economic and psychological fact of decaying capitalist society:

Whatever other criticisms might be levelled at the present society, it certainly knew how to build roads. Eight, ten and twelve-lane expressways interlaced across the continent, plunging from overhead causeways into the giant car parks in the centre of the cities, or dividing into the great suburban arteries with their multiacre parking aprons around the marketing centres. Together the roadways and car parks covered more than a third of the country's entire area...[17]

In "The Subliminal Man" Ballard did something extraordinary for him and unusual for any Anglo-American writer of science fiction: he subjected this future automobilized monopoly capitalist society to a rigorous analysis, showing how the psychology of the people within it is determined by the political economy. The vast forces of production, still ruled by capitalist social relations, become a colossal alien power, constantly producing more and more commodities and increasingly incapable of satisfying real human needs. If the commodities turned out by capitalist production actually satisfied human needs, they could be sold through rational description. Since this is clearly not the case, in capitalist society today advertising attempts to evade or manipulate our rational thought processes and to stimulate irrational desires. An entire industry spends millions of dollars annually just on research to discover new advertising techniques designed to exploit and intensify our desires for competitive success, power, riches, admiration, and sensation. In some cases less money is spent on products than their containers, which are intended to turn the aptlynamed "consumer" into a mindless robot, as Gerald Stahl, Executive Vice-President of the Package Designers Council, cogently explained: "You have to have a carton that attracts and hypnotizes this woman, like waving a flashlight in front of her eyes." In "The Subliminal Man" Ballard merely extrapolates from one advertising technique already utilized to reach the subconscious directly, subliminal messages beamed directly into the retina too fast to be recognized consciously. In a few pages, Ballard creates a nightmare vision of a monopoly capitalist society using this technique on a grand scale, successfully reducing each person to an automaton of mindless consumption, endlessly working, purchasing, and driving back and forth to jobs and supermarkets in a shiny new automobile on vast expressways under gigantic subliminal advertising signs whose shadows swing back and forth "like the dark blades of enormous scythes."[18]

The alienation of people within such a society and their increasing obsession with catastrophic death is a subject for deep exploration, and this is the primary subject of Ballard's subsequent fiction. The greatest strength of this late fiction is that it penetrates profoundly into the morbid psychology that comes from living in such a society; its most critical weakness is that in pursuing this exploration, Ballard loses sight of the underlying causation of the psychopathology of everyday life in decaying capitalism. He leaves behind his own best insights, in stories such as "The Overloaded Man," "The Impossible Man," "Build-Up," and "The Subliminal Man," which show the individual human being as the victim of an inhuman social structure, and begins to stand the world on its head, making the psychology of the individual the cause rather than the product of the death-oriented political economy.

Underlying the elaborate verbal structure of the late fiction are some fairly simple, in fact simple-minded, ideas about social reality. Indeed, the formal pyrotechnics disguise as much as they reveal of the ideational content. Clad in an elegant costume is the tired old idea that human nature is basically brutish and stupid, that people are inherently perverse, cruel, and self-destructive, and that's why the modern world is going to hell. *High Rise*, his latest novel, is virtually a parody of this notion. Such a vision, I believe, is merely a projection of Ballard's own class point of view, a myopia as misleading as the national and racial point of view in the earlier novels and intimately related to that narrow outlook.

Now some may think it unfair or inappropriate to discuss Ballard's late fiction as essentially political statement, but Ballard's recent art is profoundly political; in fact its content is most intensely political when its form is most "surreal." For example, *Love and Napalm:Export U.S.A.*, the most plotless, fragmented, surrealistic, and anti-novelistic of his long fictions, includes the following as explicit primary subjects: the Vietnam War; Hiroshima and Nagasaki; the massacres in Biafra and the Congo; the presidential candidacy of Ronald Reagan; the assassinations of Malcolm X, John F. Kennedy, Martin Luther King, and Robert Kennedy; Ralph Nader's campaign for automobile safety; the use of napalm as a weapon; and the use of sex as a commodity. An author who did not want his work to be discussed politically would (or should) choose different subject matter.

In *Love and Napalm* Ballard presents the fashionable liberal idea that "America is a land of violence"; that's the fundamental lesson, he tells us, of Hiroshima and Dallas, Los Angeles and Memphis, Hollywood and Saigon. (See, for example, the section entitled "The Generations of America," a four-page list of who shot instead of begot—whom in America.) This is summed up commonly in that cliche we've been hearing since 1963: "Oswald may have pulled the trigger, but wasn't it all that hate and violence in America that loaded the gun?" With all its fancy tricks, this is one of the dominant messages of *Love and Napalm*, which actually ends with these final words: "Without doubt Oswald badly misfired. But one question still remains unanswered: who loaded the starting gun?" The implied answer is that we did, with our morbid psychology, which will lead to the first word of the book, "Apocalypse." But is it true that Lee Harvey Oswald, as well as the assassins of Malcolm X, Robert Kennedy, and Martin Luther King, were just products of the diseased psychology of the American people? Those of us who believe there is overwhelming evidence indicating the direct involvement of the secret government of the U.S.A. in the assassination of each of these men make quite a contradictory political analysis from that offered by *Love and Napalm*. For if indeed the government must carry out assassinations of popular leaders and then engage in elaborate cover-ups based on stealth and deceit, this would certainly suggest that it does not express the will or desires of the American people. The same kind of contradiction appears for each of the other political premises of *Love and Napalm.* The book argues, for example, that the Vietnam War went on so long because it appealed deeply to the subconscious sexual desires of the American people. In a parody of consumer research, and in a kind of self parody, Ballard writes:

The latent sexual character of the war. All political and military explanations fail to provide a rationale for the war's extended duration. In its manifest phase the war can be seen as a limited military confrontation with strong audience participation via TV and news media, satisfying low-threshold fantasies of violence and aggression. Tests confirm that the war has also served a latent role of strongly polymorphic character. Endless-loop combat and atrocity newreels were intercut with material of genital, axillary, buccal and anal character. The expressed faecal matter of execution sequences was found to have a particular fascination for middle-income housewives (p.131).

But the fact is that the American people's massive and militant opposition to the war was one of the principal reasons the government could not continue to conduct it. This anti-war movement, one virtually unprecedented in history, appears in only one passage in the book:

Further tests were devised to assess the latent sexual fantasies of anti-war demonstrators. These confirm the hysterical nature of reactions to films of napalm victims and A.R.V.N. atrocities, and indicate that for the majority of so-called peace groups the Vietnam war serves the role of masking repressed sexual inadequacies of an extreme nature (pp.131-132.).

Sure this is cast as parody, but that is essentially mere disguise, for any recognition of the historical and moral significance of the anti-war movement would cause the nightmare vision of the book to dissolve just like any other bad dream.

This brings us back to the automobile, the central symbol of Ballard's nightmare. Ballard's choice of the automobile as emblem and synecdoche for the apocalypse is splendid. In the U.S., "25 cents out of every dollar spent at retail is connected with the auto... The automobile annually consumes...64.2 percent of the Nation's rubber production, 21 percent of all its steel, 54.7 percent of the lead, 40 percent of the malleable iron, 36.5 percent of the zinc..."[19] As Dutch economist Andre van Dam notes: "Each year automobiles kill 180,000 people worldwide, permanently maim 480,000, and injure 8,000,000. Car accidents account for 3% of the gross national product in the industrial nations, a huge sum that should be subtracted from the GNP rather than added to it."[20] And in the words of "American Ground Transport," a report submitted to the U.S. Senate Subcommittee on Antitrust and Monopoly: "We are witnessing today the collapse of a society based on the automobile."[21] But Ballard's failure to understand the source of this collapse, or rather his failure to carry forward the understanding he reached in "The Subliminal Man," leaves him mistaking the end of capitalism for the end of the world.

First, the Los Angelesation of capitalist society has not been primarily a product of Anglo-American mass psychology. As the report cited above thoroughly documents, it was the giant automobile companies that consciously, systematically, and ruthlessly destroyed all competing forms of mass transportation. Prior to the Depression, most large American cities had a virtually pollution-free electric railway system. Betwen 1935 and 1956, General Motors alone bought up "more than 100 electric surface rail systems in 45 cities," disposed of them as scrap, set up subsidiary bus companies with fleets of General Motors buses, and used its enormous political leverage to have the cities redesigned for automobiles and buses.[22] Los Angeles is indeed the model city for what the automobile monopoly could do:

Thirty-five years ago Los Angeles was a beautiful city of lush palm trees, fragrant orange groves and ocean-clean air. It was served then by the world's largest electric railway network. In the late 1930's General Motors and allied highway interests acquired the local transit companies, scrapped their pollution-free electric trains, tore down their power transmission lines, ripped up their tracks, and placed GM buses on already congested Los Angeles streets. The noisy, foul-smelling buses turned earlier patrons of the high-speed rail system away from public transit and, in effect, sold millions of private automobiles. Largely as a result, this city is today an ecological wasteland: the palm trees are dying of petrochemical smog; the orange groves have been paved over by 300 miles of freeways; the air is a septic tank into which 4 million cars, half of them built by General Motors, pump 13,000 tons of pollutants daily.[23]

And if the slogan of General Motors was once "What's good for General Motors is good for America," it's true that GM must long since have added parenthetically "Today America, tomorrow the world." But frightening as the spectacle may be of the world being converted into a gigantic Los Angeles, no such possibility exists in reality. Ronald Reagan's cheerful boast that "We could pave Vietnam over and be home by Christmas," with its ironies too complex to count, proved to be just as phantasmagorical as Ballard's cheerless vision of the same kind of event. The empire based on the auto economy is no longer expanding, but collapsing and dying, largely because the majority of people in the world are in the process of creating a more advanced social system.

Although Ballard's brilliant imagination penetrates deeply into the symbolic significance of the automobile, it is determined by his class outlook and therefore operates within very narrow limits. From his class point of view, automobiles exist only as objects of consumption—first economic and now primarily psychological—and destruction. In *Crash* they have come to consume and embody an anti-human sexuality. In *Concrete Island* they are not only the vehicle of self-destruction but of willful self-isolation in the cellular island prison formed by a society of speeding machines, concrete speedways, and "normal" individuals who race back and forth to work and empty relationships with other individuals. The millions upon millions of automobiles just appear ready-made on the scene. With the notable and revealing exception of "The Subliminal Man," in which Dr. Franklin has to augment his income by working Sundays as "visiting factory doctor to one of the automobile plants that had started Sunday shifts" (p.255), there is no sense whatever that automobiles and their milieu are physically constructed by the tens of millions of people around the world extracting raw materials from the earth, manufacturing steel, tires, glass, concrete, and petroleum products, and assembling the finished machines in factories designed to turn them also into facsimiles of automata. Ballard, because his outlook is that of a minority sub-class of petty bourgeois intellectuals rather than that of the vast majority of people who work in the mines, mills, factories, fields, refineries, offices, hospitals, transportation systems, stores, and forests of the world, sees the automobile only as something that is consumed or consumes. Hence the exquisite symbolic logic of the cannibalistic and ritualistic re-arrangement of the pieces of cars. In *Love and Napalm* and *Crash*, this primarily takes the form of the sexual fantasies of mingled human and mechanical parts in car crashes. In *Concrete Island* and earlier, *The Drought,* this takes the form of elaborate buildings contrived from wrecked and abandoned cars: Lomax, the Hardoon of *The Drought,* is an architect who creates a "bejewelled temple" out of the abandoned machines of civilization; when Robert Maitland, architect and protagonist of *Concrete Island*, has his man Friday build a shack for him, it is one made "out of the discarded sections of car bodies."[24]

The working people of Ballard's own society rarely appear in his field of view, and when they do, they resemble Morlocks. In fact, when Ballard imagines a society "where," he tells us, "I would be happy to live,"[25] it is the world of *Vermilion Sands*, a weird hedonistic playground and sandbox for infantile artists who resemble incipient Eloi, safely isolated from the terrors of the city and totally untroubled by the intrusion of any workers except chauffeurs, maids, butlers, and personal secretaries. The working people of the rest of the world are no longer presented as the superstitious, treacherous, terrifying savages of *The Drowned World* and *The Crystal World;* they simply have disappeared from view altogether.

Hence Ballard's imagined world is reduced to the dimensions of that island created by intertwined expressways on which individuals in their cellular commodities hurtle to their destruction or that apartment complex in which the wealthy and professional classes degenerate into anarchic tribal warfare among themselves. And hence Ballard accurately, indeed magnificently, projects the doomed social structure in which he exists. What could Ballard create if he were able to envision the end of capitalism as not the end, but the beginning, of a human world?

Joe De Bolt

The Development
of
John Brunner

Since John Brunner began to publish fiction in the early 1950s, he has produced scores of stories and novels.[1] His career may be divided into three major stages: 1953-1958, the early period dominated by traditional science fiction and an emphasis upon action; 1959-1967, the transitional period dominated by science fiction-mainstream hybrids[2] and a heightened interest in characterization; and 1968-1978, the mature period dominated by dystopian works and a preoccupation with society. Each of these stages has built upon the developments of its predecessor.

Brunner exhibited an early interest in types of fiction other than science fiction, and these various types—including fantasy, mainstream, and mystery-suspense—constitute modes which, once having branched from the parent science fiction stalk, have continued throughout his subsequent work. In addition, his science fiction itself has undergone subdivision, first into a science fiction-mainstream fusion and later into dystopias and revisions of earlier works. Because stylistic advances in his handling of each type of fiction have influenced the others, one may make the first of two broad generalizations giving order to the breadth and variety of his fiction: throughout his writing career, Brunner has exhibited continual growth in the craft of writing.

The second generalization involves Brunner's themes. Chief among these are his social concerns—war, poverty, overpopulation, ethnocentrism, greed, racism, and oppression are typical examples. Of equal importance are the behavior and capacities of the mind, including the effects of drugs; the emergence of superior mental processes; and the domination of mind over mind. He probably pays as much attention to science and technology as do most science fiction writers, but for the most part he is content to see technology

106

as a tool rather than a monster, its consequences flowing from the good or evil uses to which it is put by individuals and societies. Science is a worthy pursuit, provided humanity grows along with its knowledge; otherwise, humanity's own cleverness may do it in. Given this perspective, social concerns and the human mind assume a greater significance for Brunner than does the mere development of, or danger from science and technology.

Finally, Brunner believes in human progress; sees rationality and emotionality as jointly important for that progress; and generally embraces the liberal, democratic, egalitarian, and individually-fulfilling vision of the future long prominent in the West. He cares intensely enough about human survival and the realization of that vision to devote much of his major fiction to social instruction. His stories frequently teach, warn, moralize, and otherwise carry messages; it is to his great credit as a writer that they also entertain. Hence the second generalization: although Brunner does not offer a totally consistent philosophy in all his works, he has exhibited a strikingly consistent core of themes.

The Early Period: 1953-1958

The parent stalk of all of Brunner's fiction is, of course, science fiction. As a boy he had immersed himself in the science fiction of the times, and his early works show that influence; all of the settings of the genre are there, waiting both for action to infuse them with life and for the writer's insights and interests to shape their meanings. It was into this mold that Brunner began pouring his imagination.

The first works appeared in 1953.[3] In one of these, "Thou Good and Faithful" (1953), so many of Brunner's career-long concerns appear that it is worth dwelling on. It tells of an expedition from an overcrowded Earth searching for new planets to colonize. Action abounds as the explorers puzzle out the mystery of a beautiful park-like planet tended by advanced humanoid robots who also keep pets. There is enough ship maneuvering and technical detail to satisfy the *Astounding* reader of the times, while the robots and their pets add a touch of Simak's whimsy; but in hindsight, it is the social themes that dominate the story. Earth has been ruined by overpopulation and advanced industrialization:

...Deeley turned and stared out across the greenness of the plain to the blue hills on the horizon. He said softly, "...It's Earth as it may have been a thousand years ago, but there hasn't been room for this much peacefulness and beauty on Earth for a good many centuries. That's why I emigrated—to find a chance to be alone."

Chang nodded.... He said, "It's gotten that way on New Earth, too—where I was born. No place for beauty any more. Too much overcrowding. Too much to do and too little time to do it."

"Uh uh," agreed Keston with a touch of cynicism. "But by the same token, if this world is uninhabited our fortunes'll be made by the spill-over from those same

overcrowded planets."
"What a mess that'll make," said Adhem seriously.[4]

Moreover, the technology developed by humanity has not liberated it; rather, people still are capable of feeling that they are becoming subservient to their machines. When faced with the conclusion that the robots on the new-found planet are sentient, one of the crewmen exclaims:

"You know what this reminds me of? The time I talked to the big brain on Canopus X and XI. I wouldn't go through that again if I was paid. I was terrified."
"Why?" Deeley wanted to know.
"Well, I suppose it wasn't really fright so much as awe—the knowing that this man-made thing was ten times as intelligent as its builders and knew ten thousand times as much as any man could hope to learn in a lifetime. But at the bottom of it was always the fear that the servant would become the master."
Chang stuffed his pipe afresh, forcing himself to feel calm. He said, "Here the fear has become reality" (p.33).

But the robots have not done in their masters, nor do they pose a threat to the Earthmen. They received the planet as a gift from their grateful masters and offer it, in turn, as a gift to humanity, provided that they may serve humanity as well. Indeed, the robots so freed their original creators from discontent that they did not seek the stars in a meaningless quest for living space. Their creators turned instead from the physical sciences to the mental sciences and, becoming "pure mind," evolved to a higher level of existence, something their machines could never do. As the master computer which coordinates the world of the robots explains to the skeptical Earthmen:

"Yes, our creators outstripped us. They merged in a being as far superior to me as I am to you. They became pure mind, and they no longer needed us. But because without our aid they could not have achieved what they did, they were grateful, and though we cannot evolve, being machines without power of growth, they did what they could for us. They gave us our freedom, and a sense of beauty, and their technology which had become our technology over the years, and most important, they gave us what we most desired—this world" (p.46).

Now these machines offer their world and themselves, and the same possibility for transcendence, to humanity. For humanity, Chang, the ship's captain, accepts. Thus technology—at least that designed for positive benefit—can be a springboard for liberation and for both human material *and* spiritual progress, an antidote to the endless proliferation of people and the ensuing social problems.

"Brainpower" (1953) might appear to contradict such a view of technology, for it posits an advanced computer, built by the outer planets of the solar system as a weapon against the Earth-dominated confederation of inner planets; the computer becomes a threat to all humanity:

"The brain," said Finklman deliberately, "is too intelligent to let itself be bothered by men."

"In fact, I doubt if it will even let us survive."[5]

Despite the story's traditional Frankenstein plot of a gadget turning on its creator, one should note that the computer was created as a *weapon* and that its rebellion will at least have the consequence of uniting warring humanity against the common enemy.

Brunner returns again to the theme of mental evolution in "Tomorrow Is Another Day" (1954).[6] Mental sensitives are evolving within humanity and control human development; however, while one group, the "libido," representing "the main drives of the race," steers humanity toward progress, a second group, the "mortido," deplores the noisome byproducts of progress—the wars, pestilence, overpopulation, hunger, and poverty—and attempts to push humanity to extinction. Both sides contend for August Michel, whose unique genetic endowment may tip the balance for either side. But Michel ends by having none of their struggle, for he is true "super-consciousness" and realizes that both libido and mortido are necessary for sanity. As Michel leaves the warring parties, having willed them to forget him so that they can continue their "birth pangs of a new creation," it is interesting to note that it is December in the story, the traditional season of rebirth.

That progress is desirable is never in doubt for Brunner, although the paths for progress are generally those borrowed from the science fiction genre of the times. And if humanity, or another intelligent species, is stymied in its development, then a little outside help is always in order; Brunner is not a defender of social Darwinism. Thus, in "Armistice" (1955), aliens (or perhaps superhumans) have undertaken the task of freeing humanity from a "blind alley" of mental conformity and lost initiative and imagination imposed by the apparent necessity of governing farflung interstellar colonies:

"And in the name of government you stopped the growth of the human mind—you stifled thought? You turned men into hive-minded insects?"[7]

Indeed, it was the aliens' unusual mental processes—ones which humanity once possessed—that led to their capture on one of the colony worlds; their captor explained:

"I knew that you and Noorden could not be entirely human. You think too much. Your brainwaves weren't consistent with your pretended behavior. And men do not pretend any more" (pp. 74-75).

Most of the story is a contest of wills and words between the captive Kerguelen and his captor, the planet's "custodian-in-chief," Talbot, who is exceptional among the humans of his day. He sees the harmful consequences of human complacency but can think of no alternative. He desperately questions Kerguelen, hoping for an answer: "How do you rule chaos?" Kerguelen replies, "We have no government":

"But how can you exist without one?"

"Why should we not? What does your central control do?"

"It stopped wars. It stopped plague and famine and fear."

"It stopped humanity," said Kerguelen flatly. "We, too, once had wars and the other things you name. Now we have none, yet we have more planets and many more people than you. You created a State and made it your father and mother, your schoolteacher and even your lover. You grew so dependent on it that now you are afraid of what might happen without it. In fact, you have made everybody so scared that if you did do away with it everything you fear would probably happen because people felt it was expected of them" (p.76).

That is the crux of the problem; the status quo must be destroyed, civilization perhaps turned back to the primitive, for humanity to evolve again—this time out of its blind alley. And this is the mission of the aliens; they know that humanity's fear will prevent it from choosing this path reasonably, and its pride precludes the possibility of open help. So the work must be done secretly, and Kerguelen precipitates his own death to preserve the mission.

Perhaps, in time, it will be humanity's turn to help other species progress; this is the point of "By the Name of Man" (1956). Earthmen play God to the natives of Venus, helping the primitive villagers to improve gradually their material well being. Reciprocally, playing God makes one a better person, for "nothing makes a man mend his habits faster than having someone look up to him."[8]

Often in time travel stories citizens from the future have returned to the present era in order to guide humanity along better paths; Brunner employs this device in "Host Age" (1956). A mysterious disease, caused by a pathogen which can be cultured only on human tissue and which seems infinitely adaptable to all forms of treatments, attacks one in ten and kills one in ten of these. A troop of soldiers from the future have purposely spread the disease in the present in order to insure humanity's survival in their own time, when a strong alien enemy, the creator of the disease, has almost wiped out humankind. The alien's victory derives from future humanity's success in eradicating all diseases, thereby rendering the species extremely vulnerable to biological warfare. With the super-virus now loose in the past, medicine will never achieve such a goal, and humanity, having developed a high tolerance to the disease, will eventually be victorious over the aliens. Yet the cost to the present is the death of 1% of Earth's population and the disruption of the social order for some time. Those in the present are given no choice in paying this price, but ultimate survival for the species is assured.

Throughout this early period, and in the next period as well, Brunner continually rings changes on traditional science fiction plots. In "Visitors' Book" (1955) technologically superior aliens invading the solar system are bluffed into fleeing by the human defenders through the use of a clever psychological ploy. "Lungfish" (1957) is the metaphoric title of a story in which intended interstellar colonists, born on board the space-ark during its journey, refuse to land at trip's end; although the mission's manifest function of planetary colonization fails, the trip-born prove to be the precursors of a humanity evolved to dwell in space. The humorous unintentional consequences of a new technology are depicted in "Out of Order" (1957), when an automated designing-manufacturing-distributing system, "Supply Central," takes literally a rush order, spoken in colloquial exaggeration, to deliver the items "yesterday..." "Two by Two" (1956) is a creation story in which the sole surviving human, an astronaut saved from a solar nova by being on the side of the moon away from the sun, returns to the burned Earth in search of life. But all is dead, except for the microbes in his ship and body, and these, he realizes, will eventually replenish the Earth. Conquering the planets is the theme of "The Number of My Days" (1956), in which extraterrestrial engineers build a dome on Venus as a step in that planet's terraforming and sweat out the bane of their profession, the "death call," the statistical prediction of fatalities on a given job. "Threshold of Eternity" (serialized, 1957-1958; published as a book, 1959) is space warfare on a grand scale, as beleaguered humanity strives with every erg to drive out an alien invader. Interestingly, humanity's defense hinges on super-computers joined with human minds, a kind of ultimate human-machine symbiosis. "Eye of the Beholder" (1957) is a first contact story in which the gentle alien, a talented painter, is killed by the spaceship-wrecked humans he is trying to aid. In this parable, the killer is a woman, beautiful of body but ugly of soul, while the victim, at least in humanity's ethnocentric terms, reverses these features.

Even in these early years of his career, Brunner was interested in increasing his range and sharpening his craft. "Puzzle for Spacemen" (1955) is a murder mystery—a murder in a locked spaceship as it were—in which a spaceship's company's psychologist undertakes the investigation of an alleged suicide at a deep-space "Earth-Jupiter line-of-sight radio relay" station undergoing construction. He solves the crime but in keeping with

Brunner's themes, probably loses his job. Murder means that a huge damage claim must be paid by his company; the alternative, suicide, would cast doubt on the reliability of psychological testing, and this the psychologist couldn't allow: "Our knowledge of our own limitations is one of our most powerful weapons against the universe. We *must* be able to rely on it."[9]

Brunner chose a historical setting, medieval Europe, for "No Future in It" (1955), a comedic tale of an itinerant cow doctor who is mistaken for a wizard and finds himself trapped into producing gold for his merchant master. Unfortunately, magic doesn't work, but the magician does succeed in accidentally catching a time traveler in his pentacle. Before continuing his journey, the kindly man from the future transmutes an iron pot into gold, thereby saving the false wizard's hide. But the cow doctor has learned his lesson; as he prepares to flee his workshop, he advises his young apprentice, "Avoid magic—'tis a perilous calling, and there's no future in it."[10]

Horror is the mood of "The Biggest Game" (1956), in which a gigolo who preys on foolish women ends up himself the quarry of aliens disguised as humans. He will be stuffed and mounted, a prize trophy from this successful hunt. Of course he only gets what he deserves; in Brunner's fiction there persists a strong tendency for the virtuous to be rewarded and the evil punished. "The Biggest Game" represents a step away from Brunner's science fiction core and, coupled with "Fair" (1956) and "This Rough Magic" (1956), marks the initial appearance of a mode of science fiction-mainstream hybridization which will dominate the next period of his work. It also shares a contemporary setting with "This Rough Magic," which was later expanded into the novel *Black Is the Color* (1969). Magic works here as a powerful psychological weapon in the conflict between members of a racist conspiracy attempting to exacerbate the racial tension in Britain and a small group of integrationists who happen upon the plot.

"Fair" displays a typical Brunner theme—the overcoming of racism, nationalism, and other ethnocentric beliefs which divide humanity and threaten nuclear war—although it is more noteworthy for the sophisticated and effective writing in the first two-thirds of the narrative. The flash, color, and noise of the fair are there, of course, but so are the despair and emptiness of this gaudy world without a purpose, without a future, where the rides only return one to the starting point, where there is only escapism but no escape. This is Brunner's early masterpiece of description. A rich depiction of character appears only in Brunner's next period and in "The Whole Man" (1959).

Fantasy also splits from Brunner's science fiction in this early period.[11] Although it will never become his strongest suit, several works of merit do appear within it in the later periods. Moreover, it is the mode within which one of his most common and effective

devices—the literal and/or symbolic control of one mind by
another—is nurtured. This device, and with it the origins of his
fantasy, make their appearance in his first published novel, "The
Wanton of Argus" (1953), later retitled *The Space Time Juggler*
(1963).[12] This is a sword-and-sorcery novel into which Brunner
threw nearly every cliché in that genre. It is part of his Galactic
Emprie series, now collected in the single volume, *Interstellar
Empire* (1976), and qualifies as science fiction in that the "magic" of
Kelab the Conjurer is really the product of extraordinarily
developed mental powers. Yet in the novel's climax the battle of
minds between Kelab and the equally endowed villain takes on the
trappings and mood of fantasy as mental illusions are shaped and
shattered.

   This battle of illusions, or at least the one-sided imposition of
illusion, recurs in its literal sense again and again in his fiction,
including such works as *The Whole Man* (1964), *Father of Lies*
(1968), *The Gaudy Shadows* (1970), and *The Traveler in Black*
(1971). Equally common, however, is its occurrence in symbolic
form, where one person's will dominates that of another. This, too,
originates in Brunner's early period; "A Time to Rend" (1956;
expanded as "No Other Gods But Me" in 1966) involves the invasion
of this world, with its technologically-oriented human culture, by
the psychically-dominated people from a parallel Earth. Their
leader, Telthis, is pure evil, as are the villains in *The Atlantic
Abomination* (1960) and *The Devil's Work* (1970), all of whom share
the desire and ability to control the wills of others. Brunner has
remained strongly attracted to this theme.

   Two pure fantasies published in this early period further
illustrate the extension of Brunner's range. "Death Do Us Part"
(1955) is a humorous ghost story in which an ancient shade seeks out
a modern-day lawyer in order to obtain a divorce from his
unpleasant ghostly wife. Brunner maintains his light touch in
"When Gabriel . . ." (1956); an unsuspecting jazz musician is handed
Gabriel's trumpet by the Devil and, when he plays it in a nightclub
which had formerly been a crypt, he raises the dead.

   In 1958 Brunner's early period came to an end. He had created a
broad spectrum of science fiction, and he had branched out into both
a science fiction-mainstream hybridization and fantasy. No single
major work marks the close of this period or provides a bridge to the
next. Still, one work in this final year is worthy of attention. "Earth
is but a Star" (1958) is the story of a quest for someone to care about
the future. Later published as *The 100th Millennium* (1959) and
revised as *Catch a Falling Star* (1968), it is set in the far future when
the challenge has gone out of human life and much of the world is
sliding into decadence. The hero, Creohan, a maverick in his culture,
has discovered that a visiting star will destroy the Earth in 300

years. Very few show concern. In this novel the mind-controlling illusions occur off-stage—in the House of History, where citizens seeking escape from the present have grown addicted to visions of earlier, more vigorous ages:

> But for the rest of the people—why, they live and laugh and love and there's an end of it. They know they will be dead in any case before this disaster happens—what interest has it for them? It seems to me as though all the spirit that motivated these lusty ages the Historians flee to has been drained from our modern breed![13]

Creohan and a few companions set out in search of some present or past culture which possesses the power to turn the approaching star aside; failing that, they hope at least to find some people who will mourn for Earth. Their quest ends in failure.

Actually, the star is under the control of a culture of humans who left Earth a hundred thousand years before the time of Creohan. The Earth's apparent death will prove to be a rebirth, for the culture of these voyagers stands in marked contrast to the stagnated one of the Historians:

> They were possessed of a curiosity which at times approached an obsession; what lay at the end of their trail of knowledge-getting they never inquired—perhaps they had a vague idea it was happiness; much more likely, to Creohan's way of thinking (for he felt he understood these people), it was the satisfaction of having attained a self-imposed objective and therewith overcoming their limitations (p.106).

Perhaps Brunner shared Creohan's admiration of this point of view; certainly the works of his next period reflect it.

The Transitional Period: 1959-1967

The year 1959 not only distinctly marked the beginning of a second period in Brunner's work, it also was the first year of his still-successful career as a full-time, free-lance writer.[14] There was continuity with the initial period, as the three already established narrative modes in his work—science fiction, fantasy, and the science fiction-mainstream hybrid—continued, but two major changes did occur which demonstrate that a watershed had been crossed. First, two new modes—mainstream *per se* and mystery-suspense fictions—make an appearance almost immediately, while, secondly, major advances in craftmanship occur, particularly in terms of character development. Indeed, most of his best shorter fiction was written during this period, especially within the science fiction-mainstream hybrids. Several of his best novels were also completed during this period.

Although by far the largest portion of his writing in terms of quantity, Brunner's orthodox science fiction of this period is weakest in terms of quality; yet his writing itself continues to improve as the lessons he has learned from his other modes are incorporated into his science fiction. *The World Swappers* (1959) and *Echo in the Skull* (1959) are very much a piece with his earlier work. In the former, a creative genius, Said Counce, has invented a matter transmitter that not only makes instantaneous interstellar travel possible, but immortality as well, since recordings of persons can be used to duplicate them when they die. Counce has kept this invention secret for 300 years, using it as a nucleus about which to gather 3000 idealistic men and women in a secret organization to serve others. He perfects a scheme to insure peaceful relations between humans, especially those who were once misfits and dissidents and who fled overcrowded Earth to establish colonies on other planets, and aliens who must eventually be encountered. The plan works, although the cost of survival is high for some, such as the ten million puritan settlers on a overly harsh planet who are starved into leaving so that cold-adapted aliens can have the planet as the basis for peace. Also, the rich and ambitious Earthman, Bassett, who was used by Counce to help implement his plan, must die. His type, with such great power, has no place in a peaceful tolerant universe. Counce tells him: "You are an enemy of mankind, because your only friend is yourself."[15]

Echo in the Skull—revised as *Give Warning to the World* 1974)—involves Earth's invasion by an alien monster, a member of a race of beings spreading through the galaxy who parasitize humans in order to reproduce themselves. The offspring attach to the victim's back, forming greenish, wet patches that are "soft and yielding like a bladder filled with half-melted grease."[16] The setting is contemporary London, the chief characters are an amnesiac young woman, Sally Ercott, who is being driven mad by "visions" of life on other worlds, and a young man, Nick Jenkins, who rescues her. Together they end the threat of Brunner's version of *The Puppet Masters*. Sally's visions are really warnings from a "pool of interracial memory" derived from those who died under the monsters' yoke. Of course boy gets girl in the end.

The significant point about these two novels is that both contain lead characters with special mental abilities. Nick says of himself, "But I have an odd sort of mind...I sort of have the knack of putting two and one-and-a-half together..." (p.91). He is an inventor by occupation, and open-minded enough to guess that Sally's delusions are real glimpses of life on other worlds. Counce's mental processes seem identical; he has "the ability to stand a problem on its head, so that it loses its difficulty. It isn't a conscious talent. It's just a gift."[17] And recall that he invented the matter transmitter. These characters exhibit the prototypes of another of Brunner's favorite devices, the intuitive problem solver—of the innately lucky person, or the polymath, or the synthesist—which appears in numerous variations in such works as *Meeting at*

Infinity (1961), *Castaways World* (1963), *Enigma from Tantalus* (1965), *Stand on Zanzibar* (1968), and *The Stone That Never Came Down* (1973).

Whereas Nick Jenkins and Said Counce use their talents to save humanity and are rewarded for it, Joe Munday, of "The Trouble I See" (1959), uses a similar talent—the ability to feel if any given action will have harmful effects on him—for personal gain and is destroyed by it. The same happens to Donald Hogan, the synthesist of *Stand on Zanzibar,* whose talent is used in the service of government espionage.

In "Round Trip" (1959), it is the psychological trait of curiosity which receives attention again. Humans have traveled to the location of the original "big bang" only to find a giant space ship containing evidence that the universe is cyclical. Perfectly cyclical, for the expedition's leader discovers that an inner vault of the ship contains a doppelganger of himself, and, he explains in a touching letter to his wife, he must take his double's place to preserve the balance of things, leaving his double to return to her. Why did the first person enter the vault in the universe's first cycle?—to "verify with our direct perceptions what is predicted by our tools..."[18]

"Elected Silence" 1959) is the powerful story of a man held captive in a tiny cell by enemy aliens for twenty-eight years. Rescued by his own military forces and subjected to interrogation by mental probes without having the opportunity to adjust to human social life, he rebels and flees to his death in a life-boat almost identical to his cell. Human or alien, both were his captors, torturers of his mind. The depth of characterization is unusual for Brunner's early work, and it is clearly the focus of his attention rather than the action. This increased interest in motivation and the inner struggles of the mind find their greatest flowering, however, in the science fiction-mainstream hybridization, beginning with the character of Gerald Howson.

In "The Whole Man" (1959)—published in the same year as "Curative Telepath"—Howson, a slum child, born a misshapen dwarf and hemophiliac, is one of the world's most powerful telepaths. As an adult he uses his talent to treat the mentally ill. Unfortunately, other telepaths at times abuse their talent by linking minds with non-telepaths for whom they create vivid fantasy worlds. Such individuals enter catatonia and will die unless rescued by another telepath. "City of the Tiger" (1958)—republished in 1959 as a companion to "Curative Telepath"[19]—tells of such a rescue by Howson. Its setting is pure fantasy, a far Eastern city with emperor, dragons, swordsmen, and sorcerers; as such, this story makes a contribution to Brunner's development as a fantasy writer, for it is only in the final scene that the reader discovers that all is illusion.

The second Howson story, "The Whole Man," is the one in which the troubled personality of the crippled superman is explored as he returns to his roots in search of a place in human society. Ultimately, he discovers a satisfying new role: he gives mental concerts before thousands to whom he projects uplifting visions, thereby making both telepathy and his work with the mentally ill less frightening to the public. These two stories, revised and expanded, were issed as *The Whole Man* (1964, *Telepathist* in Britain) one of Brunner's best early novels. It marks a highpoint in the development of his craft to that date and stands far above anything from his earlier period.

One of the works profiting almost immediately from Brunner's growth as a writer—and one very much a science fiction-mainstream cross—was *The Squares of the City* (1965). Although finished in 1960, it did not see print for five years; this undoubtedly handicapped Brunner's career, for it, too, is one of his best early novels. The social relevance which Brunner sought did not find ready expression in his science fiction of those years, but by placing stories quite close to the present and using social settings in which current problems abound, he found that he could combine good fiction and social comment. This is similar to, if not the beginning of, the method he used so successfully in his later dystopian works, beginning with *Stand on Zanzibar* (1968).

The Squares of the City is set in the teeming, modernistic capital of a developing nation in South America. The hero, Boyd Hakluyt, is a traffic analyst who believes he has been brought in to clear up the congestion resulting from the hordes of homeless squatters infesting the city. Actually, he is a pawn—or more precisely, a knight—in a deadly game being played by two political leaders representing different factions of the society. They have agreed to play human chess, winner take the country, instead of having an open civil war. Individuals are manipulated by subliminal perception to perform the players' "moves." Hakluyt uncovers the intrigue, precipitates the cessation of the game, and as the city slips into war, flees the country. He returns, however, facing the fact that he has helped to create the disaster and must share in the guilt: "Anyone is guilty who has so far renounced his right to think and act rationally that someone else can press his buttons and make him dance".[20]

Brunner's social concerns also found an outlet when he began his series of mainstream works with *The Brink* (1959), a novel in which nuclear war almost erupts when a Russian space shot—their first attempt at a manned satellite—crashes near an Air Force base in Nebraska. Brunner's apprehension about nuclear weapons testing and war was of long standing; he actively campaigned with the nuclear disarmament movement in Britain, wrote a marching

song for it— "The H-Bombs' Thunder," published in *Sing* (1958)—
and helped with the journal *Sanity*. His experiences in the
movement served as the basis for a second mainstream novel,
Manalive, written about 1961 but never published. He considers that
book to be one of his best writing efforts up to that time.[21] One short
fragment of the narrative can be found in *The Book of John Brunner*
(1976), where "The H-Bombs' Thunder" is also reprinted. Perhaps
he sensed that the reading public was not yet tuned in to his brand of
social criticism, or perhaps his interests in character development
pushed such explicit social comment aside for the moment. For
whatever reasons, he turned away from overt forms of social
commentary, except in the more indirect and somewhat disguised
form typical of science fiction of the early 1960s, and did not return
to it again until *Stand on Zanzibar* late in that tumultuous decade.

Continuing to work with mainstream fiction, he produced *The
Crutch of Memory* (1964), an excellent novel probing the
consciousness of a young man suffering from impotence as a result
of childhood traumas. As the protagonist transits Europe on his
way to a holiday in Greece, he meets a sensitive and independent
young woman. The book traces their developing romance across the
splendor of the Grecian landscape. Description and
characterization blend effectively to produce an absorbing work. Its
opening lines read:

> In that country a light so pure the air itself is luminous has penetrated the earth
> and laid bare its bones. They rise ribbed and huge behind the underscore of sea.
> I shall go back into that light—but not yet. I would not dare, yet.
> I, I, I—I am a sort of a writer. Of all words, that vertical stroke 'I' comes easiest to
> me.
> But there the verticals are cypresses and they stood in groves when men sought
> counsel of oracles...It is like being one of the black figures in an optical illusion:
> perspective lines converge around you and reduce your stature. These lines converge
> to the beginning of time.[22]

This work marked Brunner's initial major exploration of the sexual
psyche; he would return to it several times again, especially in terms
of the domination of one partner's will by another's, even to the
point of depravity, as exemplified in "The Evil That Men Do" (1966),
Quicksand (1967), *Black Is the Color* (1969), and *The Devil's Work*
(1970).

The psychologically bizarre emerges in unique form in one final
mainstream work from this period, "The Nail in the Middle of the
Hand" (1965). The setting of this short story is historical, the height
of the Roman Empire; the event, the crucifixion of Christ; the
protagonist, the expert but mundane crucifier, Decius Asculus, who
takes joyful pride in his workmanship—until he glances up and
meets the eyes of the passive one who went to the cross without a
struggle. That night they find Decius in the barracks, one hand

already nailed to the table before him, pondering how to do the other one—perhaps by holding the hammer in his teeth.

Brunner launched still another mode—mystery-suspense—in the early years of this transitional period with the story "The Gaudy Shadows" (1960), revised and expanded as a book in 1970. It concerns the misuse of mind-altering drugs by their inventor. Rather than employing them for research or therapy, he uses them to entertain well-paying rich at private parties and to murder his opponents. During an attack on the story's hero, this villain inadvertently whiffs one of his own chemicals—a depressant strong enough to cause one to suicide—and is driven into a foetal ball of madness. As with the other Brunner motifs mentioned, powerful drugs appear frequently in his works: from "Put Down This Earth" (1961)—retitled *The Dreaming Earth* (1963)—where they make people disappear; through *The Sheep Look Up* (1972), where Denver trips out on nerve gas; to "The Taste of the Dish and the Savor of the Day" (1977), where an addictively delicious food bestows immortality if one eats nothing else. Brunner's speculative pharmaceutics would sustain a study in themsevles.

Brunner's second mystery, *Wear the Butcher's Medal* (1965) did not appear until five years after his first. A young American, Phil Burns, drifting across Europe, uncovers a plot by neo-Nazis to smuggle weapons into East Germany for an uprising which will perhaps trigger World War Three. Although Phil's acts are not decisive in the final crushing of the conspiracy, he does discover that he cares enough to become involved and risk his life in a just cause. And he's learned a lesson: "It's never a clash of ideas that takes men to a battlefield—it's a conflict of greed that does it."[23]

Brunner's final mystery in this period is "The Evil That Men Do" (1966)—published as a book in 1969. A perverted pornographer has used hypnosis to implant his sado-masochistic fantasies into the mind of an isolated young girl; as an adult, she repressses these memories, only to have them break out in inexplicable fugues. A young hypnotist, in training for clinical practice, tries to unravel the mystery of these waking nightmares. In the story's climax, he fights off a maddened knife attack by the woman, who has lost her senses when she discovers the rotting body of her corrupter in the basement of her abandoned girlhood home. Strong stuff, but none of these three early mysteries is the equal of Brunner's major accomplishment in this mode in his mature period: the three Max Curfew novels.

Returning to Brunner's fantasy, one finds his major achievement is *The Traveler in Black* (1971), a collection of four stories, two of which, "Imprint of Chaos" (1960) and "Break the Door of Hell" (1966), were published during his transitional period. The other two are "The Wager Lost by Winning" (1970) and "Dread

Empire" (1971). Although he claims that *The Traveler in Black* is a conscious pastiche of James Branch Cabell's work, it undeniably owes a debt to Brunner's own "City of the Tiger," "Earth Is but a Star," and, ultimately, "The Wanton of Argus." The traveler is a striking figure, a being of many names but a single nature, charged by God to bring order out of chaos, time out of eternity. As the present universe emerges out of the collapsing ancient chaos, God returns in the form of a young woman, and she and the traveler, tired from his labors, take their leave:

> "I long for rest," he said. "But—one more thing. Who is to come after us?"
> "Let him decide," the pale girl said, and took him by the hand which lacked the staff. Turning, they went together into absence.[24]

The Traveler in Black almost exhausts Brunner's fantasy, although a few lesser works can be mentioned. "Father of Lies" (1962)—published as a book in 1968—has an inverted Gerald Howson-like character, a mad boy super-psychic who has held his father's manor estate in the grip of an Arthurian illusion. "Orpheus's Brother" (1965) is an odd and gruesome piece about the destruction of the brother of a dead rock singer who has become a god (in a mythic manner of speaking). "The Vitanuls" (1967) proceeds on the premise that the current population explosion, plus the introduction of a longevity drug, has used up the entire pool of human souls and that babies are being born mindless. An Indian holy man, once a noted obstetrician, chooses death in order to free his soul for another. This is a superior story.

Although Brunner's science fiction remained voluminous during this middle period, most works suffered because they seem to lack the attention he gave to works in other modes, especially mainstream and the science fiction-mainstream hybrids. Frankly, he needed volume to pay the bills, and he used science fiction to generate that volume. A number of interesting works do occur, however, several of which express his social concerns. *Slavers of Space* (1960)—revised as *Into the Slave Nebula* (1968)—teaches a valuable lesson about racism as the reader is carried along by Brunner's typically well-executed action. Android slave labor creates affluence for humanity, while the blue-skinned androids have no rights whatsoever. Yet except for skin color, they are completely indistinguishable from people. Actually, the androids are human babies born on isolated planets who are captured, dyed blue, and then raised to believe that they have been artificially produced. Thus the slave and the master are truly brothers under their skin pigments.

Society has invented a way to end war in "Badman" (1960). The title represents a sinister figure who has attributed to him a legacy of aggression and meanness; the people hate him and all he stands or so that he serves as a negative role model. Of course, the Badman phenomenon is really a plan by the government intent on eliminating anti-social behavior. In "Put Down This Earth" the population explosion is brought under control by the United Nations; in secrecy, a euphoric drug is circulated which causes people to vanish from Earth and reappear on other habitable worlds. Again, government conspires against its citizens for their own good. The United Nations plays a central role in *I Speak for Earth* (1961); its members choose a representative of Earth to be tested by the Galactic Federation of Worlds to determine humanity's fitness as a member species. The representative is an "amalgam," a composite of six minds in one body—an American, German, Russian, Black African, Indian, and Chinese—so that he expresses the unity of humanity.

Other examples of his social concerns include "Singleminded" 1963) about ultra nationalism; "See What I Mean!" (1964), in which nuclear war is prevented; and *The Martian Sphinx* (1965), in which the hero is a low status white in a world dominated by high status non-whites. The mind and its capacities are explored in "Crack of Doom" (1962)—published in book form as *The Psionic Menace* 1963); *The Rites of Ohe* (1963), and "Enigma from Tantalus" 1964)—published in book form in 1965. However, human progress dominates much of Brunner's science fiction of this period, for time and again he optimistically points out the inevitable success of humanity, its ability to overcome any obstacle, and even its eventual evolutionary transcendence to a higher plane.

The Atlantic Abomination (1960) is a case in point. An alien super being, once an overload of Earth, threatens the enslavement of all humanity after a scientific expedition rewakens it. The arrogant creature's philosophy of rule by the naturally superior is implemented by its ability to mentally control masses of people. In the end, however, an enlightened and unified human race destroys it: "Men change their gods, and when they have changed them often enough they cease to fear their power."[25] Humanity also beats the odds against allegedly superior foes in *Meeting at Infinity* (1961), *The Super Barbarians* (1962), and *Day of the Star Cities* (1965)—revised as *Age of Miracles* (1973). Even underdogs within the human race come out ahead against their own oppressing kind, as in "The Long Way to Earth" (1966)—published in book form as *A Planet of Your Own* (1966). In it a young woman outsmarts a computer and the trap set for her by greedy businessmen. When the human race has been condemned to galactic ostracism for its past sins, as in *The Astronauts Must Not Land* (1963)—revised as *More Things in Heaven* (1973)—it can still hope for eventual salvation since real improvement does take place. As humanity tries to tailor itself biologically and mentally for expansion to the stars, plans may go awry and some groups may appear to be dead ends; yet even then there is hope, as pointed out in "Born Under Mars" (1966)-published in book form in 1967:

But for all that we graph 'progress' in terms of starships and mental patients, we're tied to the assumption that we aren't shut in an enclosed cycle which repeats and repeats and drags us helplessly up and down forever, but at worst in a sort of maze which may have a way out and certainly has paths in it that we haven't yet traversed...and when we get to the point at which we can't discover a new turning to explore, then what else are we to do if not create the sort of human beings who *will* be able to?[26]

Stagnation--the lack of challenge--is a major threat to progress according to Brunner. In *Sanctuary in the Sky* (1960) the need is for intellectual variety: "...we had hoped to meet alien intelligences with whom we could co-operate. Our own views were, we felt becoming set, predictable, reactionary—in a word, dull. And we feared that dullness might be the prelude to decadence, decay death."[27] In *The Skynappers* (1960) the threat arises from too much help. First, a benevolent government foments a revolution against itself in an attempt to end human complacency; second, a super computer supplies knowledge too easily to humanity, thereby blocking its eventual transcendence.

In addition to the works already mentioned, Brunner's science fiction of the period covers a broad spectrum. At one end are such space operas as "The Altar at Asconel" (1965), part of his Galactic Empire series, and Zarathustra Refugee Planets' novels—*Secret Agent of Terra* (1962), *Castaways' World* (1963), and *The Repairmen of Cyclops* (1965). More sophisticated are *Times Without Number* (1962), his major story of parallel worlds; *The Long Result* (1965) and *Listen! The Stars!* (1963). Among the superior stories of the period are "Report on the Nature of the Lunar Surface" (1960) "Wasted on the Young" (1965), and "Judas" (1967).

"Judas," published in Ellison's *Dangerous Visions,* indicates that by the end of this transitional period Brunner was finished with the easy optimism and naive solutions suggested by the simplified view of social reality which characterized not only much of his own work but most of the science fiction of the era. In "Judas" a man has created a super robot, a God in metal, in his own image—evil and all His attempt to destroy it only reinforces its psychological grip on humanity; the "Word Made Steel" will never be broken. And one should recall that in "The Vitanuls," also published in 1967, babies were being born mindless and without souls. Brunner's dark dystopian visions were just below the horizon and would appear within the next year.

Just as certain stories hint at his growing pessimism, so, too, do others show his increasing artistry, especially those belonging to

he science fiction-mainstream hybrids. *The Squares of the City* has
been discussed, as have the two stories leading to *The Whole
Man,* although the completed novel incorporates much new material
and extensive revision of the old. In all of these hybrids he
emphasized study of character; frequently he focused on the
internal struggles of persons caught in emotionally charged and/or
hopeless situations. The settings are usually the present or the very
near future, another hint of the dystopias to come. "Protect Me from
My Friends" (1962), for example, tells of the escape of a telepath,
isolated from people for his own protection, into a world of
overwhelming and destructive mental stimuli. The prose is
unconventional--jumbled, condensed fragments of experience as
seen through the mind's eye of the unfortunate telepath. "Such
Stuff" (1962), although written in a conventional narrative form,
involves the psychological dimension as well; a psychologist is
trapped in the projected dreams of a patient who, as part of an
experiment, has been kept from dreaming for months. "Some Lapse
of Time" (1963) is less successful as a story, but the elements of
mental illusion and the nightmare of being trapped are present; a
doctor believes that nuclear war will soon end civilization, but no
one will accept his intuitive evidence. His family and colleagues
worry for his sanity. Undertaking a desperate act to forestall the
nuclear tragedy, he is killed, his attempt to alter the future a failure.

"The Totally Rich" (1963), perhaps Brunner's best short story,
tells of an extraordinarily wealthy woman who so needs to be loved
that she surreptitiously manipulates the life of a young scientist so
that he can invent a machine to reincarnate her dead lover. The task
completed, the scientist and woman celebrate in the now deserted
village—actually a set she had built to give him solitude for his
work. In the midst of their love-making, the scientist reveals that the
machine won't be perfected until after the woman has lost her
beauty. In despair she drowns herself, and the scientist muses:

These are the totally rich. They inhabit the same planet, breathe the same air.
But they are becoming, little by little, a different species because what was most
human in them is—well, this is my opinion—dead.
They keep apart, as I mentioned. And God! Aren't you grateful?[28]

"The Last Lonely Man" (1964) is also superior Brunner. In an
age when immortality can be achieved by the sharing of one's
psyche with another following death, what of the person who can
find no one with whom to contract for the sharing? Might not the
fear of such an eventuality drive some into madness, into such
insecurity that these fears become reality? Again Brunner springs
the trap shut, locking the person and his nightmare within himself.
In contrast, ancient Rome is the setting for "An Elixir for the
Emperor" (1964), although immortality figures in it. It is a tale of

revenge in which an old and wise man maneuvers the evil senator into outwitting himself. The senator dies from poison, but the old man, reluctantly, must accept immortality as the price for his revenge.

Overpopulated society will not accept birth control or suicide although it tolerates murder in "Nobody Axed You" (1965), and television shows compete for ratings based on the number of homicides they inspire in their audiences. The star of one show, being forced to abort her child by her husband—her co-star and producer—contrives to have him murder her during the show's taping. As he sees what he has done, he sprays the set with bullets: "The show topped the thousand that week for the first time."[29] In "Speech Is Silver" (1965) a man sells his voice and image to a company which plays tapes to sleeping people to improve their psychological condition. Finding that he has sold his very self, he counterattacks with a bizarre revenge which wins back his identity and destroys the company.

Were it not for its clichéd horror-movie ending, "The Productions of Time" (1966)—published as a book in 1967—would be a superior Brunner novel. Control of the will is again the central issue, as a mysterious playwright and director, Manuel Delgado, and his band of dark-suited assistants play upon the weaknesses of a cast of actors allegedly gathered to produce an *avant-garde* play. But Delgado, a visitor from the future, is secretly recording the perverted and degraded activity of the actors offstage, as they are guided deeper into decadence and the collapse of their wills. The jaded future audiences will never see this effort, however, for one of the actors overcomes his alcoholism and destroys his tormentors.

Destruction of the will is again examined in *Quicksand* (1967), which, together with *The Crutch of Memory* (1964), is probably Brunner's best novel published prior to 1968. In *Quicksand*, the hero himself, as in many of Brunner's works, contributes to his own destruction. He is Paul Fidler, a psychiatrist treating a young woman—Urchin—found naked and without memory in the English countryside. Faced with intolerable family and professional pressures, Fidler flees with the woman, escaping into her expert sexual care. Jealousy and despair soon follow, and the suffering Fidler finally takes both their lives. The novel is a perfect blend of science fiction and mainstream, for it is never made clear whether the woman is a time traveler from some future world of tyranny and decadent eroticism—as she claims—or simply the victim of psychosis. The high craftsmanship, broadened view of human personality, and social pessimism of *Quicksand*, "Judas," and "The Vitanuls" appropriately end Brunner's transitional period and prepare the stage for his most mature work.

The Mature Period: 1968-To Date

One must remember that Brunner remains a full-time writer who lives by his writing. This fact explains some of his work, particularly the tendency already seen to revise works and/or to expand shorter ones to book-length. After 1967 while the fantasy tends to disappear, he produced five novels in the mystery-suspense mode, two of which were revisions of earlier works. Only one mainstream novel appeared. He revised nine science fiction novels[30] from the earlier periods and produced six new ones, as well as a handful of short stories. Although all of his work illustrates his increased artistry, his major accomplishment of this last period is the dystopian novels.

His new science fiction shows an interesting mixture of what he had gained from his experience during his career. There is, for example, "The Product of the Masses" (1968), a humorous story of an aloof female scientist whose repressed sexuality leads her to commit a basic error in animal biology. A mechanical beast being used to study a species in the field ends up being chased by all the males; after all, the scientist designed it as an attractive female, and it is spring on that particular planet. "Pond Water" (1968) is a parable about a super robot, Alexander. Built as a defender of humanity, Alexander disdains its puny human creators and conquers the galaxy. When it seeks more worlds to conquer, it finds only one, that of "the imagination of man"; since it can never acquire that world, it falls dead. Then there is "Factsheet Six" (1968), in which a man uses psychic powers to wreak vengeance on the industrialist whose shoddy products crippled him and killed his wife and child.

Brunner's outstanding science fiction achievement of 1968, however, remains the novel, *Bedlam Planet*, his best study of planetary colonization. It is an intriguing work, for while the theme of human transcendence and progress is reiterated, the ecological logic of the novel runs deep and may be seen as a suggestion of concerns to come. Settlers on the new world to perpetuate the old Earth's ways, but they are failing. One by one they go mad after eating the native food, but out of their madness comes the solution to living on the new world. Brunner evokes the theme several times: "No, what sanity consists in is doing what *the planet you live on* will accept."[31] "Man isn't a rational being. He's a rational *animal,* and unless the animal and human parts of us are perfectly integrated we shall always live here as strangers" (p.146). "Your body is wiser than your mind; it's been around longer, and carries memories in its cells which we've barely begun to guess at" (p.147).

In contrast, Brunner returns to fairly straightforward entertainment in *Double, Double* (1969), which concerns a deadly, shape-changing alien monster destroyed by a small group of resourceful British locals and scientists. *Timescoop* (1969) lampoons the search by a wealthy executive for a distinguished lineage. His supposedly illustrious ancestors turn out to be an unwholesome lot when they are snatched from the past by a time machine and put on public display in the present.

Some of the better short stories from the 1970s include:"Out of Mindshot" (1970), in which an isolated telepathic woman must kill a sadistic man who has hunted her down to use for his personal gain; "Easy Way Out" (1971), which focuses on two men, a doctor and a playboy, who survive a spaceship crash and face the temptation of mentally escaping from their predicament by using an illusion-creating device; "Who Steals My Purse" (1973), a Vietnam War-inspired story, suggests bombing a belligerent, third-world country with a billion dollars worth of needed goods; "What Friends Are For" (1974), in which aliens teach human children to be "better at being human;" "Bloodstream" (1974), which proposes that modern cities are a newly evolved kind of super organism and their inhabitants only the cells needed for their functioning.

Of Brunner's three remaining science fiction novels, *The Dramaturges of Yan* (1971) is about myth, with which he had dealt previously in *Bedlam Planet* and "Orpheus's Brother." For the Yan species progress had produced a stable society and culture for thousands of years. Development had stopped. As a result the planet Yan possesses a single consciousness which is "simply not various enough to cope with the universe."[32] Ultimately, Earthmen precipitate the destruction of the Yanish culture, the species, and the planet itself; yet this was the Yan's own choice:

So, for the first time, we have seen a species pass away. It grew old. It had done its best. It wanted to be remembered for its best. And even if in the end it leaves no trace but a few poems, those will carry on, in their fashion (p.156).

This same concern for the extinction of a race dominates *Total Eclipse* (1974). A group of scientists have traveled to Sigma Draconis III in order to discover why an advanced race there has died out. They hope to avoid the same fate for Earth, which is threatened by social problems and war. An anthropologist discovers the cause by taking the role of one of the extinct aliens; they were greedy, like humans, and acted against their own best interests, favoring one small group rather than the species as a whole. In an unusual twist, the scientific expedition never gets the chance to report its findings to Earth. Slowly spores and other tiny bits of alien life kill the team members until only the anthropologist remains. His written record, the novel's final chapter, is exceptionally moving.

In "Web of Everywhere" (1974), the invention of the "skelter," a matter transmitter, has fundamentally altered humanity's way of life, for every individual is but a step away from anyone else. War, social upheaval, and the death of two-thirds of the population follow. After locks—called "privateers," which prevent unauthorized use—are developed for the "skelters," things settle down, and Earth is ruled by a small intellectual elite. In the novel Brunner makes effective use of his own poetry as section introductions. The poems are allegedly the works of Mustapha Sharif, a blind poet, who is one of the narrative's two chief characters. The plot deals more with emotion and personal motivation than with action. Driven by guilt and despair, Sharif's companion, Dykstra, kills himself; the poet has the final word:

> You
> stood before the skelter
> thinking it was new and strange
> to confront so many options
>
> You
> overlooked the fact
> that every dawn since time
> began
> has lighted uncountable
> choices.[33]

Although Brunner's science fiction of this period is marked more by a darkening mood than by explicit social commentary, his mysteries and dystopias voice his concerns. Even the minor, revised mysteries reflect this: *The Gaudy Shadows* (1970) hits hard at the misuse of mind-altering drugs, while *Black Is the Color* (1969) makes an explicit attack on racist South Africa. But the three Max Curfew novels serve almost as political primers.

When Curfew, a brilliant Jamaican Black trained in espionage in the Soviet Union, becomes disillusioned by the East, he returns to the West, for whom he holds no brief either, although he is used by their intelligence services. In the first novel, *A Plague on Both Your Causes* (1969)—American title, *Blacklash* (1969)—Curfew upsets a Rhodesian-style white supremacist government in an imaginary African state. Next, in *Good Men Do Nothing* (1970), he confronts the right-wing military government of Greece, where he is imprisoned and tortured. Finally, in *Honky in the Woodpile* (1971), Curfew challenges an oppressive Black government in the West Indies. The series thus contains various situations allowing Brunner to protest against political tyrannies; most importantly, no race has a monopoly on virtue.

The following passages illustrate something of the works' political tone. In *A Plague on Both Your Causes*, after Curfew has saved an African country from white apartheid domination and his white British government employers have rejected him for failing them, he reflects:

When he had gone I sighed and poured another drink, and sat down to think about the mind of the buckra boss class. There's a sickness there somewhere, and it's going to take a lot of education and probably some unpleasant discipline before it's cured.[34]

After escaping from the Greek police state, Curfew and his friend, the Contessa Vittoria, discuss life in *Good Men Do Nothing*:

"You sound as though you know all about it!"
"I do. I know all about rape, murder, arson, torture, sabotage, lies, deceit, treachery--all the things I hate most, Vita. All the things I hate most."
She kept looking at me.
"And it doesn't matter what you do, there's always more of them. Risk your life, put your neck in the noose, bait your own trap—there's always another Petronelli, always another sweet-talking Fidori."
"But most people don't do anything about them," Vita said.
"I know. That's what's mainly wrong with the world."[35]

In *Honky in the Woodpile,* Fierro, black leader of his island nation's government in exile, explains to Curfew what politically motivates people:

"And why we failed," Fierro said simply, "was because before people will rise to protest against the way they are cheated and lied to and deprived, they must understand what would happen if they were not so treated. I learned that from my brother, who went to live in those dirty shacks up the hill, who slept with the animals and drank the foul water and ate the food with dead insects in it. But we could never explain it to our friend Carlos, who had such dreams of glory and wished to achieve the kind of victory that eluded Che."
I waited. After some thought he added the clincher. "You know, my brother has sometimes said that the happiest people he has ever met were up the hill on Grand Madrugada. Because like dogs, not like human beings, they had the scraps from the table of the rich man, and if they grew unhappy and miserable they could be sure the Sabatanos would put them down."[36]

Despite the quantity of Brunner's work, most attention has been given his dystopian visions of the near-future. This is quite proper, because they are his major artistic and thematic accomplishments, the mode of his mature period into which he poured the most work and creativity. Yet as should now be apparent, they did not emerge from nowhere. Brunner's fifteen years as a working writer preceded their appearances, and they benefited from the lessons Brunner had learned from thinking about the future in his science fiction, from the expansion of his artistry through his excursions into mainstream fiction, and from his continual—and growing—interest in the social condition, human consciousness, progress, and the social applications of technology. One may refer to them as a literature of social influence rather than simply a literature of ideas, as that concept is usually applied in science fiction; moreover, they re a deliberate product of a conscious artistry, not mere entertainments. A great deal has been written about his major dystopias, *Stand on Zanzibar* (1968), *The Jagged Orbit* (1969), and *The Sheep Look Up* (1972).[37]

By definition a dystopia is a cautionary tale, as all of these works are; in addition, each is set in the very near future and in a major industrial country, either the United States or Britain. *Stand on Zanzibar* explores the psychological, social, and political effects of overpopulation, big business and big government, and of advances in the manipulation of genetic inheritance. It is a large book, with many characters and subplots, a trait it shares with *The Jagged Orbit, The Sheep Look Up,* and *The Shockwave Rider* (1975); Brunner maintains coherence throughout the narrative both by introducing his version of techniques previously developed by John Dos Passos and by a media-oriented mind-set inspired by Marshall McLuhan. In a sense, at the time Brunner's innovations represented one solution to the perennial problem in speculative literature: how to describe a world alien to the reader and to attain some degree of character development without stopping the story's action to the point that the reader loses interest.[38] The failure to accomplish these goals resulted in the stuffiness associated with so many other— especially earlier—utopian and dystopian works. Brunner is most successful in *The Sheep Look Up*, where the chief character, as it were, is the society itself.

The warning of *Stand on Zanzibar* is not all that strong when compared to those of *The Jagged Orbit* and *The Sheep Look Up.* (His dystopian works generally become increasingly pessimistic through *The Sheep Look Up*, but then the mood lightens somewhat, ending on the more optimistic notes of *The Stone That Never Came Down* (1973) and *The Shockwave Rider.*) *The Jagged Orbit* is his most experimental work; he copies selections from the day's newspaper directly into the narrative and lets these determine the direction of the story.[39] The urban hell is worse than that of *Stand on Zanzibar*. Arms manufacturers fan racial hostility in an urban environment divided into black and white armed-camps. People live privatistic, defensive lives, and even the predominant theory in clinical psychology of the day holds isolation as the basis for treatment. Yet the overall effect is still less real, less socially coherent than *Stand on Zanzibar*. Like that novel, too, the ending of *The Jagged Orbit* seems contrived and unsatisfying. Voices of wisdom—Chad Mulligan, radical sociologist in *Stand on Zanzibar,* and Xavier Conroy, dissident psychologist in *The Jagged Orbit*— speak throughout both books and contribute to the somewhat "happy" and spurious endings. None of this occurs in *The Sheep Look Up*. In it the voice of wisdom belongs to ecologist Austin Train, but he is first driven underground, then framed for kidnapping, and

finally martyred by one of his own, unwanted followers. Ecologica
disaster is clearly triggred by a dysfunctional social system in th
United States, which is finally destroyed in the novel's conclusion
It is a brutal, shocking, and effective book.

While these three novels have received widest attention, the
are not the only works belonging to Brunner's dystopian mod-
Between *The Jagged Orbit* and *The Sheep Look Up*, he publishe
"The Inception of the Epoch of Mrs. Bedonebyasyoudid" (1971) an
The Wrong End of Time (1971). The former is a powerful short stor
detailing a series of terrorist attacks in New York City made by
group of multi-racial American radicals led by a Vietcong officer. A
the story ends, tanks are rumbling through the streets; the war ha
been brought home. This is, obviously, Brunner's most explicit ant
Vietnam War statement. Concomitantly, *The Wrong End of Tim*
(1971) is Brunner's most scathing attack upon the culture an
politics of the United States; however, this attack is less visible an
its criticism somewhat more muted than that of, say, *The Shee*
Look Up, for it is swathed in layers of stock devices. Thus, the wor
presents an awkward blend of realistic social extrapolation an
farfetched science fiction gimmicks. The former includes th
following: the Soviet Union has grown somewhat more liberal whil
the United States has become increasingly reactionary and "craze-
with neurotic insecurity"; the military-industrial complex runs th
country, maintaining its grip by represssive police and securit;
forces; racism is rampant, as well as a hatred and suspicion o
anything foreign; the entire country has tightly closed its borders
hiding behind the world's most dangerous nuclear weapons system
repression of speech and thought is ubiquitous, paranoia is th
norm, and the overpopulated nation is increasingly polarized int-
the rich and the poor; nuclear holocaust has only been avoidec
because Soviet intelligence has been able to obtain all America;
military secrets.

Tempering the edge of this critique are a number of scienc-
fiction devices: an alien ship has appeared to Russian spac-
explorers on the edge of the solar system and seems to be warnin;
them that an alien attack on the United States is imminent; a secre
agent is sent into the United States to find a way of defusing tha
country's paranoia so that an alien attack will not trigger blind
geocidal retaliation; the agent meets a young black who possesse;
clairvoyance and who manipulates the situation so that the agen
discovers the truth of the alien message. Out of fear, all have read
the message backward, for the aliens came from an antimatte
universe where time is reversed; the repression of external behavio
in the United States leads to the emergence of such internal talent;
as that possessed by the clairovoyant black; the country's paranoi;
results from its past pre-eminent role in world affairs; for unable to

grow and fearing decline, the society has grown stagnant and repressive, caring more about its own selfishness and greed than about anyone else. In the end, the alien's message discloses that humanity's progress will lead it to the stars and beyond.[40]

Two other dystopian works form an interesting parallel with "The Inception of the Epoch of Mrs. Bedonebyasyoudid" and *The Wrong End of Time*. In the short story, "The Protocols of the Elders of Britain" (1975) the governments of Britain and other countries conspire to manipulate their citizens; for Britain, the establishment of a "disciplined efficient corporate state" is expected prior to 1980. A computer repairman uncovers these facts when he is called upon to repair the faulty machines. He is confined in a mental hospital and given electroshock to rid him of his "delusions of persecution."

Set in the Britain of the 1980s, *The Stone That Never Came Down* (1973) depicts a society of rampant inflation and unemployment, wandering mobs of vicious religious fanatics (part of the repressive religious frenzy gripping the Western world), strike-breaking by the military, and worsening race relations. Moreover, World War Three is threatened by emerging conflict in Europe within the collapsing Common Market. But one of Brunner's favorite science fiction devices arrives on the scene and eventually saves the day. Here it takes the form of a self-replicating molecule, perhaps symbolically named "VC," which increases human intelligence. It also makes selective inattention difficult, creates greater sensitivity to sensory input, and gives total recall. A small group accidentally exposed to the chemical use it to end the military crisis and begin the movement toward a new society where all will be "advanced" humans like themselves. Again, a simplistic philosophy—people can save themselves if they are just smart enough and science may be able to provide that intelligence—blunts the edge of an otherwise cogent dystopian social extrapolation.

Two final works complete Brunner's dystopian tradition to date. The realistic story, "The Berendt Conversion" (1975), portrays the effects of a future famine; Brunner's intention both to warn and to extrapolate are clearly evident, for he adds an afterword in which he gives the sources, actual cases from past famines, upon which he bases the effects of hunger in his story.

Alvin Toffler's *Future Shock* inspired Brunner to write *The Shockwave Rider* (1975), which in tone, style, size, and seriousness must be ranked with Brunner's three earlier major dystopias. It is not the achievement of *The Sheep Look Up*, but Brunner's ironic humor, although muted, is still present, as is his fertile inventiveness. The times had changed; the rebellious and liberating late 1960s, which no doubt had influenced the genesis of Brunner's dystopias, were long past and a longing for a return to "normal" times was in the air. Dystopias were going out of fashion, and *The*

Shockwave Rider, itself influenced by these trends, may be Brunner's last effort in this mode.

In summary, it tells the story of Nickie Haflinger, a kind of polymath and genius at computer manipulation, who flees from the government training center, Tarnover, where his talents were being developed by the state for their own purposes. Eventually, Haflinger turns the computer system, which integrates and controls the entire society of North America, against the government. The final blow is a plebiscite in which the votes of citizens will instruct the computers whether or not to restructure society. There are two propositions: "1. That this is a rich planet. Therefore poverty and hunger are unworthy of it, and since we can abolish them, we must. 2. That we are a civilized species. Therefore none shall henceforth gain illicit advantage by reason of the fact that we together know more than one of us can know."[41]

The Shockwave Rider is also unique in that it contains a utopia within it, the village of Precipice, inhabited by mentally and morally superior persons who reject the empty, wasteful luxury of the consumer society and the stultification of imposed social conformity. In such a community, built on a human scale and in harmony with the environment, humanity is able to resist the poundings of future shock. And such an elite of the calm and self-assured can be the nucleus for eventual social reform.

Looking back on Brunner's numerous treatments of society and social change, one can finally discern the theoretical model which underlies much of his work. It might best be described as Toynbeeish; social progress occurs, although individual societies rise and fall, provided the stimulus of challenge is present and the creative elite does not forsake its social responsibilities. Knowledge accumulates which, when in the hands of an informed public, allows reasoning people to democratically solve their problems and continue to advance; violence only begets violence, and, in the long run, evolution, not revolution, is the path of success. The enemy of progress is human greed and selfishness, which, as Brunner has Nickie Haflinger point out, gives rise to evil in the modern world; "If there is such a phenomenon as absolute evil, it consists in treating another human being as a thing" (p.236).

The moral implications of this are explored by Brunner in *The Devil's Work* (1970), his only mainstream novel to date in his mature period. The story is one of horror, as young Stephen Green, fresh from boarding school, has his will destroyed by Barron Someday, a prince of big business who deals in oil, armaments, aircraft, chemicals, and devil worship. The work is highly symbolic, as a few of the character and place names indicate: it is set in the village of Limborough; P.R. Unthank is Rector of the local church and Jimmy Lavender is his effeminate curate; Jack Wilderspin is the motorcycle riding leader of a local youth gang; Stephen Green's home is on a street bearing the sign, "No Through Road." The writing techniques are similar to, but more controlled than those found in *Stand on Zanzibar*. Overall, it is a powerful and impressive novel. The plot involves Stephen's growing financial, psychological, and social dependence on Someday, who has built on Stephen's existing problems—his estrangement from his widowed father and his inability to find a place among the youth in his community—in such a way that Stephen eventually has no choice but to accept his position with Someday. Thus, Stephen finds his freedom of choice taken away, rendered powerless for life; the horror of it lies in his realization that this has come to pass. As Shaw stated, "To break a man's spirit is devil's work."

This review of Brunner's works ends in mid-1978. He has not published a novel since 1975, and it is not certain what path his future work may take. One new direction may be indicated by his present writing task, a large historical novel about a riverboat race on the Mississippi set in the heyday of the American South; after more than a year's work, it is half completed. Of Brunner's four recently published stories, the three appearing in *The Magazine of Fantasy and Science Fiction* exhibit the polish typical of the mature Brunner, along with a sophisticated blend of science fiction, mainstream, and suspense elements. "The Taste of the Dish and the Savor of the Day" (1977) utilizes Brunner's extensive knowledge of gourmet food as background in a French-laced, erudite story about an exquisite dish, invented 200 years ago by a cook who dabbled in alchemy, which bestows immortality provided one eats nothing else—a price too dear if one wants to fully experience life rather than simply have it. "The Man Who Could Provide Us with Elephants" (1977) and "The Man Who Understood Carboniferous Flora" (1978) chronicle the adventures of Mr. Secrett, the chief librarian of the "Royal Society for Applied Linguistics" and purveyor of extraordinary information. Reminiscent of Sterling E. Lanier's exploits of Brigadier Fellows and of Arthur C. Clarke's White Hart tales, these science fictional tall stories mix humor and horror to render pleasant entertainment.

With "The Suicide of Man" (1978) in *Isaac Asimov's Science Fiction Magazine,* Brunner returns to science fiction. Despite its title, the story is optimistic and, interestingly, deals with human transcendence, a theme of his first American tale, "Thou Good and Faithful" (1953). Again, technology is an aid to that transcendence; off-stage machines recreate the persona of Lodovico Zaras, a 1978 cancer victim who chose suicide, as a "collective precept," an entity given substance through its perception by a humanity thousands of years in the future. In effect, Lodovico is a ghost. This future humanity, just as did the alien creators of the robots in "Thou Good and Faithful," created utopia on their world. As Lodovico observes:

"Every ideal of my time seems to have come to pass. Between any person and any other there is peace. There is no jealousy, nor greed, because there is enough to satisfy everyone. Nobody lacks the chance to attempt, if not accomplish, his or her ambitions."[42]

Yet not all ambitions can be fulfilled, for people, still bound by their material bodies, cannot explore the depths of space, nor can they escape death. But Lodovico is immortal, being an "incorruptible, indissoluble, inerasable image upon the consciousness of all mankind" (p.178), and he is to explore space and return to tell humanity what it is like. These voyages are accomplished at the cost of great pain to Lodovico; he is damaged time and again, but returns to Earth to be healed. Was all his suffering worthwhile? Yes, answers Lodovico: "Because what has been wrong with humanity since the beginning is not wrong with me. We have always had the imagination that belongs with immortality, but we have been trapped in destructible substance" (p.183). This is the signal which humanity awaited:

"We created you to help us determine whether our species has engendered as much consciousness as is proper to it. The fact that you are as-you-are is the evidence we wanted. The ambition of a rational, intelligent species is not as-much-as-possible, but *enough*" (p.185).

Now humanity could fix the date for its suicide, and all those presently alive, as well as those who had ever lived, could be "recalled" and "re-perceived" to wander the universe at will, immortal, to experience all of it and survive to remember. This is the same fulfillment offered humanity in "Thou Good and Faithful".

"So in ripe time it was done, and mankind died as a material species. But its hordes of ghosts were billions strong, and went to compare notes with strangers who had made the like discovery, to confirm or disprove what they had found out about the universe, and often enough learned they had been wrong.
Often enough to keep them curious and intrigued for at least the current cosmic cycle. Even immortality cannot shrink the gap between the galaxies" (p.185).

Thus, after 25 years Brunner yet remains true both to his science fiction origins and to his thematic core of social concerns, the capacities of mind, the utility of technology, and human progress. Moreover, whatever his future, Brunner, only in his mid-forties, has at least two major achievements to his credit: a number of fine science fiction-mainstream hybrids and a masterful series of dystopias. This judgment ignores the wide diversity of his other highly competent, entertaining, and frequently thought-provoking fiction.

Self-effacingly, Brunner has described himself as merely a

raftsman whose major forte is that of *pasticheur*,[43] but he is much
1ore than that in the development of modern speculative literature:
n important innovator, an extender of the range and quality of
peculative literature, and an instructor of our social conscience. As
Robert Scholes points out:

But surely the task which several centuries of scientific progress have forced
pon us is that of founding a new morality and a new politics upon our new
nowledge of the cosmos and the human situation in it... In recent years, no writers
nside the field of science fiction or outside of it have done more to create a modern
onscience than John Brunner and Ursula K. Le Guin.[44]

And there is still tomorrow.

Patricia Warrick

Mack Reynolds: The Future as Socio-economic Possibility

Science fiction for Mack Reynolds is political fiction. He constantly filters man's present and future worlds through the prisms of socio-economic theories and political ideologies. He creates an array of images, each suggesting what might be possible if man alters some element of his political or economic world. His paradigms of the future balance between despair and promise. He uses the lens of magnification to suggest the dystopia that could result if man's present political structures become static and fail to respond to technological developments. But he also imagines a bright millenium, the year 2000, when man lives harmoniously with his fellow men, his technology, and his environment. Encounters with alien creatures, cosmic adventures, inner psychic journeys, new possibilities in science—all these staples of science fiction are of no concern to Reynolds. Only the dynamics of the political and economic world, where man is both shaper and shaped, interest him.

Brian Aldiss notes in *Billion Year Spree* that it was Mack Reynolds who brought "passionate left-wing debate to *Analog*."[1] This is not surprising because he was nurtured on leftist politics. He was born in California in 1917 to parents who were radical in their views. His father was a Wobbly in his youth, and later became a member of the Socialist Labor Party (the DeLeonists). In 1924 his father was the vice-presidential candidate for the Socialist Labor Party and became its presidential candidate in the 1928 and 1932 elections. As Reynolds grew up, he was surrounded with socialist thought. He recently wrote: "I am the child who at the age of four or so asked, 'Mother, who is Comrade Jesus Christ?' In my home, I had never heard of anyone who was not addressed as Comrade."[2]

Later as a young man he joined the Socialist Labor Party and served first in 1940 as the public relations man for the Party's candidate and then as a national organizer, traveling around the

136

country and giving lectures and radio addresses. He eventually resigned from the Party because he felt it had become antiquated in its program. He did not, however, renounce his political philosophy. Of it he has stated:

I continue to consider myself a radical in my socio-economic beliefs. Although I know of no organization at this time [1975] that I feel I could affiliate myself with, I am a Marxist only in the sense that I believe him to have been the outstanding scholar of political economy of the nineteenth century, and certainly the father, with Engels, of the socialist-communist movement. Since he did his work a century ago there have been many developments, and much of his work (for instance, the *Communist Manifesto)*, is antiquated.[3]

Reynolds now lives and writes in Guanajuarta, Mexico, but from 1955 to 1965 he served as foreign travel editor for *Rogue Magazine*, an assignment which took him to Europe, the Near East, North Africa, the Orient, and Latin America—a total of over sixty countries. That makes him one of the most widely traveled contemporary science fiction writers. He often draws upon this extensive experience to create backgrounds for his stories set on the Earth in the near future. Although he has read widely in political economy, history, and anthropology, the importance of his travels cannot be underestimated, for he has directly observed a wide range of politico-economic systems:

Fascist countries, such as Spain and Portugal; monarchies, such as the Arab states; Communist dictatorships, including all the European ones, save only Albania; off-beat experiments, such as Israel; pseudo-socialism, such as that of Scandinavia; various levels of capitalism, from more or less classic Switzerland to the state capitalism of the United States and Great Britain; not to speak of the Chaotic mish-mashes to be found in the newly liberated colonies.
Through that period [of his travels], from time to time I found myself in the midst of this military revolt, that minor war, the other attempted revolution.[4]

Reynolds' interest and experience in socio-economics are reflected in all his fiction. He extrapolates into the near future, speculating about what might happen if anarchism, industrialism, feudalism, technocracy, state capitalism, syndicalism, fascism, communism in all its variety, or socialism were established. He holds that the world's prevailing political and economic systems are antiquated and in need of radical change. He accepts technological innovation as a given. His concern is that changes in political and economic structures occur so slowly that they are not able to deal constructively with technological development. He holds that war is a monstrosity which can be ended and that poverty could easily be eliminated on a worldwide basis.

In contrast to many recent science fiction writers, he is not antitechnology. He believes that present social problems are caused not by technology itself but by the economic systems which utilize technology. He particularly attacks what he calls State Capitalism—a system where the state owns and controls the means of production. This system, he maintains, manifests itself differently in various countries, but its effect is the same. To the average citizen, it makes little difference whether the means of production are owned by corporations, as in America, or by the state, as in Russia.

Since he began writing at mid-century, he has produced over forty novels and at least a hundred short stories. Six different categories emerge from my reading of his longer works.[5] Each pictures a different world, and very often the same protagonist appears in the several novels of a category. I have identified the following:

1. Third World Series: *Blackman's Burden* (1961), *Border, Breed, Nor Birth* (1962), *Black Sheep Astray* (1973). These three works share the same protagonist, El Hassan; they portray North Africa in the near future, attempting to industrialize. The tension and conflict in the novels grow out of the encounter of primitive with industrially advanced cultures.

2. Joe Mauser, Mercenary: *The Earth War* (1963), *Mercenary From Tomorrow* (1968), *Time Gladiator* (1969). This trilogy focuses upon Joe Mauser, a mercenary soldier who attempts to fight his way to the top of a highly stratified class structure. The setting is the United States and Europe early in the twenty-first century. The novels follow the expanding consciousness of Mauser as he becomes increasingly aware of the deadly stasis of the capitalistic class structure and finally attempts to instigate a quiet revolution in the system.

3. Year 2000 Series: *After Some Tomorrow* (1967), *The Cosmic Eye* (1969), *The Five Way Secret Agent* (1969), *Computer World* (1970), *Looking Backward from the Year 2000* (1973), *Commune 2000 A.M.* (1974), *Satellite City* (1975), *The Towers of Utopia* (1975), *Tomorrow Might Be Different* (1975), *Ability Quotient* (1975), *Equality in the Year 2000* (1976), *Roll Town, Roll* (1976), *Day After Tomorrow* (1976). This group contains the largest number of novels, and it is the one to which Reynolds has given the most recent attention. All share in common an Earth setting in the year 2000 in a post-industrial civilization which is fully computerized and automated. He explores various possibilities of this future technological culture: international data banks, drugs, religion, technocracies, communes. His essential technique is to extrapolate from some present trend to create a possible future world.

4. Interplanetary Novels: *The Space Barbarians* (1960), *The Rival Regelians* (1967), *Computer War* (1967), *Galactic Medal of Honor* (1976). A thousand years prior to the opening of these stories, the galaxy has been seeded by Earth with humans, one hundred

persons per planet. Each planet has been allowed to develop its economic and political systems unmolested, and the novels explore the varied results of that development. Each individual story allows Reynolds to examine one or more socio-economic systems: feudalism, anarchy, capitalism, fascism, socialism. He makes use of both primitive and technologically advanced societies.

5. United Planets, Section G Series: *Planetary Agent X* (1965), *Dawnman Planet* (1966), *Amazon Planet* (1975), *Section G: United Planets* (1976). These novels portray a future in which 2,435 planets are loosely organized by a political structure known as the United Planets. Its constitution stipulates that 1) the organization will not interfere in internal political, socio-economic, or religious institutions of any planet; 2) nor will any member planet be allowed to interfere in the internal affairs of another planet. The novels share a protagonist, Ronald Bronston, an agent in the Commissariat of Interplanetary Affairs. He travels throughout the system, investigating possible violations of the constitution. One of the most interesting societies is the totally feminist one described in *Amazon Planet.*

6. Humor and Miscellaneous: *The Case of the Little Men* (1951)—first novel; *Code Duello* (1966); *After Some Tomorrows* (1967); *Earth Unaware* (1968)—also published under the title *Of Godlike Power; Once Departed* (1970); *Depression or Bust* (1974).

Recently twenty-two of his short stories have been collected in *The Best of Mack Reynolds* (1976). Although he is a very uneven writer, most of the stories in this collection are excellent. He has produced a number of stories—both short and long—which provide the thinnest of adventure entertainment or the dullest of socio-economic lectures. I will examine here only a half dozen novels substantial enough to be taken seriously and a number of short stories which deservedly have become classics of science fiction.

The Encounter Between Primitive and Advanced Societies
One of Reynolds' most successful novels, *The Space Barbarians* (1960), portrays the meeting of a primitive society with a technologically advanced culture structured on the capitalistic free enterprise system. At the narrative's beginning the reader assumes that the hunting and gathering culture on the planet Caledonia is the barbarian society, but he finds as the novel progresses that Reynolds shares the view Thorsten Veblen expressed in *The Theory of the Leisure Class.* Modern man, under his gloss of civilization, is only slightly removed from his barbaric ancestors. The technologically sophisticated culture is quite as predatory and savage in its seizure of goods without working for them as are the uncivilized tribes of Caledonia. Although the novel is set in another planetary system a thousand years in the future, it echoes the

destruction of the American Indian culture when European civilization invaded the American continents. Reynolds makes the details of his fictional world sufficiently different, however, so that the story seems fresh.

As it begins, Caledonia is shown to be inhabited by a large number of clans loosely organized into a confederation. It had received its seed of human life centuries earlier when a ship from Earth bearing Scottish colonists crashed after it had been thrown off course. The hunting and gathering society regulates itself through traditions, bans, and an honor code observed by all the clans. Raids to seize horses and women are commonplace, but killing is at a minimum because of the practice of counting coup on an enemy to signal his defeat. Private property is minimal, and the clans have never conceived of the private ownership of land.

The story is told from the viewpoint of John, leader of the clan Hawk. Through his eyes the reader views the arrival of a spaceship from the advanced planet of Sidon. Exploring for minerals, its crew discovers large deposits of platinum, and John of the Hawks realizes that an invasion of his land will inevitably take place. He realizes, too, that his people cannot defend themselves against laser weapons with their single shot carbines, but his first reaction is to lead the tribes in a courageous, though futile, defense.

The Sidonians come in numbers and set up mining operations. They bring priests who are followers of the religion of Lord Krishna and convert many of the natives. Part of the religious ritual involves taking the drug, soma, which pacifies the natives. With their aggressive natures thus neutralized, the Caledonians are forced to work in the mines. John of the Hawks leads a small group who retreat to the hills; they set up guerilla operations to harass the mining operations and dream of attacking Sidon City. To reconnoiter the city successfully and plan the strategy of attack, John undertakes the subterfuge of seeming to allow himself to be converted and going to work in the city.

There he encounters firsthand a modern, computerized electronic society. Discovering a remote terminal which gives him access to the city's electronic data files, he begins to study and assimilate this strange culture; as he does, he realizes two things. First, in its improved standard of living, its health care, and its educational system, it represents a great advance over his own culture. Secondly, technological innovation and progress are inevitable; the society which resists change and remains static will not survive.

The Space Barbarians is particularly successful in dramatizing its ideas rather than merely talking about them—a feat Reynolds does not always achieve. Told from John's viewpoint, as noted, it is a tale of his expanding consciousness as he comes to understand a new culture. His journey to awareness is a painful and often tragic one. It costs him both the love of his new bride and his position as honored head of his clan. Reynolds does not oversimplify, nor does he romanticize. According to his view, technological progress brings cultural change—which may or may not mean improvement. Whatever the consequence, however, the historical process is inevitable. To survive, man must change. Certain values of primitive Caledonia which are worthwhile may be lost, but there will be balancing gains as John's people move toward a post-industrial society. Life and process are synonymous for Reynolds.

Three novels set in northern Africa concern themselves with the same theme—the encounter of primitive and advanced cultures. *Blackman's Burden* (1961), *Border, Breed Nor Birth* (1962), and *Black Sheep Astray* (1973) can be read as a single tale which pictures the attempt of a five-man-team of American blacks to hasten the process of industrialization in underdeveloped African countries. The Reunited Nations African Development Project sponsors the team and insists that the nations of the world must industrialize together. Since the Africans were slow in starting, they must be helped. Once again the assumption that technological development is inevitable underlies the stories. The trilogy might well be termed political fiction instead of science fiction because it is essentially in the realistic mode and set in the present. Reynolds draws upon his experience in North Africa to sketch an authentic background for his action, but the narrative is presented from various points of view and uses a variety of settings and a rather large cast of characters. It thus lacks the tight plot of *The Space Barbarians*; still, it is good fiction, and Homer Crawford, the black American sociologist who becomes El Hassan, the hero required to unite the North Africans, is one of Reynolds' more successful characterizations.

The Joe Mauser Trilogy

Even though he has written a number of interplanetary novels, like *The Space Barbarians,* which afford him imaginary models to explore his theories, the immediate future of Earth intrigues Reynolds far more than galactic adventures thousands of years from now. His most successful fiction narrows in on the year 2000 and speculates about what Western culture will be like as it enters the twenty-first century. Unlike so many of his contemporaries, Reynolds proposes both utopian and dystopian alternatives. He extrapolates from present trends which he regards as threatening to the majority of the population; by this method he creates fictional societies which are critical of our present one. He has stated that he "endorses a Marxist view of change"[6]; in the Joe Mauser trilogy he examines class consciousness and the historical process, but he does not see the class struggle unfolding in the way Marx predicted.

In *The Earth War* (1963), *Mercenary From Tomorrow* (1968) and *Time Gladiator* (1969), the society of Joe Mauser is totally computerized; the work of production and service is no longer done by humans but by various automated devices. The problem of poverty has been eliminated; each individual in the United States— now called the Ultra-Welfare State—receives enough financial credits to assure his basic survival without working. Economic affluence and automation make such subsidy possible; they also make it necessary, for automation has eliminated most jobs. Money no longer exists; a universal credit card identifies each individual and all financial transactions are handled by computers. The International Data Center stores complete information on each individual: his financial, police, educational, medical, and employment records. Rapid mass transportation is underground with hovercraft available for surface travel when necessary.

Problems of overpopulation, pollution, and war have been eliminated—or at least brought under control. Internationally political spheres of influence have divided the world into four areas West-world (the Americas), Common-world (the western European countries), Sov-world (the eastern European countries), and Neutworld (the developing nations). The first three power blocks are locked in a permanent state of cold war. Despite their official differences in political and economic ideologies, however, the masses of people in West-world and Sov-world find life pathetically the same. Both groups are alienated, passive consumers. A character in *Time Gladiator* remarks that Marx had never envisioned a time when ninety percent of the population would become his "*lumpen* proletariat," but in Reynolds' fictional world this is exactly what has happened.

The classless society has not come into being, nor has government withered away. In the People's Capitalism of the United States there prevails a strict caste system instituted in the past for their own advantage by "a fraction of a fraction, hereditary aristocrats"—the so-called "Uppers," who will tolerate no change. The actual administrative and decision-making processes have been turned over to the small middle class—no more than nine percent of the population. Because of automation the labor of the masses—ninety percent of the population—is no longer needed. "Don't educate the lower castes," decree the Uppers, "they might become restless. Give them bread and circuses instead."[7] The proletariat do not read, nor do they have an interest in political affairs. They are entertained by television and regularly given a pacifying drug. They are content in their pale consumers' version of happiness, and that's the problem, for they do not see how meaningless their existence is, nor do they want to revolt. One observer in *Time Gladiator* who worries about the static condition of society reflects:

In the past revolutions were put over by enraged majorities, in mutiny against what they considered a parasitical ruling minority which was oppressing them. The masses were moved to revolt by desperation. However, today there is no desperation, either in the West-world, or the Sov-world. The second industrial revolution with its automation and other techniques has solved the problem of production of abundance. There simply is no starving lower class.[8]

This fact is what has disrupted the forward movement of history which Marx thought to be inevitable. Affluence has assured the existence of the proletariat by means of the guaranteed annual wage.

Yet the masses are exploited as consumers. As noted, the drug *trank* keeps them passive. Their desire for violence is fed by television. A world whose appetite had been whetted by violence in sports and newscasts of the Vietnam War is now given the *fracas*. It is a kind of national trial by combat used to settle differences between competing corporations, disputes between corporations and unions, and disputes between unions. Each party hires a limited army of professional soldiers who fight under tightly controlled conditions. The combat takes place in a restricted area designated as a Military Reservation, and only weapons developed prior to the year 1900 may be used. (Because all nations have recognized the deadly nature of atomic weapons, their use has been banned by international treaty.) The winner of the fracas is the winner of the dispute.

The fracas entertains the masses much as the Roman circuses did. Sitting in front of their TV's in the comfort of their living rooms, they can watch real killings, for numerous cameras have been strategically placed in the Military Reservation to give a full view of the carnage. The heroes of the lower caste are those mercenaries most successful in the business of war. A mercenary may be killed, but he may also become a hero who is often jumped in caste and showered with gifts and money.

What is the solution to the problem of an ossified society where the bulk of men have been reduced to an alienated, inhuman level of existence? The plot of the three novels unfolds Reynolds' proposal. He focuses on Joe Mauser, a fighter and man of action--the typical protagonist in Reynolds' best fiction. Portrayed against the background of the passive society, his heroes are men whose primary characteristic is their ability to act. More importantly, they achieve a new awareness when, pushed into an extreme situation, they must use a changed mode of action to survive. As a result of that new action, their situation is altered; with that alteration comes a new consciousness. Thus throughout the trilogy one observes Joe's growth of consciousness, growth of awareness.

In the first novel, *Mercenary from Tomorrow*, he is an ambitious young American in his twenties who aspires to fight his way out of the lower caste into which he was born. He wants to achieve money and status. Because of the rigid stratification of society, only two options are open to him: a religious career or the professional military. He selects the latter, obviously, and becomes a mercenary in the national war games—the fracas. The narrative follows 1) Joe's zig-zag, adventurous course up the ladder of caste in the United States; 2) his rejection of the whole static caste system; 3) his realization that class and status are an international problem; 4) his development of an awareness of the historical process; and finally, 5) his recognition that some form of revolutionary action is necessary to break up the intolerable societal structure and set history in motion again. But the revolution proposed at the end of the trilogy is not the violent uprising of the proletariat which Marx predicted.

For Joe, as for Marx and Reynolds, the function of consciousness is important because it defines for the individual the outer reality in which he lives. Marx felt that men could gain a true consciousness—one that lay beyond the awareness of each class—only if the means of production were destroyed and private property done away with, for these factors produced the alienation of the masses. The proletariat must unite and rise against its oppressors. But Reynolds does not believe that the revolution will come through the efforts of the proletariat. The largest percentage of them have become dehumanized. As noted, they do not read, so they cannot be educated to an awareness of their condition. The only way of reaching them is through television, now controlled by the small minority who are the upper class. They must maintain the status quo. Thus, as Reynolds envisions it, a slow, nonviolent revolution can be accomplished only by the middle caste who are increasingly taking over the task of running the bureaucracy. The revolution will face the opposition of both the upper and lower castes.

In the final scene of *Time Gladiator*, the managers in the various international power blocs decide that cooperation of all those in the middle class having a revolutionary spirit—regardless of their nationalities—is necessary if society's ossification is to be dissolved. Representatives of the West-world and the Sov-world meet to plan secretly a strategy which will transform society and set the historical process in motion again. Both Reynolds and Marx insist upon the desirability of change; the trilogy dramatizes the process by which Joe Mauser reaches that same conclusion.

When one moves beyond the desirability of change, the views of Marx and Reynolds diverge. Marx rejected the cyclic theory of history, maintaining that history does not repeat itself but moves forward linerally. He optimistically suggested that the new society would of necessity be a better society. Reynolds suggests another possibility: if it has not been permanently halted, the historical process may be tragically delayed. In the twentieth century radical technological innovations have occurred which could not have been anticipated a century ago. Their effect has been so significant that the historical process, as Marx saw it, has been altered. In his trilogy Reynolds treats three such innovations: the atomic bomb, computers and automation, and television. In his future the development of the bomb has eliminated war. Sociologists have noted that national conflicts, while unacceptable from a humanistic view, have nevertheless accelerated the productive capacities of nations. In Reynolds' future world the impetus to change is gone. Also absent is the impetus of the working class to revolt against the exploitation of their labor; automation and the Guaranteed Annual Income have removed this pressure for change. Finally, the impetus to change which might arise from achieving a "true consciousness" has also vanished, for television and drugs have imprisoned the consciousness of most people and made it nonfunctional. Yet Reynolds and Marx do agree on the desired end: man's liberation— both from things and other men—so that he can become a creative human being rather than the exploited, divided and alienated creature he now is.

The Five Way Secret Agent

Secret agents figure in much of Reynolds' fiction, usually those novels which are his weakest. The agent tends to be a mere observer of the political and economic scene he visits, carrying on his job dispassionately, oscillating with stereotyped repetition between fighting and giving or receiving stock lectures on economic theory. *The Five Way Secret Agent* (1969) proves to be an exception. It projects an emerging world economic system in which multinational corporations and formal governments vie for power on an international level. The interests of the governments of the United States and the Soviet Complex will be furthered if national identity and power are maintained, but the multinational corporations will benefit by blurring of national identities and winding down of hostilities between nations. Reynolds describes five different groups seeking power, and he ties them together by having each one attempt to hire the same secret agent—quite possibly the first five-way agent in international intrigue fiction.

The first power group is International Communications, a global corporation which Reynolds calls a "cosmocorp." Running it as a meritocracy, its managers believe that it can grow and evolve into an effective world government as technological advances occur in both communication and transportation and the sciences continue to proliferate.[9] They reject the Reunited Nations as a viable organization for world government because the participating states never rise above national interests. Supranational in purpose, the cosmocorp hopes to make contact with its counterpart in the Soviet complex, feeling certain that the meritocracy there must be just as disillusioned with the inefficiency of governmental bureaucracy. Together they may be able to move rapidly toward a harmonious world enterprise.

Three groups seek to prevent expansion of the cosmocorps. The first of these, nationalistic interests in America who control the bureaucracy and the military machine, wishes to maintain the status quo. A parallel structure in Russia also wants to preserve nationalistic structures. The third organization, made up of third generation descendants of the Mafia, has organized a cosmocorp of its own and does not want to see a rival become dominant. A fifth group, similar to the supranational meritocracy of International Communications, wishes to see the emergence of a cosmocorps which is a meritocracy whose top managers are elected democratically. In short, they envision a structure similar to that proposed by the Technocrats of the 1930s who based their theory on Thorsten Veblen's *The Theory of the Leisure Class* and *The Engineers and the Price Class.*[10]

Examining *Five Way Secret Agent* with several other novels in "Science Fiction Models of World Order Systems," political scientist Dennis Livingston concludes:

> Science fiction allows authors to use their informed, creative imagination to speculate about alternative futures. The models that result may be closely reasoned extrapolations from present trends...or they may be formulated out of any combination of social elements of which the author can conceive. Unlike academic forecasting which must be restricted to the realm of the feasible or the possible, science fiction has no compulsion to be respectable. As long as stories maintain an aura of credibility, a matter of the internal consistency of the plot, the author is bound only by the limits of the conceivable, not by the limits of the possible: World government, postnuclear societies, and technological breakdowns are all possibilities for the future. Indeed, if it is true that forecasters implicitly take for granted their own cultural standards as the base lines for projections, then the more outlandish concepts in science fiction may come closer to the actual shape of future events.[11]

Looking Backward From the Year 2000

In 1973 Reynolds published *Looking Backward from the Year 2000*, a utopian vision which pulls together many ideas he had examined separately in his Year 2000 series. It is one of his longest novels, a substantial attempt in the realistic mode to picture the good life in America thirty years from now. To prepare for writing his work, he did an impressive amount of reading and research, drawing on a wide number of contemporary social critics and futurists: Herman Kahn, John K. Galbraith, Robert Heilbroner, Arthur C. Clarke, Isaac Asimov, Erich Fromm. But his major source is Edward Bellamy's 1888 novel, *Looking Backward: A.D. 2000-1887,* for he borrows Bellamy's plot and characters *in toto,* writing a revisionist socialistic tract.[12] He incorporates those technological innovations not anticipated by Bellamy, but essentially he agrees with the value systems underlying Bellamy's society and modifies Bellamy's social structures only as he thinks they are likely to be different in the post-industrial society toward which modern technology is directing the world.

Bellamy's novel was one of the most widely-read books of its time, has never been out-of-print, has been translated into more than twenty languages, and has influenced such social critics as Thorsten Veblen and George Bernard Shaw.[13] It is, of course, the story of the wealthy young Bostonian, Julian West, who awakens to find a world from which the poverty, social unrest, labor strikes, and violence which haunted the late nineteenth century world have disappeared. The storyline—Julian's love for and betrothal to the great-granddaughter of his fiancee in nineteenth century Boston—is a weak thread often unable to sustain the long lectures on the economics and political philosophy of the good society. It succeeds better as a social document than as a work of fiction.

Bellamy held that man's nature is essentially good and the ills of society result from the perversion of his nature by social institutions, especially the economic structure of his society. Correct the economic inequality, and the changes will yield a utopia. These assumptions parallel those of Marx, although Bellamy apparently had not read Marx at the time he wrote *Looking Backward.* His views disagreed with those of Marx regarding the necessity of violent revolution to overthrow the capitalistic system. Instead, he solved the problems of the day through instigating economic equality and nationalizing the production of goods. Bellamy's faith lay in the belief that an industrial society has the productive means to guarantee the basic necessities of life to everyone—and beyond that, to provide a high degree of affluence.

Reynolds shares almost all of Bellamy's underlying beliefs and agrees with the economic system Bellamy designs to implement these values. Only in a few areas does Reynolds disagree. In contrast to Bellamy's emphasis upon a high level of affluence, Reynolds sees limited material consumption as essential to the good life. His utopia has only a few large cities; most people live in small communities. Bellamy's good life, on the other hand, is achieved in large cities. Reynolds advocates a decentralization of the industrial bureaucracy, contrasting sharply with Bellamy's Industrial

Army—a highly bureaucratic, regimented structure in which masses of workers function in robot-like obedience. Bellamy was probably more highly motivated by religious ideals in designing his utopia than is Reynolds. Neither stresses religion in his design, but elsewhere, in *The Religion of Human Solidarity*—published in 1940—he defines a philosophic system strongly influenced by Christianity. In both Reynolds and Bellamy, government has essentially "withered away" in much the fashion Marx proposed.

As noted, the design of Reynolds' utopia differs from Bellamy's chiefly in those areas where twentieth-century technological innovation has created possibilities not available to Bellamy. Community technology, the computer, improved transportation, automation of industrial processes, unlimited energy sources through nuclear fission, space exploration and settlement—all these new developments make possible a utopia which requires no alteration of Bellamy's value system but instead does offer the means for even greater fulfillment of the human potential. Computers, especially, are a major influence in bringing about Reynolds' utopia. They have accomplished the automation of industry so that, consequently, the labor of two-percent of the population produces affluence for an entire society. The remainder of the population happily uses its leisure time in a variety of creative ways. Corporations contribute annually to a huge fund called United States Basics, which is used instead of gold to back the economy.[14]

Through a series of nightmares Julian relives the problems facing the United States in the 1960s and 1970s: the Vietnam War, political corruption, drug abuse, ruthless competition in the business world, prostitution, violence in the streets. Each time he awakens with relief at discovering himself in a world where automated technology—wisely used—assures everyone of a basic income, free transportation, education, health care, and freedom from the threat of war. The development of multinational corporations has resulted in the repudiation of military action as a means of solving international difficulties; it is no longer advantageous to the corporations to settle disputes in this way (p.89). At one point Edith brings Julian a copy of Bellamy's book, asking him to read the famous parable of the coach where a few ride in luxurious comfort while most of humanity toils in the harness to pull the stagecoach. She points out the difference between Bellamy's and Reynolds' worlds: "The coach itself is nuclear-powered, and there is no driver. It's automated. And everybody rides now. There are seats for all" (p.73).

It is not easy to evaluate Reynolds' accomplishment in writing his utopian vision of the near future. Utopias have been out of style in the literary world for much of the twentieth century. Only two have received wide recognition: B.F. Skinner's *Walden Two* (1948) and Aldous Huxley's *Island* (1962). The prevailing dystopian mode is a reaction against the plethora of facile and simplistic utopias poured out in the decades before World War One. It also reflects the disillusionment with the perverted use made of technology to produce nuclear warfare, with conspicuous consumption, with environmental pollution, and with totalitarian social control. But signs indicate a reaction—this time against the seemingly endless avalanche of doomsday books flooding the fiction and non-fiction markets. Individual voices are beginning to suggest the need to create again positive images of the future: Buckminster Fuller's *Utopia or Oblivion* (1969) and Rose Dumont's *Utopia or Else* (1974). Robert Boguslaw notes in *The New Utopians* (1965) that systems design is starting to examine seriously the kind of future which is desirable now that technology makes almost anything possible.

Reynolds may thus be the first of a new wave of utopian thinkers to use science fiction. The form lends itself effectively to modelling a proposed social structure and sketching the various subsystems—economic, educational, familial—which make up the larger design. On the other hand, the limitation of the utopian form is severe, for conflict is inappropriate in the good society so that the author is hard-pressed to find a means of sustaining his plot. He must describe in detail a great many social structures, and this is likely to make dull reading for the individual seeking entertainment. Then, too, as Vernon Louis Parrington emphasized, one utopian novel tends to read like the next because there are only so many ways to escape to and explore the future world.[15] Given these limitations, Reynolds succeeds well in *Looking Backward from the Year 2000*. His use of Bellamy's novel as an underpinning points up what he is attempting—utopian image-making—and dramatizes the radical technological revolution of the twentieth century. He has been thorough and thoughtful in collecting ideas expressed by a variety of contemporary futurists and in assimilating those ideas into a coherent and reasonably complete model of a desirable society available to us in the near future. As always, he accepts the inevitability of change and continued technological development: he suggests this can be beneficial if competition and conspicuous consumption are eliminated; and he refuses to be lured back to the simplicity of a pastoral world. His utopia is a dynamic, not a static one.

The Short Fiction

The Best of Mack Reynolds (1976) contains among its twenty-two short stories a few which are outstanding and one, "Compounded Interest" (1956), which has been recognized as a classic story of time travel. As with the novels, the shorter narratives catch the essence of Reynolds' political views. "Freedom" (1961), for example, dramatizes the ideological conversion of Colonel Simonov, originally one of the most reliable undercover agents of the Russians. When he is assigned to investigate the virus of revolt which is infecting Czechoslovakia, his superior tells him. "You are being given the most important assignment of your career, Ilya. This rot, the ever growing ferment against the Party, must be cut out, liquidated. It seems to fester worst among the middle echelons of . . . what did the Yugoslavian Djilas call us? . . . the *New Class*. Why? That's what we must know."[16] Almost immediately after his arrival in Prague, he discovers in his aircushion car a pamphlet. Its title is *Freedom* and it begins:

> Comrades, more than a hundred years ago the founders of scientific socialism, Karl Marx and Frederick Engels, explained that the State was incompatible with liberty, that the State was an instrument of repression of one class by another. They explained that for true freedom ever to exist the State must wither away.
> Under the leadership of Lenin, Stalin, Krushchev, and now Zverev, the State has become ever stronger. Far from withering away, it continues to oppress us. Fellow Russians, it is time we take action! We must. . . (p.53).

Simonov meets a fellow Russian, Catherina Panova, who tells him of the growing, restless demand by the intellectuals for more freedom now that the Soviet complex is highly industrialized. The people have a high standard of living, and the economic promises of the Party have been kept. Shocked to find that she agrees with the demands for freedom, he sends her name along with others back to his superiors in Moscow. Later, as his friendship with Catherina deepens into love and he attends more lectures and events in the open atmosphere of Prague, he begins to agree with those Czechs who argue for more freedom. He comes to realize that man's drive toward freedom cannot be suppressed.

> Man never achieves complete freedom. It's a goal never reached, but one continually striven for. The moment as small a group as two or three gather together, all of them must give up some of the individual's freedom. When man associates with millions of his fellow men, he gives up a good many freedoms for the sake of the commuity. But always he works to retain as much liberty as possible, and to gain more. It's the nature of our species, I suppose. (p.74).

As in the case of Joe Mauser, the reader watches Simonov's consciousness grow and change. He decides to return to Moscow to try to recover the lists of names of aberrant thinkers which he has forwarded to his superiors. He realizes that such an effort is highly risky and may cost him his life, but it is necessary. He is shot and killed. The Russian plainclothesmen who stand over his body wonder what could have made one of the Party's best agents turn against his superiors; they have no way of knowing that he has fallen in love with freedom.

In "Utopian" (1970), whose opening recalls Bellamy, Tracy Cogswell awakens to discover that during his long sleep radical social change has occurred. He learns that the third world countries have industrialized and that oppressive governments have been overthrown. The dreams of the movement which he had headed in his earlier lifetime have been fulfilled. All should be well, but it isn't, the new leaders tell him; man must learn how to live in Utopia:

The human race is turning to mush, Tracy. Something must be done. For decades we've had what every Utopian through history has dreamed of. Democracy in its ultimate form. Abundance for all. The end of strife between nations, races, and, for all purposes practical, between individuals. And, as a species, we're heading for dissolution.[17]

"Pacifist" (1964) is the story of Warren Casey, a member of a small underground organization, the Pacifists, who are dedicated to the prevention of nuclear war. They claim they represent a new kind of realism in pacifism: "We are willing to fight, to kill and to die, in order to prevent war. We are not interested in the survival of individuals; we are of the opinion that another war will destroy the race, and to preserve humanity we will do literally anything."[18] Among their members are able experts in charting world development. As the story opens, they have concluded that a United States senator must be stopped, for if his policies are continued, they will lead to war within three years. Casey visits the senator, and threatens to kill the members of his family one by one if he does not resign. He next must threaten a scientist whose research is judged dangerous. The Pacifists' logic holds that it is better to kill some individuals than to allow the destruction of the race, but the scientist points out to Casey the fallacy of that position:

You make a basic mistake in thinking this a matter of individuals. To use an example, in effect what you are saying is *kill the dictator and democracy will return to the country.* Nonsense. You put the cart before the horse. That dictator didn't get into power because he was so fabulously capable that he was able to thwart a whole nation's desire for liberty. He, himself, is the product of the situation. Change the situation and he will disappear, but simply assassinate him and all you'll get is another dictator (p.161).

Increasingly sickened by all the killings he has done in the name of peace, surrounded in a police ambush as the story ends, Casey allows himself to be killed rather than even trying to escape.

"Revolution" (1960) also examines the psychology of violence. As did "Pacifist," it concentrates upon the consciousness of a secret revolutionary who changes his view of his activities. He is sent by the United States to Russia to make contact with the underground and channel Western financial aid to its members. He joins the organization and together they plan a revolution. This dramatic situation requires a discussion of other revolutionary attempts, what caused them, and the factors that influenced their success. Reynolds handles this well, avoiding the split between gratuitous violence and economic lecture which mars some of his fiction. As the months pass, the fervor of the revolutionaries increases as they become true believers in their cause. So does their ruthlessness in planning how they will maintain control once they seize power. The protagonist realizes that revolution will not solve the problem of governmental oppression; it will merely replace one set of officials with another.

All in all, one feels that Reynolds is more successful with his short stories than with his novels. Too often in the longer narratives he uses stereotyped characters and plots, invariably of the cloak-and-dagger variety. He also depends on excessive violence to move the plot forward. Intermittently, he stops the storyline to give his audience long political-economic lectures. On the other hand, in novels like *The Space Barbarians* and the Joe Mauser trilogy, he avoids this disjunction of idea and action, particularly because he tells the story from the point of view of the central character. The dramatic tension grows from the inner conflict the protagonist experiences as his original political ideology is called into question by new insights arising from his experience. Disappointingly, however, even in this fiction which succeeds dramatically, Reynolds often writes without literary style and grace. Certainly the task he has undertaken in writing political science fiction is not an easy one. Irving Howe has taken note of the difficulty in his *Politics and the Novel:*

One of the great problems, but also one of the supreme challenges, for the political novelist is to make ideas or ideologies come to life, to endow them with the capacity for stirring characters into passionate gestures and sacrifices, and even more, to create the illusion that they have a kind of independent motion, so that they themselves—those abstract weights of idea or ideology—seem to become active characters in the political novel.[19]

Mack Reynolds deserves recognition as one of the first writers to present a viewpoint not often found in American magazine science fiction—a radical left criticism of capitalism. He also is one of the few contemporary writers who retains a faith in the possibility of a utopian society achieved through science and technology. He must be regarded as a significant figure in the development of political science fiction, for he does for the social sciences what "hard" science fiction writers have done with the ideas of those disciplines. They have shown how the theories and achievements of physics, chemistry, and biology—applied through engineering technology—may shape and alter man's future. Reynolds does the same for economics and political science. He asks how theory, applied through social engineering, may change man's present social institutions. And it is to his credit that he is not doctrinaire, for he offers a range of possible answers, although all are predicated upon the dignity of man as an individual.

Susan Wood

Discovering Worlds:
The Fiction of Ursula K. Le Guin

Ursula K. Le Guin makes maps. The worlds she presents to her
readers are various: Rocannon's World, where golden-haired
warriors ride winged cats; Gethen, where ambisexual humans have
built a civilization perfectly adapted to perpetual cold; Earthsea,
where innumerable islands are home to wizards and dragons,
goatherds and kings; Anarres, where anarchists strive to maintain
life in the desert, and freedom in that life. Yet all the exotic, complex
and varied societies Le Guin presents are really aspects of one world:
ours, now. In the nine novels and numerous short works which she
has written between 1962 and 1976, the exploration of imaginary
worlds has provided a framework for an exploration of the varieties
of physical life, social organizations, and personal development
open to human beings.[1] At the same time, this richness and variety
suggest the ethical concept underlying her work: a celebration of life
itself, through a joyful acceptance of its patterns. This concept is
expressed not only in the works themselves, but in her vision of the
artistic process which brought them forth.

It is easy to think of the science fiction and fantasy writer as a
god: one who can create a world, fill it with life for the readers'
amusement, and rest on the seventh day. Le Guin's working mode,
however, is organic and intuitive, rather than planned; she acts like
one of her League ethnographers, observing and reporting on the
life form of new planets. She explains, for example, that she had no
outlines, no plans of the island-world Earthsea and its languages,
when she began to write her fantasy trilogy. She discovers people
and places as they exist—in the writer's subconscious, in the truth
and reality of their own being:

> This attitude towards action, creation, is evidently a basic one, the same root from
> which the interest in the *I Ching* and Taoist philosophy evident in most of my books
> arises. The Taoist world is orderly, not chaotic, but its order is not one imposed by
> man or by a personal or humane deity. The true laws—ethical and aesthetic, as surely
> as scientific—are not imposed from above by any authority, but exist in things and
> are to be found—discovered.[2]

In turn, the discovery of this intrinsic order, on a personal level, forms the action of Le Guin's major works. In general, her characters are engaged in a quest, both a physical journey to an unknown goal which proves to be their home, and an inward search for knowledge of the one true act they must perform. The development of the plot, then, takes on a deeper significance than is usual in science fiction, with its emphasis on action for the sake of entertainment. The Le Guin character often initiates actions which have personal and social consequences. The student-wizard Ged, in his pride, looses a spirit of unlike; the Ekumen envoy Genly Ai refuses to trust the one person who trusts him: and the fates of whole worlds are altered, as surely as they are by George Orr, who, in an effective dream, can wipe out six billion people. More important than the pattern of plot, however, is each character's movement to an understanding of this pattern: to an acceptance both of the integrity of each individual life, and of the place of each individual within the overall pattern of life.

This metaphor of discovery, of course, has limitations. A romantic definition, perhaps overly so, it appears to de-emphasize the importance of skill and craft in writing fiction. Discoveries, after all, may involve a slow and patient search for the right word: perhaps, as in the Earthsea trilogy, for the true name which will control the essence of the thing. Le Guin's work resonates with such definitive words: in *City of Illusions,* the presentation of the Shing stronghold, Es Toch, as a city "built across a chasm in the ground, a hollow place," (p.159), both a literal chasm and a moral "abyss of self-destruction" (p.196), a self-deluding lie; in *The Lathe of Heaven,* the description of George Orr in terms that recall *Tao* 37, as "a block of wood not carved," perfect in its integrity (p.95). A central and recurrent image is that of life as a pattern or web, with individual points of life joined by lines of communication. This image, with its strong ethical overtones—each life is, like a Gethenian, "singularly complete," but none exists in isolation—is echoed in a variety of symbols: the patterning frame, a foretelling device in *City of Illusions;* the web of tensions and communications woven by the Foretellers in *The Left Hand of Darkness;* the spells woven of words, movements, and human understanding in the Earthsea Trilogy; and the description of the Ekumen, the framework of human communication which Le Guin's future worlds evolve, as a "network" for trade in goods and ideas (p.26). Overall, the books are unified by the patterns formed from seeing black and white, darkness and light, self and other, death and life, not as opposites but as necessary complements in the harmony of existence. These recurrent image patterns, significant in themselves, serve also to describe and reinforce the underlying concepts of integrity and interdependence. All Le Guin's fiction works through imagery as well as content to question what a character in *The Left Hand of*

Darkness sees as "the whole tendency to dualism that pervades human thinking" (p.68).[3]

In fact, Le Guin's fictions themselves are webs, woven of words, recurrent images and thematic patterns, moving always closer to an expression of a human truth, a vision of life. Her central figures—scientist, wizard, designer, or traveller—embody aspects of the artist seeking truth and expressing its patterns. Any full appreciation of her work, then, must embody an appreciation of its conscious craft: the patterning of *The Left Hand of Darkness* around the myth of its own world; the balancing of *The Dispossessed* between two planets and one movement of discovery; the careful cadencing of sentences. Le Guin's apparent delight in language becomes another means of celebrating human life. Thus style and structure are important elements of her work; her skill at handling them is a major contribution to the maturity of the field.

Le Guin's weakness is a paradoxical tendency to impose moral and ethical patterns on her work, so that form and content work against her philosophy. This didacticism is most evident in "The Word for World Is Forest" (1972), "The Ones Who Walk Away from Omelas" (1972), and passages of *The Dispossessed*. The author's statement of values precludes their discovery, in contrast to the process, most notable in the Earthsea books, whereby the reader shares naturally in the characters' growing awareness of the right direction of their lives. Such a tendency is inevitable, however, given Le Guin's serious concern with human experience and conduct. It is this concern, usually embodied convincingly in individuals' actions and perceptions, which has made her one of the most notable writers to choose science fiction as a framework for discovery.

Ursula Le Guin's work, then, is mature art: rich and varied in content, skillful in presentation, joyous in its celebration of life, and, above all, thoughtful in approach, rooted in and developing a significant personal philosophy. The maturity is literal as well as literary.

Ursula Kroeber Le Guin was born in 1929, the daughter of anthropologist and author, A. L. Kroeber, and writer, Theodora Kroeber. The self-portrait she gives in an autobiographical essay in the British sf journal *Foundation* is that of a child happily surrounded by people who appreciated both other cultures and the spoken and written word as an augmentation of life.[4] She collected her first rejection slip when twelve, from John W. Campbell, then editor of *Astounding*. The following twenty years included a Master's degree in French and Italian literature from Columbia, marriage to historian Charles Le Guin, the birth of three children, and the production of several published poems and unpublished novels. By the early 1960's when Cele Goldsmith Lalli began to buy such fantasies as "April in Paris" (1962), "The Word of Unbinding"

(1964), and "The Rule of Names" (1964) for *Fantastic* and *Amazing*, Le Guin was an accomplished writer, expressing valuable insights with grace and humour.

Her rapid development as a writer from that point is best seen in *The Wind's Twelve Quarters* (1975), a collection of seventeen short stories first published betwen 1962 and 1974, highlighted by "Winter's King" (1969), "Nine Lives" (1969), and "Vaster Than Empires and More Slow" (1971). All are notable stories in which scientific extrapolations—sub-lightspeed travel and alien biology in the first and third stories, cloning in the second—provide a framework for powerful psychological studies.

In Le Guin's first three novels, *Rocannon's World* (1966), *Planet of Exile* (1966), and *City of Illusions* (1967), innovative and entertaining fictions develop on the solid conceptual basis of human values affirmed. *The Left Hand of Darkness* (1969) confirms its author's status as one of the major forces in contemporary science fiction. A work of great emotional power, impressive technical skill, and genuine social and psychological extrapolation, it won both the 1970 Nebula award of the Science Fiction Writers of America and the Hugo award of the 28th World Science Fiction Convention as the best novel of the year. It presents a new world in the distant future to challenge our view of the present, in particular our assumptions about male and female roles, about sexuality and love.

The next novel, *The Lathe of Heaven* (1971) brings readers back to an all-too-possible near-future Earth: polluted, disease-ridden, self-destructive. Yet it avoids easy "relevance" to offer, again, a genuine alternative for human life: not a social blueprint, but a personal philosophy of right living. "The Word for World is Forest," which appeared in 1972 in Harlan Ellison's *Again, Dangerous Visions,* is unfortunately less successful in avoiding the limitations of moral outrage at contemporary problems. In Le Guin's most recent sf novel, *The Dispossessed* (1974), two worlds, the anarchist society of Anarres and a capitalistic nation on its sister-planet Urras, are tested through a scientist's search for truth, a couple's discovery of joy.

By 1975, Ursula Le Guin was acknowledged as a leader of the science fiction field: winner of three Nebula awards and three Hugo awards,[5] she was the Guest of Honour at the 33rd World Science Fiction Convention in Melbourne, Australia—which presented her with a fourth Hugo for *The Dispossessed*. It seems fitting, however, that the major work of this mature writer, who is bringing a new adult concern with the living of life to science fiction, should be a work nominally for children: the Earthsea trilogy, composed of *A Wizard of Earthsea* (1968); *The Tombs of Atuan* (1971), a Newbery Honor Book; and *The Farthest Shore* (1972), winner of the National Book Award for Children's Literature. This work, which has won praise and professional honours, reconfirms the importance of fantasy as a timeless vehicle for examining basic human concerns: growth, maturity, and death.

The central concerns of Le Guin's work are evident in her first novel, *Rocannon's World*. The genesis of this colourful heroic fantasy is a short story, "The Dowry of Angyar," published in *Amazing* in 1964 and reprinted as the novel's Prologue. This story, Le Guin writes, became "the germ of a novel" when a minor character asserted his importance: " 'I'm Rocannon. I want to explore my world.' "[6] It also introduced thematic concerns and characteristics of style developed in the later novels.

Most notable, perhaps, is the richness and variety of the world presented. Fomalhaut II is seen in a dual perspective, through the superficial "objective" summary of the League's *Abridged Handy Pocket Guide to Intelligent Life-forms* and the romantic presentation of Semley's heroic culture, scanned and dismissed by the League investigators. That culture is a tapestry of proud warriors on winged cat-like steeds; beautiful golden-haired women; laughing elfin creatures of sunlight, the Fiia; and lumpish troll-like creatures of night, the Gdemiar or Clayfolk—or, to the League scientists who so casually interfere with the destiny of planets, "the trogs."

The story unfolds with tragic inevitability. Semley, a highborn Angyar lady, seeks her dowry, a legendary necklace of sapphire and gold. Courageous, yet blindly arrogant, she trusts herself to the Clayfolk, whose technology she refuses to comprehend; thus she remains unaware that they have sent her on a sub-lightspeed flight of sixteen years to the nearest League world, Ollul. Here, Rocannon gives her back her necklace. Returning home after one subjective night, Semley discovers the cost of her quest: her husband long dead, her daughter grown, her dowry the burden of loss and madness. The mythically appropriate pattern of her fate is achieved (as is Argaven's in "Winter's King") by the scientific realities of sublightspeed travel; time, like other human truths, is subjective, mutable.

Semley's action, then, has consequences for herself and her kinfolk; and Le Guin, in her awareness of these consequences, finds the beginning of her novel. Semley's situation, in turn, had been partly created by League interference in her world. Rocannon, whose reading of the cursory League summary of the planet's cultures is ironically counterpointed by his growing interest in Semley, interferes in his turn with the planet's destiny—and so is claimed by the "tragic myth" Semley suggests to him (p.24). He forbids League contact while he mounts an ethnographic survey; and thus, in the years which elapse while he makes his sublightspeed journey, the unprotected planet is over-run by rebels who wipe out his expedition.

Rocannon, acknowledging his responsibility for events, undertakes a destructive quest for revenge. Like the Le Guin heroes who follow him—Falk, Estraven and Ged, especially—he becomes part of a mythic pattern, his destiny linking past and future to present. Seeking across unmapped continents for his enemies, he learns the secret of "mindhearing," a form of telepathic communication which enables him to complete his mission. Yet, like Semley, he must pay with the loss of that "which you hold dearest and would least willingly give," his friend Mogien's life (p.118). Mogien, however, is a warrior who senses, and joyfully accepts, the heroic death which fate holds for him. Moreover, Rocannon, in losing everything—friends, possessions, even his identity—is reborn from Zgama's fire as Olthor, the Wanderer, a hero of Angyar legend. His mission completed, he gains a new home on the world ultimately give his name. Where, then, does the freedom of individual action end, and the pattern of consequences merge into the pattern of fate or of myth? "How can you tell the fact from legend, truth from truth?" asks the storyteller beginning Semley's tale (p.5). The question foreshadows the specific opening of *The Left Hand of Darkness,* with its strikingly similar plot of journey through annihilation of self and sacrifice of life to new awareness and integration. It also announces one general thematic concern of Le Guin's novels: the nature of truth.

The most important element of *Rocannon's World,* as of *Planet of Exile* and *City of Illusions,* is not, however, philosophical speculation, but the richness and variety of the life presented. A whole novel could be written, for instance, about the telepathic Fiia, a humanoid race who "chose the green valleys, the sunlight, and the bowl of wood" when their kin, the Clayfolk, chose "night and caves and swords of metal"—and who know they have, by this choice, made themselves incomplete, "the Half-People" (p.108). (In fact, the choices suggested here do gain fuller development in the fallen-Eden tale of "The Word for World is Forest.") Even within the limits of a short formula narrative, Le Guin exhibits a remarkable ability to communicate the essence of a culture--as, for example, when she sums up the proud Angyar as "lacking any first-person forms for the verb 'to be unable' " (p.45).

The language, too, complements the world it depicts. The ritual beauty of the Fiia's greetings of Semley—"Hail, Halla's bride, Kirienlady, Windborne, Semley the Fair" (p.12)—contrasts effectively with Ketho the League curator's mumbled "She wants something we've got here in the museum, is that what the trogs say?"(p.21). As the prosaic account of Rocannon evolves into the heroic tale of Olthor the Wanderer, the language becomes more rich and cadenced. Thus he is first seen looking at a "very tall, dark-skinned, yellow-haired woman" accompanied by "four uneasy and unattractive dwarves" (p.6). He is last presented in language no more ornate, but subtly different, as he is different—the stuff of legend:

When ships of the League returned to the planet, and Yahan guided one of the surveys south to Breygna to find him, he was dead. The people of Breygna mourned their Lord, and his widow, tall and fair-haired, wearing a great blue jewel set in gold at her throat, greeted those who came seeking him. So he never knew that the League had given that world his name (p.136).

Though Le Guin's style has evolved towards simplicity, it is still characterized by this flowing quality, a skillful use of cadence and sound patterns, and a flexible use of compound and complex sentences to state, elaborate, and qualify the variations of life and truth.

The exile's quest, a journey which leads physically home and spiritually to harmony, becomes Le Guin's basic narrative pattern. In *Planet of Exile*, the movements to integration are biological, as Terran genes slowly adapt to the alien world Werel; social, as Terrans and native Teverans ally at last against their common enemies, the marauding Gaal and the 5,000-night-long winter; and, most important, personal, as Jakob Agat and Rolery defy cultural taboos to marry. Both races, both individuals, thus gain a new "chance of life" in the midst of death (p.119). This life is affirmed in the sequel, *City of Illusions*. Here the exile Falk crosses a far-future North America, in the process stripped, like Rocannon, of every shred of his past life, including his name. His goal is the city of the Shing, his enemies who give him back his true name—Ramarren, Agat's heir, a leader of the high civilization his hybrid race has evolved on Werel. As the dualminded Falk/Ramarren, he resists Shing mind control, and thus exposes the lie by which they rule on Earth. Ramarren's return to Werel will bring, in turn, freedom back to the home world Terra, and to the League.

Another aspect of Le Guin's concern with harmony is her emphasis on communications devices and techniques, both for themselves and for their symbolic importance. Sub-lightspeed travel can bridge the abyss of space. The ansible, a device which "will permit communication without any time interval between two points in space," allows ideas to "leap the great gaps" of space-time."[7] Mindspeech, or paraverbal communication, bridges the isolation of individuals "like a touch across the abyss."[8] All these suggest, finally, the state of being "in touch": that primary communication within the self, the integration of conscious and unconscious minds and the self-knowledge which, repeatedly, enables the central character to cross the abyss of despair, to "get through nothingness and out the other side."[9]

The multiplicity and inter-relationship of these concepts, and the flexibility of the image expressing them, provides a useful insight into Le Guin's process of exploring ideas. *The Dispossessed*, for example, opens with Shevek crossing the void of space like a flung stone, an image suggesting his social and physical exile by recalling both the rocks flung at him as he leaves and his last sight of Anarres as "a ball of white stone falling down into blackness." His awareness of this isolation plunges him into a depression, presented in images corresponding with his physical situation aboard the interplanetary freighter: "For hours or days he existed in a vacancy, a dry and wretched void without past or future. The walls stood tight about him. Outside them was the silence." The abyss is thus associated with the book's local image of the ambiguous wall, the created and chosen prison cutting off all human communication. In fact, Shevek's primary isolation here is from his own sense of integrity, the awareness of freedom and accompanying responsibility basic to Odonian society. He feels that "he had given up his birthright of decision. It was gone, fallen away from him along with his world, the world of the Promise, the barren stone." Despair is deepened by a fever in which he hangs "in a limbo between reason and unreason, no man's land" (pp.5-8).

The flung stone, however, also suggests Shevek's independent discovery of Zeno's Paradox, and thus his role as physicist. By asserting his right to work and to share the results of that work, he transcends the abyss of despair—and gains freedom to create. In turn, by transcending the "prison" of provable theory, he achieves the vision in which he sees the fundamental unity, not only of two apparently opposed views of reality, but of the universe itself; "at this instant the difference between this planet and that, between Urras and Anarres, was no more significant to him than the difference between two grains of sand on the shore of the sea. There were no more abysses, no more walls. There was no more exile. He had seen the foundations of the universe, and they were solid." In personal and scientific terms this vision of "simplicity which contained in it all complexity" is "the way clear, the way home, the light" (pp.247-248). Its practical application is the ansible which makes possible the League of All Worlds and the Ekumen, webs of communication stretched across the abyss of space and cultural difference.

Le Guin's science fiction also presents a future history consistent with its philosophy in stressing both the interdependence of life and the variety of its possible forms. Intelligent human life, in this cosmography, arose millenia ago on the planet Hain, which established innumerable colonies. Each colony-planet became "the world" to "the men" after Hainish civilization collapsed. By 2300 A.D., which Ian Watson postulates as the date of *The Dispossesed*,[10] a revived Hainish culture possessing sub-lightspeed travel has contacted eight worlds. The ansible facilitates creation of the League of All Worlds, a trade union and super-government. In "The Word for World Is Forest," scientists of the eighteen-year old League end Terran exploitation of Athshe. "Vaster Than Empires and More Slow," set in "the earliest decades of the League," shows the Terrans, who resent the fact that Hainish "not only founded but salvaged" their civilization, mounting expeditions to seek "truly alien worlds." In an effective image, the misfits of the Extreme Survey crew are pictured entering their vessel by wriggling through the coupling tube one by one "like apprehensive spermatozoa trying to fertilize the universe."[11] What they discover is a perfectly integrated alien intelligence, the tree-world 4470; what they learn from it is the need, not to dominate the universe, but to accept and love another being unreservedly. "Nine Lives," also set in the early years of Terran expansion, presents the same discovery as two mining engineers isolated on a hostile world, learn to respond to an alien/human being, the ten-clone John Chow, and in turn teach love of the other to one unit of that clone. In its extrapolation of the psychological implications of a biological advance, as well as in its characterization and skillful narration, this is probably Le Guin's finest short story.

Rocannon's World, set some 300 years after the League's foundation, chronicles two major developments. The League appears to have developed as an authoritarian government, levying taxes on new worlds to equip forces against the mysterious alien Enemy; inevitably its unthinking use of power breeds rebels. On the positive side, however, Rocannon does learn the teachable skill of mindhearing, with its potential for creating true understanding. In *Planet of Exile*, set in "year 1405 of the League of All Worlds," the Terran colony on Werel has been isolated for 600 Earth-years by the Shing advance; in *City of Illusions,* 1200 years later, the end of this isolation begins when Werel sends an expedition back to the home-world. As Zove tells Falk, the latter's mission is to restore hope to a world which fears its own past greatness as much as it fears the Shing: "We keep a little knowledge, and do nothing with it. But once we used that knowledge to weave the pattern of life like a tapestry across night and chaos. We enlarged the chances of life. We did man's work" (p.18). In *The Left Hand of Darkness*, the Hainish worlds have been undertaking this work for 1491 Ekumenical years.

The Ekumen, like the viable anarchistic society of Anarres, reveals Le Guin's power to envision genuine alternatives to present human organizations. Genly Ai, the Ekumen envoy, describes the government he serves as "not a kingdom but a co-ordinator, a clearing-house for trade and knowledge" uniting 3,000 nations on eighty-three worlds, seeking an alliance with the Gethenian nations for many reasons: " 'Material profit. Increase of knowledge. The augmentation of the complexity and intensity of the field of intelligent life. The enrichment of harmony and the greater glory of God. Curiosity. Adventure. Delight' " (p.25). Ai's own experience of exile and acceptance enables him to understand the Ekumen and its reasons for sending him to Gethen alone:

> Alone, I cannot change your world. But I can be changed by it.... Alone, the relationship I finally make, if I make one, is not impersonal and not only political: it is individual, it is personal, it is both more and less than political. Not We and They; not I and It; but I and Thou. Not political, not pragmatic, but mystical. In a certain sense the Ekumen is not a body politic, but a body mystic. It considers beginnings to be extremely important. Beginnings, and means. Its doctrine is just the reverse of the doctrine that the end justifies the means. It proceeds, therefore, by subtle ways, and slow ones, and queer, risky ones; rather as evolution does, which is in certain senses its model (pp.185-186).

The promise of this "mystical" and individual relationship with the human community of the Ekumen motivates Estraven to sacrifice his life to further Ai's mission. This promise finds its expression in the love which bridges the abyss between Ai and Estraven; its fulfillment in "the delight, the courage" with which individual Karhiders welcome "the coming of men from the stars" (p.221); and its symbol in the bridge whose keystone is mortared with blood.

The future Earths of other works—notably *The Lathe of Heaven* and "The New Atlantis" (1975)—exist in different cosmogenies. They are, however, broadly consistent with the post-collapse Terra of the League's formative years, a "discord" in which life continues only through "the absolute regimentation of each life towards the goal of racial survival."[12] More important, the action and underlying values of the non-Hainish works, especially of the Earthsea trilogy, always point to the same philosophy of harmony and balance.

Le Guin's Hainish future history resembles, in broad outline, the pattern of spaceflight-Galactic Empire-Interregnum-Rise of a Permanent Galactic Civilization which Donald Wollheim identifies as basic to science fiction.[13] Yet the very fact that Hain, not ruined Terra, is the prime world challenges readers' assumptions. Even the League involves not domination of the universe by our descendants, but acceptance of a larger pattern of life. The Ekumen, in turn, offers a genuine alternative to the standard idea of the military/economic empire evolving to "challenge" creation.

Criticism of xenophobia, the racial expression of fear of the other, is implicit in Le Guin's future history. The opening pages of *Planet of Exile*, for example, call into question the nature of "humanity." The centre of consciousness is Rolery, a native woman exploring, with fear and fascination, the city "imagined by alien minds." These others, the "grinning black false-men" with their eyes of an "unearthly darkness," are soon revealed to be "human" in the reader's terms (pp.6-9). They are Terran colonists who, even after 600 years, hold aloof from the natives whom they regard contemptuously as non-human, "just hilfs" (p.29). The separation of these races, and their potential for union, is powerfully suggested when Rolery and Jakob Agat touch light palm to dark palm in "the salute of equals" (p.14). Specifically the gesture recalls Agat's rescue of Rolery from the abyss and foreshadows their communication in love and mindspeech "like a touch across the abyss" (p.83). Generally it foreshadows the interbreeding of races to produce the new civilization which restores the League. This basic human gesture of touching hands recurs throughout Le Guin's work. In *The Lathe of Heaven*, for example, Heather Lelache confirms her liking for George Orr with a handshake which reminds her of her mother's SNCC button, black and white hands joined.

The Left Hand of Darkness, in particular, questions the nature of "humanity" by challenging assumptions about sexuality and sex roles. King Argaven rejects alliance with "all those nations of monsters living out in the Void" as "a disgusting idea... I don't see why human beings here on earth should want or tolerate any dealings with creatures so monstrously different" from the Gethenian ambisexual norm (pp.25-26). Here, too, the action presents Genly Ai—specifically presented as "earth-coloured," darker-skinned than the Gethenians—learning to accept and "touch" one member of an alien race. The wholeness in dualism which Gethen offers is, in turn, expressed through images of touch in Tormer's Lay:

> Light is the left hand of darkness and darkness the right hand of light. Two are one, life and death, lying together like lovers in kemmer, like hands joined together, like the end and the way (p.168).

The touch confirming the acceptance of the other, then, is part of the larger image pattern of light and darkness, opposition and integration, which resonates throughout Le Guin's work. In specific terms, it signals a social and personal harmony. Thus the movement of *Planet of Exile* is a joyous one, culminating in Agat's realization that "these were his people. He was no exile here" (p.126). The counterbalancing movement is tragic, tracing the consequences of disharmony in dislocation and breakdown. In "The Word for World Is Forest," notably, the world-dominating Terran culture is represented by the soldier Don Davidson. Disastrously insecure in his identity, he believes that "the only time a man is really and entirely a man is when he's just had a woman or just killed another man."[14] Davidson is so completely unbalanced that he can only continue to exist by imposing his will on the external world, clearing the forest which he fears and killing the Hainish-stock humanoid natives whom he dismisses as sub-human "creechies." In contrast, the Athshean world is harmonious. The forest presents a delicate ecological balance of trees and water, shadow and sunlight; its people maintain sanity "not on the razor's edge of reason but on the double support, the fine balance, of reason and dream" (p.114).

Inevitably, Davidson's insanity grows; the paranoid conviction that every living thing is his enemy leaves him in a mental isolation confirmed by physical exile to the Terran-made desert of Dump Island. The real tragedy, however, is not his fate but the perpetuation of his madness in Athshean culture. Led by Davidson's counterpart, the dreamer Selver, the Athsheans learn to preserve themselves by exterminating their killers—whom they identify, ironically, as non-human "yumens." Their real fall into the world of experience comes, the story suggests, not with the actual acts of murder but with the prior process of objectification. This produces a split betwen the I and the not-I, and thus makes the idea of murder possible. If, as Northrop Frye suggests, the basic reaction of the (Western) human mind is to "see the world as objective, as something set over against you and not yourself or related to you in any way,"[15] then Le Guin's novels in all their elements—cosmography, imagery, character development, resolution—offer an alternative to that process.

It is evident, then, that Ursula K. Le Guin's work possesses a thematic and conceptual interdependence consistent with her philosophy. Discussion of any one element, or any one novel, quickly leads to a branching network of cross-references and examples. Nevertheless, within the overall pattern, each work explores a unique aspect of the human problem of right living, on and in response to a unique world.

Gethen, named Winter by the Ekumen's investigators, is the most richly detailed of Le Guin's worlds, and the strangest. Here, human beings have evolved complex civilizations which have been profoundly influenced by two factors: a physical condition of almost perpetual winter, and a human condition of periodic ambisexuality. These realities, in turn, provide metaphors which echo the central movement in from imbalance to harmony, as the alien/human Genly Ai, Ekumen envoy to Gethen, learns to accept the winter-world, to love one of its alien/human people, and to know harmony and joy within his divided self.

The first Investigators named the new planet Winter, and noted that "the dominant factor in Gethenian life is not sex or any other human thing: it is their environment, their cold world. Here man has a crueler enemy even than himself" (p.70). Life exists in a precarious balance with death. Individuals move as tiny dark shadows across a blinding backdrop of white, and move through their society in the complex prestige-relationships of *shifgrethor,* a term which "comes from an old word for *shadow*" (p.177). They seek refuge from the "bright winter, bitter, terrible and bright" in the warm dark circle of the communal Hearth, whose unity forms their primary social organization (p.154). The Hearth's fires exist, however, "to warm the spirit and not the flesh," since the Gethenians rely on adaptation, "physiological weatherproofing," rather than central heating (p.21). In thirty centuries of technological progress, they have developed electricity and other efficient devices like the Chabe stove, which emits heat and light; yet change proceeds slowly, carefully, and Winter remains "a world where a common table implement is a little device with which you crack the ice that has formed on your drink between drafts" (p.8). Gethenians are, however, losing this precarious balance. Having evolved to some degree of control over their world, they are becoming each other's enemies: family Hearths are uniting into the large rival nations of Orgoreyn and Karhide, abandoning their local feuds to mobilize for war. Love of one's own country is becoming "hate of one's uncountry" (p.152). Estraven, Prime Minister of Karhide, the only Gethenian who trusts Ai, welcomes him for bringing a "new option": unity for Gethen within the diversity of the Ekumen. Yet, ironically, the Envoy sent alone to form a personal bond with Gethen is an individual unable to make that rapport. "I've been cold ever since I came to this world," he tells Estraven, walking away from their crucial meeting "cold, unconfident, obsessed by perfidy, and solitude, and fear" (pp.14-15). Self-alienated, he can only see Estraven as an alien, and mistrust him on, ultimately, the basis of his own sexual confusion.

Estraven, as a Gethenian, is potentially ambisexual, a man (a wielder of power) who is also a woman. Ai, even after two years on Gethen, can only see a Gethenian "self-consciously...first as a man, then as a woman, forcing him into those categories so irrelevant to his nature and so essential to my own." Yet human women are truly aliens to him. Thus he mistrusts Estraven, regarding those signals and actions which arise from the complications of shifgrethor as a "womanly" performance, "all charm and tact and lack of substance, specious and adroit. Was it in fact this soft supple femininity that I disliked and distrusted in him? (p.9)

Gethenians, in fact, are neither men nor women, but potentially either. Sexually neutral and androgynous most of the month, each regularly enters an estrus period, *kemmer,* becoming male or female as hormone changes dictate. Thus sex roles and their corresponding social behavior cannot exist; and responsibilities, notably parenthood, are shared. Dualism becomes not the sexual alienation

Ai feels, but the basic relationship of "I" and "thou."

Yet the dualism persists for the reader. Prime ministers and secret agents, pulling sledges, wearing breeches in the cold, represented always in Ai's narrative by the masculine/generic pronoun "he": the Gethenians too easily seem men who, jarringly, are sometimes women. "The king was pregnant" (p.72). The reader's own preconceptions, plus Le Guin's admitted failure to show "the 'female' component of the Gethenian characters in *action*,"[16] make it too easy to envision a Gethenian as Ai does, forcing each into the "irrelevant" categories of man and woman.

It is not possible, as David Ketterer suggests, to paraphrase the action of *The Left Hand of Darkness* adequately without mentioning Gethenian ambisexuality.[17] That action, echoing the novel's central concepts, is unified, a circle; yet it is also dual, internal, and external. Genly Ai completes his journey from Karhide, through Orgoreyn, over the Ice, back to Erhenrang where—with dramatic rightness, but perhaps unconvincing haste given his earlier hesitations—he completes his mission by welcoming the Ekumen ambassadors to the planet. This action fuses the archetype of the winter-journey through death to rebirth with specific Gethenian myths of "The Place Inside the Blizzard" and "Estraven The Traitor": tales of betrayal and higher loyalty which, in turn, find literal expression in Estraven's own fate. In this fusion, the action unites the inner and outer worlds. Ai's journey is not just a simple hero-tale of Man against Ice, though the physical hardships are effectively presented, as the thermometer drops each morning to "somewhere between zero and -60°" and the sledge sticks yet again (p.173). Rather, the shared exile and danger of that journey enable him to move, at last, to an understanding of Gethen, made possible only by an acceptance of the individual's, Estraven's, sexuality.

Genly Ai, like most narrators, unconsciously reveals his own character in his observations about others. The reader assumes the Ekumen envoy will be wise, experienced. It is a shock to realize that Ai is only thirty, and naive, especially in his dealings in Orgoreyn. His chief limitation is the ignorance and fear of female sexuality which lead him to mistrust, not just Estraven but most Gethenians, seeing them as males with certain negative traits he identifies as female. Thus he describes his building superintendent, father of four, as "my landlady, a voluble man," an individual "feminine in looks and manners" with "a soft fat face and a prying, spying, ignoble, kindly nature" (pp.35-36). His profound mistrust of Estraven continues even after the latter has rescued him from certain death in Pulefen Voluntary Farm. Both sit, exiles, aliens, in a tent on the Ice, in warmth and light surrounded by death: alone. Ai muses:

What is a friend, in a world where any friend may be a lover at a new phase of the moon? Not I, locked in my virility; no friend to Therem Harth, or any other of his race. Neither man nor woman, neither and both, cyclic, lunar, metamorphosing under the hand's touch, changelings in the human cradle, they were no flesh of mine, no friends: no love between us (p.153).

Yet just as the reality of Gethen shaped its societies and the myths by which its people express human truths, so the actual experience of the winter-journey enables Ai to accept Estraven, to forge the personal bond uniting worlds. His awareness of the Gethenians as "isolated, and undivided" on a hostile world lacking even highly-evolved animals, leads to an understanding of their holistic worldview and Terran dualism: matters which do "go even wider than sex..." He also begins to recognize his own sexual alienation. Significantly, the episode is presented from Estraven's point of view, emphasizing the isolation of each individual, their growing understanding (pp.167-168). When the physical realities of tent life force the two to deal with the sexual tension between them, Ai is finally able to accept Estraven as the latter has always accepted him: as a whole human being. Their trust and love are confirmed not by sexual contact which "would be for us to meet once more as aliens," but by the subtler touch of mindspeech: "a bond, indeed, but an obscure and austere one, not so much admitting further light (as I had expected it to) as showing the extent of the darkness" (p.182).

Finally, when Ai tries to walk in the white void of shadowless snow, the place "inside the blizzard" where even the senses are traitors, he fully comprehends the dualism which complements Gethenian wholeness. "'We need the shadows in order to walk'" (p.191), even though each shadow, in the Orgota creation myth, is the death which follows each mortal over the eternal ice of the world (p.171). Ai sees the Gethenians as uniting all opposites, like the Terran yin-yang symbol: "'Light, dark. Fear, courage. Cold, warmth. Female, male... Both and one. A shadow on snow'" (p.191).

Unfortunately Ai's insight, like his rapport with Estraven, remains incomplete. By the novel's end he can accept Faxe the Weaver as a "person," but, like Gulliver, he rejects his fellow human beings as "great apes with intelligent eyes, all of them in rut, in kemmer" (p.221). Ironically, it is as a self-made alien again that he brings the unique humans of Gethen into the fully human community of the Ekumen—an action confirming that dualism and harmony which only Estraven fully understands. In turn, these concepts, central to Le Guin's work, arise naturally from the interplay of action, setting, metaphor and myth.

The narration which Ai presents embodies another of Le Guin's concerns. "I'll make my report as if I told a story, for I was taught as a child on my homeworld that Truth is a matter of the imagination," he begins. Indeed, his viewpoint influences the reader's view of the Gethenians. Moreover, as he adds, "The story is not all mine, nor told by me alone" (p.1). Balancing perspectives are provided, for example, by the scientific, yet inevitably personal, comments of the Investigator Ong Tot Oppong in Chapter 7. The introduction of Estraven's journal, beginning with the chapter "One Way Into Orgoreyn," alternating with Ai's account of the same events, starting with the chapter "Another Way Into Orgoreyn," creates irony and suspense. It also develops the theme of communication, as misunderstanding, mistrust, and misplaced trust build to their crisis. Most important, Estraven's diary develops an understanding of his character as he methodically records their progress and reviews his life—all the while making his own winter journey to the death which will end his exile from Estre, which will reunite him with Arek his brother and lover whose "shadow" follows him through life (p.55).

The introduction of the Gethenian myths lifts the individual actions on which they comment into the wider context of human truth. In what sense, for example, was Estraven a "traitor"? In what sense was his fate freely chosen (and possibly, in Gethenian terms, a contemptible suicide)? In what sense was it the inevitable end of a pattern of conflicting loyalties and loves, since, as he writes, "I was born to live in exile...and my one way home was by way of dying" (p.54)? In what sense is the whole account another journey made by Genly Ai, trying to rediscover the joy he knew on that painful journey which was "the real center of my own life" (p.172)?

All of Le Guin's major novels, in fact, present protagonists who are trying to find the "real center" of their lives. George Orr of *The Lathe of Heaven* loses his intrinsic balance when, involuntarily, he begins to create worlds. The novel's opening view of an overcrowded, polluted, rainwashed Portland of April 2002 is depressingly plausible. Yet it is also Orr's creation. Since puberty, he has had "effective" dreams—dreams which become reality. He alone possesses the knowledge of other truths. One is of a world which ended in nuclear holocaust in April 1998: the reality of the void, in which there is "nothing left. Nothing but dreams." Heather Lelache, who loves him and has stood with him at the center of reality as worlds shifted, denies this truth in a fury of fear:

"Maybe that's all it's ever been! Whatever it is, it's all right. You don't suppose you'd be allowed to do anything you weren't supposed to do, do you? Who the hell do you think you are! There is nothing that doesn't fit, nothing happens that isn't supposed to happen. Ever! What does it matter whether you call it real or dreams? It's all one— isn't it?' (p.106)

The novel's crisis develops as Orr's worlds cease to be "one," losing their continuity as the psychiatrist William Haber plays God with his dreams.

George Orr, the dreamer, is "the man in the middle of the graph," whose perfect balance may be seen as either "self-cancellation" or "a peculiar state of poise, of self-harmony" (p.137). His proper occupation is as a designer, one whose talent is "the realization of proper and fitting forms for thing" (p.125). His effective dreams may follow this function; but if they are manipulated, they create chaos. Characteristically, Orr recognizes his power, and his "obligation" to "use it only when I must" (p.148). Heather Lelache, needing strength, is drawn to Orr, recognizing in him the "wholeness of being" of "a block of wood not carved... He was the strongest person she had ever known, because he could not be moved away from the center" (p.95). Yet even she, who believes like Orr that "there is a whole of which one is a part, and that in being a part one is whole," is moved by compassion to undertake the "unimaginable responsibility" of using his power (p.107). Her interference precipitates the Alien invasion, which brings immediate disaster and ultimate aid.

To an individual with "no center to him," who (like Don Davidson) defines himself "solely by the extent of his influence over other people," Orr's power is irresistibly tempting. William Haber represents the rational, progressive Western mind, trying to "make a better world" (p.81). His arguments sound so familiar, so acceptable that even Orr doubts himself, and so yields up responsibility to his irresponsible "bear-god-shaman" (p.163). "What's wrong with changing things?" Haber asks. Orr can only reply that:

"We're in this world, not against it. It doesn't work to try to stand outside things and run them, that way....There is a way, but you have to follow it. The world is, no matter how we think it ought to be. You have to be with it. You have to let it be." (pp.138-139).

His words, like Heather's perception of him, unconsciously paraphrase the Tao, though as a true sage he has no formal knowledge of the Eastern philosophies Haber so contemptuously dismisses.[18] The Taoist philosophy of unaction infuses the novel; quotations from Lao Tsu and Chuang Tse introduce specific chapters; yet *The Lathe of Heaven* is not a philosophic tract but a novel whose characters and events illustrate the wisdom which Orr and the Aliens know: "What comes is acceptable" (p.153).

Haber, in his "conscious, careful planning for the good of all," dismisses individuals: Orr, whom he despises as a tool; Heather, whose death he, chillingly, welcomes. Thus the worlds he creates are all flawed, lacking freedom, joy and, finally, validity. They reflect the "void" at the center of his being, which, in his "effective nightmare," spreads to engulf reality. In this crisis Orr, by the power of will, which is indeed great when exercised in the right way at the right time," acts as he must. Supported by the love he shared with Heather, and "a little help from [his] friends" the Aliens, he moves through the void to end the breakdown caused by Haber's dream (pp.172-174). Following his necessary way through certain loss, he finds that, as E'enemenen Asfah observes, "There are returns"—to Heather, and to joy (p.184).

When Gaveral Rocannon, in despair, asserted that "In times like this...one man's fate is not important," his companion Mogien retorted: "If it is not...what is?" (p.43) Each of Le Guin's novels shows the importance of individual life. In *The Lathe of Heaven,* as in *The Left Hand of Darkness,* form works with content, as the constantly changing point of view allows Haber and Heather Lelache (who is intensely alive in some worlds, non-existence in others) to add their interpretations of reality to Orr's. The style, too, emphasizes the ordinary, the human. When Heather, rediscovering Orr, asks if "this mess" is the best world he can dream, he replies: "It'll have to do" (p.184). The exchange is typical, phrased in the everyday language of real people—in contrast with the heightened language with which Le Guin describes Orr's heroic, necessary act. The characters move through events of increasing drama and unreality, but it is their lives, and not those events, which matter after all. Thus Orr and Heather, in the wilderness, debate the nature of reality. However, it is by scrupulously sharing the five eggs which his depopulated dream-world has provided for them that they assert reality—the validity of individual perception and experience.

Local images drawn from the novel's world, and from nature, also serve as ties to a basic reality. (Significantly, though the political and social situations Haber creates by his manipulations grow worse and worse, human nature and the shape of the continents remain unchanged.) The erupting volcano, Mt. Hood, literally and metaphorically suggests the destructive force of Haber's irresponsible will to power. The constant Portland rain and mist suggest the uncertainty, the fluidity of life itself. Another recurring image is that of the sea, of time and the unconscious, in which the turtle-like Aliens, who can control effective dreaming, swim in their element. Orr, to Haber an irresponsible "moral jellyfish" (p.147), is also at home in this sea, like a fragile creature which "has for its defence the violence and power of the whole ocean, to which it has entrusted its being, its going and its will" (p.1). *The Lathe of Heaven,* like Le Guin's other novels, shows that this chosen surrender is the right "way" for human life to follow.

"To go is to return," observes E'nemenen Asfah; and Odo, whose search for freedom begins a revolution, also knows that "True journey is return."[19] The Odonian Shevek of Le Guin's most recent novel, *The Dispossessed,* crosses other oceans of space and time, following his way home. His story, in structure and in theme, can in fact be represented by the green Circle of Life, symbol of the Odonian movement.

The controlling image of *The Dispossessed*, however, is the divisive wall of uncut rocks surrounding the spaceport on Anarres. For the Odonians, the anarchists whose ancestors colonized the planet seven generations before, the physical boundary represents the ideological wall separating them from the anarchist societies of their homeworld, Urras. "Like all walls it was ambiguous, two-faced. What was inside it and what was outside it depended upon which side of it you were on" (p.1). Thus the wall functions as a political, social, and personal symbol, not of the absence of freedom, but of the rejection of freedom. Choice, and the acceptance of human commitments, are basic to Odo's vision of freedom. Thus "a promise is a direction taken," fidelity a chosen limitation "essential in the complexity of freedom" (p.216). Yet the world of the Promise has become a world of imposed denial: of truth, of the past, of the future. The Odonians are taught, from 150-year-old films, to reject Urras utterly as "disgusting, immoral, excremental" (p.38). They will not return from their self-exile to offer Urras the hope of their new society; nor will they let Urrasti individuals or ideas cross their walls. Thus Odo's ongoing revolution goes nowhere: "To deny is not to achieve" (p.79). In general, the Odonians increasingly are rejecting freedom, in particular freedom of thought, for the rule of custom and of bureaucracy. Equally, the Urrasti have rejected the future represented by the Odonians, hiding them on the Moon just as they hid poverty and misery under the gracious trappings of their world.

Individual Odonians, too, reject freedom by denying responsibility for their actions. Sabul, who steals Shevek's ideas and blocks his development, is a self-aggrandizing hypocrite. Shevek, too, gives up his book to Sabul and his freedom to the Urrasti, accepting an authority he does not recognize as valid; as a result he becomes psychologically incapable of creating until he reasserts his own will. Thus the walls are not built by any failure of Odonian theory, but by flaws in human nature, especially "the will to dominance [which] is as central in human beings as the impulse to mutual aid is" (p.149).

Shevek and the other members of the Syndicate of Initiative are unique in their commitment to the autonomy of conscience, and in their acceptance of the social ostracism with which Odonians punish the unofficial crime of "egoizing" or being different from the group. Shevek's social function as a dissident proceeds, as it must, from his personal experience of imprisoning a fellow-student and learning how "disgusting" such power over another could be. Even earlier, the wall became a nightmare symbol for him, triggered by a teacher's rejection of his creativity but associated also with his mother Rulag's denial of her promise to him and her partner. In the nightmare, the wall vanishes when a "voice of dear familiarity" shows him "the cornerstone...the primal number" and he knows with a "rush of joy" that he is "home" (p.30). The episode foreshadows the vision which enables him to see the unity of time and, in a visionary and literal way, go "home."

Thus Shevek's actions as a scientist and Odonian are rooted clearly in individual experience. Like George Orr, he derives the strength to act from the personal bond of human love. He and Takver share a partnership which brings them deep suffering when the social emergencies of the Famine separate them; but which also brings them, in their reunion, "joy...the completion of being." This joy brings Shevek a wider social vision of human beings stepping outside the selfish search for pleasure--"a closed cycle, a locked room, a cell"--into "the landscape of time, in which the spirit may, with luck and courage, construct the fragile, makeshift, improbable roads and cities of fidelity: a landscape inhabitable by human beings." On the intellectual level, this suggests Shevek's scientific theory, which, like loyalty, binds "time into a whole" (p.295). On the political and philosophical level, Takver and Shevek's partnership is mirrored in and by the Odonian experiment itself, in which individuals, working in solidarity, have transformed the desert into a human world. In fact, Shevek, like Odo, embodies the anarchist ideal. Takver suggests that the Syndicate of Initiative should walk away from the wall of convention and "go make an Anarres beyond Anarres, a new beginning" (p.334). Shevek offers the Urrasti revolutionaries, and all the Hainish worlds, his freedom to "be the Revolution" (p.265). His success is signalled when the Hainish officer Ketho accepts the risks of walking through the wall on Anarres, to experience freedom for himself.

The multileveled symbol of the wall, then, like the single figure of the man Shevek, ties together the complex strands of the stories Le Guin presents: of the man growing up to find his true way, of the partner affirming his fidelity, of the anarchist embodying an ideal of freedom, of a scientist developing a theory which, in practical terms, will unify human civilizations. This interwoven structure suggests and reflects the unity of Odonian society, composed of complex and multileveled bonds between the self and others.

Dualism, the self-exiling division between self and surrounding world, is also an important idea which provides Le Guin with a structural concept. Most of the important background information is presented in debate: for example in Shevek's discussion with Oii's family in Chapter 5. The initial discussion between Shevek and Kimoe establishes the sexism and social inequality of Urras, the equality of Anarres. Bedap's angry debate with Shevek in Chapter 6 clarifies the flaws in Odonian society. The book begins with the physical clash at the spaceport wall as the Odonians attack the traitor/revolutionary Shevek. It culminates in the violent confrontation between the Urrasti marchers and the armed government forces; and in the personal confrontation between Keng and Shevek, who forces her to abandon the inertia of despair for the commitment of hope.

Above all, *The Dispossessed* employs an overall structure of opposition and reconciliation. The first chapter presents Shevek leaving his home; the last, his return, "the promise kept," to Anarres. Like Rocannon, Falk/Ramarren, and especially Genly Ai—who brings the end of the old world "with him in his empty hands (p.63)—Shevek appears as the messianic "'Forerunner...a stranger, an outcast, an exile, bearing in empty hands the time to come'" (p.205). Between, the even-numbered chapters chronicle his growing disillusionment with Urras; the odd-numbered chapters, in a long flashback, tell the parallel story of his disillusion with Anarres, so that the moment of his decision to go to Urras is presented immediately before his return. As the Australian critic George Turner observes, this structure not only allows a point-by-point comparison of the two culture, but points to a general political/philosophical concern: how can a strong individual like Shevek fit into *any* system, or successfully reconcile the public and private morality?[20]

Though *The Dispossessed* seems to imply that the individual and social worlds, like Anarres and Urras, cannot be united, its tone is not despairing. Perhaps its finest achievement is its tough-mindedness, the willingness to pose difficult questions, accept the impossibility or failure of solutions, and still, with hope, seek answers. Anarres is neither a utopia, an impossible no-place, nor a dystopia; rather it is a functioning, and convincing, society. Shevek and Takver are recognizable Le Guin characters—the truth-seeking scientist, the artist and complete person who intuitively senses the unity of life. Yet they are individuals, shaped by Odonian society, which comes alive through them.

The Dispossessed is an ambitious novel, attempting to present an individual, two societies, and an ideal of human life. Inevitably, Le Guin cannot maintain equal control and depth throughout; and so the idea dominates. Urras, the ur-world, is much less convincing than Anarres. Too arbitrarily the antithesis of Odonian ideals, too closely a critique of contemporary North America's flaws, it cannot present an effective challenge to test Anarres. Moreover, it is presented entirely through Shevek's extremely limited perceptions; the uprising in Nio Esseia surprises him, and fails to convince the readers.

Shevek's speculations on government and on human relations,

too, often become uncomfortably didactic—or move into generalized discussions and analyses. The novel moves in a confusing manner between center-of-consciousness narration with an individual voice presenting ideas rooted in specific human actions and perceptions, to omniscient narration from an undefined point of view and background, presenting generalized observations. For example, a three-page discussion of partnership within Odonian society contains such general statements as:

To maintain genuine spontaneous fidelity in a society that had no legal or moral sanctions against infidelity, and to maintain it during voluntarily accepted separations that could come at any time and might last years, was something of a challenge. But the human being likes to be challenged, seeks freedom in adversity (p.218).

This is less convincing than, and made redundant by, the succeeding presentation of Shevek and Takver's four-year separation, their acceptance of it and their reactions. *The Dispossessed* relies too heavily on the idea expressed and analysed rather than embodied and shown. Despite powerful emotional scenes, particularly those between Shevek and Takver, it evokes a distanced intellectual appreciation of its theme and structure rather than the intuitive understanding of shared human feeling characteristic of Le Guin's other novels.

Conversely, Le Guin's best work, the Earthsea trilogy, derives its great strength from the direct translation of ideas into shared experience. Fantasy is, as Le Guin recognizes, "a journey into the subconscious." The truth found there can be communicated directly, without the intervening barriers of social and philosophical constructs; but first the writer must find an appropriate style, one exhibiting the "permanent virtues" of clarity and simplicity.[21] The Earthsea novels clearly exemplify this ideal.

The patterning of the Earthsea trilogy is that of a human life: growth, the acceptance of power, mature action, the abdication of power, death. Within this circle of experience, each book presents another pattern: a quest through death's realm to adult knowledge and power. Like the magic of Earthsea itself, the books draw their strength from the specific knowledge of individual things. The life they present, while universal in its implications, is always particular: that of the mage Sparrowhawk, whose true name is Ged.

Though *A Wizard of Earthsea* opens in the context of legend, it moves quickly from the evocation of the shadowy figure "who in his day became both dragonlord and Archmage" (pp.11-12), to the daily life of the goatherd boy of Gont as he discovers his power to call down hawks and to shape the fog. The complementary patterns of *The Tombs of Atuan* and *The Farthest Shore*, too, are firmly rooted in the individual stories of Tenar, Priestess of the Nameless Ones who becomes White Lady of Gont, and Arren, prince of Enlad who becomes King of All the Isles. Ged, in these books, is presented from the outside as a mature and somewhat enigmatic figure of power, performing actions whose significance the young protagonists can only half comprehend. Yet he remains a sharply-realized individual: the Sparrowhawk indeed, with his "reddish-dark" face, "hawk-nosed, seamed on one cheek with old scars," and his "bright and fierce" eyes (p.4). He and his companions eat dry bread, and suffer hunger; they sail the world's seas and are parched by its sun; they act rashly and, when they must call on magic to restore the balance they have upset, they suffer exhaustion and pain. Their actions have the inevitable rightness of myth, always supported by the credibility of human feeling.

Earthsea, too, like Gethen and Anarres, is a fully-realized world. From the actuality of its wave-washed islands comes its strength as metaphor. An archipelago, Earthsea stretches some 2,000 miles from the cold North Reach south to the warm waters of the raft-people, the Children of the Sea; and another 2,000 miles from Selidor where the skull of Erreth-Akbe lies amid the bones of the dragon Orm, east to the semi-barbaric Kargad Lands. These islands hold many kingdoms and several races; the trilogy presents each particular of life—fisherman and sorceress, goat and dragon, appletree and sparkweed—in all its richness. Yet Earthsea is a finite world. The Children of the Sea still dance the midsummer Long Dance, "one dance, one music binding together the sea-divided lands" (p.69). Yet they move on fragile rafts above, and upon, a waste of limitless ocean, in celebration of the human spirit whose dance of life always moves "above the hollow place, above the terrible abyss" (p.136). Ged sails Earthsea from edge to inhabited edge, seeking beyond the world for the shores of death's realm. Thus the physical islands of Earthsea exist in a delicate balance with the sea; the known human world lies surrounded by the unknown; and all life exists defined by death. This balance is central to the magic, and the meaning, of Earthsea.

Though secular rulers, kings, and lords govern the people of Earthsea, true power rests with the mages: men whose inborn power is augmented by long study to know the essence of each created thing, the "true name" by which it can be controlled. Though they can summon and use "the immense fathomless energies of the universe," (p.68), the most important aspect of their art is the recognition of its natural limits, of "the Balance and the Pattern which the true wizard knows and serves" (p.16).

Magic is an art which must be learned, patiently. A Wizard of Earthsea and The Farthest Shore show gifted apprentices at school on Roke Island, learning to weave spells with gestures, unseen powers, and the words of the Old Speech now spoken only by wizards and dragons. Le Guin's wit, and a gift of humor rare in fantasy, find full scope in the School of the Island of the Wise, as Gamble teases Prince Arren with tales of enchanted dinners, and Ged shoots arrows made of breadcrumbs and spells after Vetch's chickenbone owls.

Magic must not be used lightly, however; for evil, in Earthsea, is a "web we men weave" by the misuse of power (p.14).In *A Wizard of Earthsea,* Ged, who believes that a mage is "one who can do anything," must, like Le Guin's other protagonists, learn painfully that "as a man's real power grows and his knowledge widens, ever the way he can follow grows narrower; until at last he chooses nothing, but does only and wholly what he *must do*..." (p.87). In pride and anger, he summons a spirit of the dead; and so he lets a dark spirit of unlife enter the world. To name, to control that Shadow, he must journey over the oceans of Earthsea, into his own spirit, to confront and accept his "black self" (p.201). His companion Vetch, watching, understands that Ged:

by naming the shadow of his death with his own name, had made himself whole: a man: who, knowing his whole true self, cannot be used or possessed by any power other than himself, and whose life therefore is lived for life's sake and never in the service of ruin, or pain, or hatred, or the dark (p.203).

In the later books of the trilogy, Ged's power is founded in abnegation; he has learned to "'desire nothing beyond my art,'" and to do only "what is needful"—even to relinquish that art (p.150).

In contrast to the heroic sweep of *A Wizard of Earthsea,* with its sparkle of sun on waves and roar of dragons, *The Tombs of Atuan* offers the narrow, intense focus of psychomyth: Le Guin's own term for her explorations in the timeless regions of the human mind.[22] With its single action, setting, and central character, the novel powerfully suggests the claustrophobia of its controlling metaphor: the dark labyrinth beneath the Tombs, the dark passages of the human spirit inhabited by the "'powers of the dark, of ruin, of madness'" (p.118).

The narrative opens with a symbolic death as the child Tenar becomes Arha, "the Eaten One," priestess of the Nameless Ones. The impersonal ritual of her sacrifice effectively suggests the denial of human life in the world of the Tombs. Tenar exists behind stone walls in a barren desert, her life and sexuality expressed only in ritual dances before the Empty Throne: celebrating death as the Long Dance celebrates life. Her only freedom is to wander her labyrinth, "the very home of darkness, the inmost center of the night," a place of corrupted power suggesting the fear, hatred, and utter loneliness which imprison her spirit (p.35). Her only right is to kill the men imprisoned there—and then live with her terrible nightmares of guilt.

Ged comes to the labyrinth seeking the Ring of Erreth-Akbe with its lost Rune of Peace, bringing the gift of "life in the place o: death" (p.69). Just as the light of his wizard's staff reveals beauty ir the dark caverns, so his wizard's knowledge reveals Tenar's true name. When he, in turn, shares his true name with her, the gift o: human trust is complete: a treasure more potent than the restorec Ring. By its power, Tenar can choose freedom for them both. The novel ends with rebirth, as she walks from the crumbling Tomb into "the huge silent glory of light" (p.140), accompanying Ged into the human world "like a child coming home" (p.163).

The Farthest Shore completes the trilogy with Ged's third and final journey through the realm of death, accompanied by Prince Arren who thus fulfils the prophesy of Maharion: "*He shall inheri: my throne who has crossed the dark and living and come to the far shores of the day*" (p.20). Its action is a sombre, ironic balance to that of *A Wizard of Earthsea*. Just as the Archmage Nemmerle gave his life to close the door which Ged, by his rash act, opened betweer life and death, so Ged gives his power to close the door which the wizard Cob opens in his attempt to escape death. Death is not, in itself, evil; rather, it is necessary, "the price we pay for our life, and for all life" (p.204). Cob's denial of death, however, has evi: consequences, for he denies life and thus destroys the essential balance of creation.

Le Guin suggests the evil effects of Cob's action in vivid, specific terms: Hort Town's foul disorder; the former wizard Hare's drugged ramblings; and especially the creeping mistrust, the numbing despair, which slowly dim Arren's shining devotion to Ged. Enduring these symptoms of imbalance, Ged and Arren come to their cause: the open door through which the light and joy of the living world flow into the lands of death. Again, the controlling images are resonant archetypes, evoking the sterility of denial and despair: the Dry River where only night flows, the Dry Land filled with "dust and cold and silence" (p.205). Yet though even "the springs of wizardry have run dry" (p.8), the human love and faith which are "the springs of being" do not fail (p.175). Arren, by his courage and devotion, leads Ged over the Mountains of Pain; and both regain life once more. The trilogy ends, not with triumph as Arren is crowned, but in a more appropriate mood of serenity. Ged, dragon-borne, vanishes from the world of action; and his story returns, full circle, to the timeless cadences of legend.

Peter Nicholls, in common with many critics, has praised Le Guin for her "telling precision of imagery," her ability to achieve "the strongest emotional reasonances...by capturing the individuality of a particular situation or character," as in the account of Arren's descent among the dead:

All those whom they saw—not many for the dead are many, but that land is large—

stood still, or moved slowly and with no purpose...They were whole and healed. They were healed of pain, and of life. They were not loathesome as Arren had feared they would be, not frightening in the way he had through they would be. Quiet were their faces, freed from anger and desire, and there was in their shadowed eyes no hope.

Instead of fear, then, great pity rose up in Arren, and if fear underlay it, it was not for himself, but for all people. For he saw the mother and child who had died together, and they were in the dark land together; but the child did not run, nor did it cry, and the mother did not hold it or ever look at it. And those who had died for love passed each other in the streets.[24]

Yet it is not just the details—the mother not looking at her child— which make this section moving. The simplicity of the language, its directness, and the sonorous cadencing of phrase and sentence into a timeless lament all combine with the specific images to make the passage unforgettable.

In Le Guin's work, even lamentation becomes a celebration of life, of the human spirit's power and desire to express its uniqueness.

I must go where I am bound to go, and turn my back on the bright shores. I was in too much haste, and now have no time left. I traded all the sunlight and the cities and the distant lands for a handful of power, for a shadow, for the dark.' So, as the mageborn will, Ged made his fear and regret into a song, a brief lament, half-sung, that was not for himself alone...[25]

Like the mageborn, Ursula K. Le Guin also finds words of power, and weaves them into complex evocative patterns of human truth. In the limitless imaginative world of science fiction and fantasy, she finds:

precise and profound metaphors of the human condition...the fantasist, whether he used the ancient archetypes of myth and legend or the younger ones of science and technology, may be talking as seriously as any sociologist—and a good deal more directly—about human life as it is lived, and as it might be lived, and as it ought to be lived.[26]

This seriousness of purpose, combined with rare skill and a determination to continue "pushing out toward the limits—my own and those of the medium"[27] have established Le Guin as a major artist, exploring a unique vision of human life.

Joe Sanders

Zelazny: Unfinished Business

One hallmark of Cele Goldsmith Lalli's rejuvenated *Amazing* and *Fantastic* in the early 1960s was her encouragement of new writers, like Piers Anthony, Ursula K. Le Guin, and Thomas M. Disch. Short stories by another newcomer named Roger Zelazny appeared in the August 1962 issues of both *Fantastic* and *Amazing.* They were only the first of a host of stories Zelazny was to sell to *Amazing* and *Fantastic* in the next year—fourteen of the seventeen he sold in that time.[1] So prolific was Zelazny and so well established was the magazines' reputation for using house pennames for fiction, that Ms. Goldsmith asked Zelazny for an autobiographical sketch be included in the editorial for *Amazing* in December 1962.[2] But Zelazny clearly established that he was real as, in following months, his stories displayed more than routine competence. How much more, Zelazny showed in such stories as "A Rose for Ecclesiastes" (1963), Hugo nominee, selected by the Science Fiction Writers of America for inclusion in *The Science Fiction Hall of Fame;* "The Doors of His Face, The Lamps of His Mouth," (1965), Hugo nominee, Nebula winner; *"He Who Shapes,"* (1965), book version retitled *The Dream Master,* Nebula winner; *". . . And Call Me Conrad"* (1965), retitled *This Immortal* for book publication, Hugo winner; *Lord of Light* (1967), Hugo winner; *Isle of the Dead* (1969), French edition winner of Prix Apollo, 1972; and many more.[3] In an almost incredibly short time Zelazny became established as a major science fiction writer. He remains so today.

What is the source of Zelazny's remarkable success? Though the limits of this essay preclude a full analysis, we can examine a few facets of Zelazny's work to suggest what he has tried to do and how well he has succeeded.

First, Zelazny's style has always been the most immediately striking thing about his work.[4] Even his very early short shorts, in however uneven fashion, show both stylistic control and a wide range of special devices. The first paragraph of "Horseman!" (1962) shows part of that range:

> When he was thunder in the hills the villagers lay dreaming harvest behind shutters. When he was an avalanche of steel the cattle began to low, mournfully, deeply, and children cried out in their sleep.[5]

Here Zelazny focuses upon a concrete subject, a part that vividly represents the whole. Instead of writing about "the people" or "the sleepers," he picks out representative groups to stand first for the oblivious, routine order of life, then for the more sensitive, vulnerable individuals. He tries to make the sensory impact as immediate as possible. Doing so, he concentrates his language by metaphor ("he was thunder in the hills...an avalanche of steel") and by omitting inert words, the stickum of everyday communication, as in "dreaming [of] harvest." And yet the interest generated by vivid word choice and skillful stirring of emotion (a possible threat to children and animals) is enough to carry the reader over gaps in the wording or in the flow of the narrative. Anything that moves along so surely *must* have meaning.

Another aspect of Zelazny's style is shown in the opening paragraph of "Passion Play" (1962):

> At the end of the season of sorrows comes the time of rejoicing. Spring, like the hands of a well-oiled clock, noiselessly indicates this time. The average days of dimness and moisture decrease steadily in number, and those of brilliance and cool begin to enter the calendar again. And it is good that the wet times are behind us, for they rust and corrode our machinery; they require the most intense standards of hygiene.[6]

Here the style is less concentrated and terse. The writing is admirably clear, but much less emotionally charged, showing a curious emphasis on machinery and on changes that seemingly are registered by dispassionate observation. Figures of speech are more restrained—as in the simile "Spring, like the hands of a well-oiled clock." And yet this follows an opening sentence that speaks of "sorrows" and "rejoicing." The reader continues, confident that the careful, rational speaker is not utterly emotionless. In each piece, the style is appropriate to the story, which in one case shows a world about to be blasted by an overwhelming visitation and in the other a religious ritual performed by the machines who have survived man. Obviously, from the very beginning of his writing career, in his first professionally published stories, Zelazny could effectively control style in his writing, applying it deliberately to different purposes.

From this start, Zelazny has gone on to develop his stylistic control. As circumstances demand, a Zelazny story may seem a completely straightforward, direct narrative, or it may be told in the fussy tones of a leather-elbowed lecturer—but at any moment it may stab right through the unsuspecting reader like a bolt of lightning. The key, always, is Zelazny's sense of what the story demands. The potential for abrupt change in the style, as the story changes, always exists; Zelazny delights in giving his readers unexpected jolts or at least in holding opposites in perilously tense balance. Many of his characters carry the same balance within themselves. One of Zelazny's characteristic modes is forced *casualness*, in which characters who barely can master some extreme emotion do a graceful verbal dance to display their self-control. As an example of stylistic control, the conversations in *Jack of Shadows* (1971) are literally as different as night and day. In the always-daylit side of that planet, ruled by science and closely resembling our world, people speak very much as they do in our everyday experience. On the dark side, ruled by magic, the characters talk in a highly formalized, artificially restrained manner. Here, as an example of tensions gracefully displayed, is Jack, the main character, forcing the Colonel Who Never Died, his father-in-law, to commit suicide:

"Poison is very good," he said. "But the effects vary so from individual to individual that it can sometimes prove painful. I'd say that your purposes would best be served by sitting in a warm bath and cutting your wrists under water. This hardly hurts at all. It is pretty much like going to sleep."

"I believe I'll do it that way then."

"In that case," said Jack, "let me give you a few pointers."

He reached forward, took the other's wrist and turned it, exposing the underside. He drew his dagger.

"Now then," he began, slipping back into a tutorial mode of speech..."do not make the same mistakes as most amateurs at this business." Using the blade as a pointer, he said, "Do not cut crosswise, so. Subsequent clotting might be sufficient to cause a reawakening, and the necessity to repeat the process. This could even occur several times. This would doubtless produce some trauma, as well as an aesthetic dissatisfaction. You must cut *lengthwise* along the blue line, here," he said, tracing. "Should the artery prove too slippery, you must lift it out with the point of your instrument and twist the blade quickly. Do not just pull upward. This is unpleasant. Remember that. The twist is the important part if you fail to get it with the lengthwise slash. Any questions?"

"I think not."

"Then repeat it back to me."[7]

Zelazny's stylistic differentation is highly purposeful in *Jack of Shadows:* it shows two separate worlds that must be brought together in the novel's last page. And as if that were not sufficient challenge, in the same novel Zelazny throws in pathos, mysticism, and farce--as in the complaint of Jack's soul, when Jack rejects it:

"That's a hell of a way to treat a soul. Here I am, waiting to comfort and caution you, and you kick me out. What will people say? 'There goes Jack's soul,' they'll say, 'poor thing. Consorting with elementals and lower astrals and—'" (pp.156-157). Zelazny loves to take such chances. Who else, in a story with a serious point, would try to set a scene with the words "Quick, a world in 300 words or less! Picture this . . ."[8] or prepare for a climax with "The day of the battle dawned pink as the fresh-bitten thigh of a maiden "[9]; or describe a crucial event "Then the fit hit the Shan"[10]—and get away with it? In fact, the appropriateness of Zelazny's style is not the only reason it attracts attention. Rather, the style calls attention to itself because it is not only striking and flexible, but because it varies so unexpectedly. One cannot settle into a comfortable position and watch the story reel by; Zelazny will throw zingers at any moment, unexpected, highly-charged passages that bounce the reader out of one mental set and leave him bewildered but deeply moved. Some time *afterward*, a reader can say that the style varied to fit the content as he now grasps it. At that time, however, all one can do is stay alert and ride with the story.

We seem, in these last observations, to be talking about more than style. True. If, as Ben Shahn says, style is simply the shape of content, then the manner in which Zelazny tells his stories must reflect what the stories are about. Before we consider content, though, let me offer one further signpost for our destination, in the form of a paradigm for Zelazny's fiction: a plot structure that recurs throughout his work. Two qualifications: first, a paradigm is not a template. I am not suggesting that Zelazny's stories reproduce exactly the same story pattern endlessly—or that they will continue to do so. On the contrary, Zelazny's talent and willingness to take chances already have created striking variants of this pattern. It is merely that Zelazny's concerns tend to express themselves in the same forms. Second, a working model is not a yardstick for critical evaluation. I intend simply to examine how Zelazny controls the expression of content in his work, and how, in another sense, content has shaped the whole body of his work.

A Zelazny story typically begins with the reader thrown into the company of a seriously disoriented character, a man who feels (and is) out of his natural place and time. His origin usually is somehow questionable, obscured. (Typically, also, Zelazny's style reflects this dislocation, and the story is told in or interrupted by cryptic, fragmentary glimpses that the reader must strain to pull together since the character is too busy trying to save himself.) The character is usually either forced or chooses (or both) to play a complex, baffling role in order to survive. As part of his role-playing, he undertakes a mission involving danger to himself but intended to culminate in an act of violence directed at someone else. His overall purpose is to gain or demonstrate power; more specifically, he often is carrying out a mission of revenge. (This is sometimes complicated by the revelation that he himself is at least partly responsible for the actions he must avenge.) As part of his role-playing, however, the character discovers some fundamental truth about himself. Typically, he discovers that the role actually fits, that he is not (merely) the man he believed. Beyond that, the truth often involves the realization that being out of *one* time actually permits a man to live more widely than does the limited herd around him; he is free to draw on a vast living tradition. Often the truth also involves the discovery that with this relative omniscience and with the relative omnipotence he has obtained in undertaking the mission, he has unknowingly acquired a kind of godhood. And with that comes recognition of the responsibility of divinity. Finally, a Zelazny story typically is open-ended; rather than a neat resolution, the reader is shown the character open to new possibilities, ready to reach out for whatever comes.

This pattern does not, of course, preclude the chance of tragic failure if a character does not grasp the drift of the action in time. Render, the hero of *The Dream Master* (1966), is a neuro-participation therapist capable of entering his patient's mind but unaware of how deeply he is becoming involved with his blind patient Eileen Shallott. He understands the implications of his role too late to prevent his own conscious personality being submerged, becoming Tristram to Eileen's Iseult, and at the end of the novel he uses his great powers to defeat those who would heal him. Nor does Zelazny's pattern mean that interference cannot short-circuit an action. Just so, in "The Graveyard Heart" (1964), Unger's frustrations ruin Moore's chance to control his life, to get back into the flow of events while there is still time to seize mastery. In a similar dilemma, John Auden, the undying but unloving central character of "The Man Who Loved the Faioli" (1967), commits himself to full life so that he can experience love even at the cost of death; however, his choice is interrupted by the curiosity of his beloved Faioli, who desires to see what he was before he changed— and who thus returns him to the coldly logical state in which he now chooses not to die, even though he wonders whether his decision is correct or not. But the *full* pattern, as explained above, is more typical of Zelazny's stories.

As with Zelazny's mastery of style, his use of this pattern can be seen in the very early stories as well as the mature works. In "A Museum Piece" (1963), the only one of the *Amazing/Fantastic* short stories Zelazny chose to preserve in the collection *The Doors of His Face, The Lamps of his Mouth* (1971), the pattern is developed as good-natured farce. Jay Smith, unsuccessful artist, poses as a statue in the art museum until he meets a nice girl, who also is pretending to be a statue while she recovers from a blighted romance. The two reaffirm their devotion to Art and Love, and return to the outside world, first escaping from a group of retired art critics—disguised as statues of Roman senators so that they can "spend their remaining days mocking the things they have hated"[11]—with the aid of an extraterrestrial who has been hiding in the same museum, disguised as a mobile. Told in an exaggerated version of Zelazny's forced-objective style, with speeches like "Thanks for eating the lion" (p.197), the story is pleasant fluff.

"A Rose for Ecclesiastes" (1963) is much more than that. It also, incredibly, is one of Zelazny's earliest stories, written a year or so before his first professional sale but withheld from submission for some time because Zelazny feared his Martian setting was too scientifically inaccurate for the story to be taken seriously.[12] But its intellectual and emotional force carries the reader past dubious technical details. "A Rose for Ecclesiastes" is the story of Gallinger, a prizewinning poet and gifted linguist chosen to accompany an expedition to Mars so that he can translate the literature preserved by the last surviving Martians and analyze their culture. However, though Gallinger can acquire languages easily and has familiarized himself with many cultures on Earth, he skillfully alienates the other members of the expedition. He expresses his concerns eloquently only through his poetry; in person, he communicates only antagonism. Gallinger's family background created this paradox. His father, a fundamentalist minister, demanded that his son use his "gift of tongues" to become a preacher of "the Word," while the boy was absorbing languages because he loved the poetry of *different* words. Gallinger never could denounce openly his father's plan for his life, but he could never accept the ideas or the man himself. He cannot even remember what his father looked like: "I can't see his face now; I never can. Maybe it is because I was always afraid to look at it then."[13] Because he could never face his father, literally or figuratively, Gallinger cannot rid himself of his father's presence, loving but threatening, cursing his son's self-directed efforts. In Gallinger's thoughts, his alienation from his father shades into alienation from the God his father served. Remembering how his father would be disappointed in how he has lived, Gallinger thinks: "*—Lord, I am sorry! Daddy—Sir—I am sorry!—It couldn't be...*"(p.76). In his poetry, he preaches a personal "word" that he never could while his father was alive; poetry is thus an affirmation of his values against those of his father. But he is still haunted, still unable to find satisfying personal relationships.

On Mars, Gallinger is welcomed by the Mothers, matriarchs who govern the rituals of the humanoid Martians. He soon masters the Martian classical tongue and becomes deeply immersed in their sacred books, whose deep pessimism reminds him of Ecclesiastes:

all is vanity, mere mortal life is worthless.... For his personal satisfaction, he begins a translation of Ecclesiastes into Martian. He reads of an inexplicable disaster of centuries before that apparently rendered the Martian males impotent, the females sterile. But when he is introduced to Braxa, who has mastered the dances that are part of Martian religious ritual, he is seduced by her and she become pregnant by him. After Braxa runs away, Gallinger overtakes her and is told that the Martians—convinced that they had already exhausted the possibilites of experience and steeped in their religion's negative outlook—reacted to their apparent doom by deciding that they must simply wait stoically for extinction. Thus, the Mothers would destroy Braxa's child. Personally equating their religion and his father's, Gallinger decides to draw on the strange respect the Mothers show for him and to read his translation of Ecclesiastes to prove that humanity is capable of producing the same eloquent expression of despair—and then capable of transcending it. He speaks, first defending his race:

"...ours is not an insignificant people...Thousands of years ago, the Locar of our world wrote a book saying that it was. He spoke as Locar did, but we did not lie down, despite plagues, wars, and famines. We did not die. One by one we beat down the diseases, we fed the hungry, we fought the wars, and, recently, have gone a long time without them...

"But we have crossed millions of miles of nothingness. We have visited another world. And our Locar had said, 'Why bother? What is the worth of it? It is all vanity, anyhow!"

"And the secret is," I lowered my voice, as at a poetry reading, "he was right! It *is* vanity; it *is* pride! It is the hubris of rationalism to always attack the prophet, the mystic, the god. It is our blasphemy which has made us great, and will sustain us, and which the gods secretly admire in us" (p.104).

Gallinger succeeds. The Martians fully accept him as the holy man sent to fulfill a prophecy of racial rebirth at the hands of a man sent from the heavens to save them. Gallinger first rejects the role he has unknowingly been filling, until he realizes that Braxa never loved him but was only acting out her part in the prophecy. Then the truth hits him, as one of the Mothers says:

"...and we will never forget your teachings"...

"Don't, " I said, automatically, suddenly knowing the great paradox which lies at the heart of all miracles. I did not believe a word of my own gospel, never had (p.106).

Gallinger attempts suicide, but is revived after the spaceship leaves Mars. He is l k with the human race, no longer aloof and isolated, for he has paid his debt to his father at last—and soul-wrenching though the participation in that role was, it has broken the alienated pose that had trapped him earlier.

This is a much more substantial story than "A Museum Piece" because Gallinger's growth through anguish and puzzlement comes through so well. Style works to that end. When Gallinger is first summoned to the captain's cabin and takes his sweet time getting there, the captain acidly remarks "That was fast. What did you do, run?" Gallinger reacts in the following passage:

I regarded his paternal discontent.

Little fatty flecks beneath pale eyes, thinning hair, and an Irish nose; a voice a decibel louder than anyone else's . . . . .

Hamlet to Claudius: "I was working."[14]

The presentation of sensory detail is vividly immediate, Zelazny leaps into it without a simple transition, such as a colon. The reader has to catch on fast that it is a person and not a bowl of chili being described. Gallinger *wants* to see the captain as less than human. Actually, of course, Gallinger's alienation from the captain is simply another reflection of his alienation from his father; the captain is a stepfather that Gallinger deliberately sees as a thing, objectifying the facts of his appearance as he could never do with his living father. Much later in the story, Gallinger is again forced to see the captain, and he first responds by repeating the objective description, adding that the loud voice is the captain's "only qualification for leadership":

I stood there, hating him. Claudius! If only this were the fifth act. (p.95)

He later explodes: "'Yes!'...Yes, *Claudius! Yes, Daddy! Yes, Emory!*" (p.96). Zelazny breaks this private mood by an intense but non-stylized conversation that reveals the captain as a sympathetic man and thus prepares Gallinger for his final development. But style primarily reinforces the displacement and eventual painful reintegration at the story's core. And that, again, is largely a function of the pattern of ideas and images characteristic of Zelazny's work.

Why does Zelazny use this pattern? Dealing with the results in his writing, which is all we can consider here, we find some immediate advantages. For one thing, it aids the development of very highly charged emotion, since the central character is forced to question the basis of his identity, a most personal concern. Along with this, the form allows for great intellectual complexity, as a whole world view is called into question. When used by a writer with real emotional perception, intellectual breadth, and stylistic versatility, the results can be highly satisfying. As here.

One more example of Zelazny's mastery of shorter fiction, from

a slightly later time, is the novelette "For a Breath I Tarry" (1966).¹⁵
The story takes place after man has wiped himself out, leaving his
machines in charge of the Earth. Solcom, the supercomputer
originally placed in charge, is locked in combat with Divcom, an
alternate controller that was activated when Solcom was briefly out
of order and now refuses to switch itself off. Only some outside
source, such as a man, could settle the dispute. Lacking this ultimate
judge, the two decide to test their rightness by permitting Divcom to
tempt Frost, the machine Solcom created to control the northern
hemisphere—although "an unprecedented solar flareup" rendered
Solcom unconscious while it was completing work on Frost and
Frost is thus "the finest, the mightiest, the most difficult to
understand" of Solcom's creations (p.6). Most of the story's action is
centered on Frost. Able to perform his duties in relatively little time,
Frost employs "an unaccountably acute imperative that he function
at full capacity at all times" (p.8) by obsessively studying the few
remaining traces of man he can locate. Frost is approached by
Mordel, a servant of Divcom, who offers more information about
man in return for Frost's switching allegience. Frost ponders the
unknowable nature of man, his superiority to mechanical
measurement because he can consider all qualities—cold, beautiful,
important—in relation to himself. But Frost is sure that he can solve
any conceivable problem, and he strikes a bargain: he will serve
Divcom if he is unable to *become* a man. Monitored by Mordel, Frost
absorbs all surviving human knowledge, experiments with human
sensory apparatus, visits the empty city built by the last men, and
tries to create art—all without becoming human. Eventually he hits
on the idea of growing human bodies from the cells of a few frozen
corpses and transferring his consciousness into one. He succeeds,
sets the machines about their proper tasks, and starts the human
race going again.

   But a plot summary cannot begin to suggest the story's
emotional weight, created by style and content working together.
Most of the story is told in Zelazny's cool, pseudo-objective style,
which seems appropriate since machines are not supposed to feel
emotion. The lack of surface emotion is deceptive, however, since
Solcom and Divcom carry on mannered dialogue while viciously
destroying each other's projects. Of all Zelazny's shorter fiction,
"For a Breath I Tarry" is the most effective at letting the reader
imagine emotion that is not expressed openly. And recognition of
the characters' unacknowledged emotion stirs profound reaction in
readers. It is a very quiet but very deeply felt story. The story also is
notable for the subtle way Zelazny shows Frost growing into a role
he desperately wants to fill. The climax, for one thing, is deceptive.
The fear and despair Frost feels after the transfer into a human body
are supposedly the proof that he is human at last. Actually, just

before the transfer, Solcom orders Frost to stop his experiment, and Frost replies:

> "Supposing I succeed in what I have set out to achieve?"
>
> "You cannot succeed in this."
>
> "Then let me ask you of your plan: What good is it? What is it for?"
>
> "Frost, you are fallen now from my favor. From this moment forth you are cast out from the rebuilding. None may question the plan."
>
> "Then at least answer my question: What good is it? What is it for?"
>
> "It is the plan for the rebuilding and maintenance of the Earth."
>
> "For what? Why rebuild? Why maintain?" (p.33)

Frost is, in fact, showing the subjective, non-mechanical measurement that Mordel has earlier called the identifying mark of man. We may further ask why, earlier in the story, Frost has been obsessed with "becoming" a man—or why, from the beginning, of all Solcom's creations Frost is given a personal pronoun (p.7). And we may also ask how the Beta machine became ready for a human body at the story's conclusion.... In all, we must conclude that "humanness" means more than occupation of a flesh and blood body that *forces* an intelligence to make measureless, personal judgments. Rather, something about the intelligence itself must be unmeasurable, capable of growing unpredictably. As readers of the story, we too become involved in a very subtle process of discovering what it means to be human. "For a Breath I Tarry" has real emotional weight, real human significance. It is a heartbreakingly good story.

Zelazny's stories thus involve a character going through a process of growth, leading not so much to certainty about what he *is* as to a realization that, since he is so much more than ever known or admitted before, he can go on growing. As Francis Sandow, hero of *Isle of the Dead* (1969), concludes, "I have been a coward, a god and a son of a bitch in my time, among other things. That is one of the things about living for a very long time. You go through phases."[16] Remember, this is not to say that all Zelazny's heroes succeed, though I believe that the tragedy of failure is intensified by the real possibility of success implicit in his works. Nor does Zelazny take himself with deadly seriousness. He can write very amusing fiction; for example, "Devil Car" (1965) is skillful self parody, and portions of several novels are quite funny. Nor, finally, does Zelazny aim at one set of direction of growth, some new frozen orthodoxy. Most representatives of orthodoxy, like Nitri in *Lord of Light,* are obviously monomaniacs. Characteristically, Frost asks *questions* in the confrontation with Solcom quoted above; "A Rose for Ecclesiastes" does not conclude with Gallinger neatly reconciled to his father's God but groping his way into direct expression of personal feeling. A Zelazny hero is not as apt to preach to others as he is to remind them of their freedom and then to go about his business.

The chief thing Zelazny is able to do in his novels that he cannot do in his shorter work is *more*. A novel's length gives him more room for experiment—more risks, more thrills—and more exploration of his theme-pattern. One of the novel's chief advantages is the Zelazny can introduce false, or partial analogies of the central character to complement his growth. Even Zelazny's first novel, *The Immortal* (1966), uncertain in plot though it is,[17]contains the renegade doctor, Moreby, who has gone out to research the mutated savages but has joined them instead. He abuses his knowledge and skills—instead of growth he encourages elegant stagnation: "there I was with a wealth of customs, superstitions, taboos—from many cultures, many eras—right here at my fingertips.... Man—even half man...is a ritual-loving creature, and I knew ever so many rituals and things like that. So I put all of this to good use and now I occupy a position of great honor and esteem."[18] He dies horribly. As a partial analog, Red Wig-Diane is able to respond sympathetically to Zelazny's hero and to comment in passing that striving is more important than the result—"It's not the [golden] fleece that's important...it's the getting"(p.155). But she is too obsessed with her past suffering to respond fully to new chances for loving—and growing. She lives miserably. Not so with Conrad, Zelazny's hero. Thomas Monteleone faults Zelazny's characterization of Conrad because as an immortal he is too little concerned with his relationship with the world that changes and grows old around him.[19] But the references that Conrad constantly makes to his own and humanity's past show that he is aware of his special position. What he does not do is *brood* about it. He has too many other things to do.

Lord of Light, Zelazny's best novel to date, is an especially clear example of the story pattern's full expression. The setting is a distant planet at a distant time, our Earth almost forgotten. The planet was colonized by the spaceship Star of India, but members of the ship's crew have used the technology available to make themselves virtually immortal and to assume godlike control over the passengers' descendants. One of the crew, Sam, sees the selfishness of what the others are doing and decides to wreck their system. Accordingly, he sometimes goes among the people in different roles, such as a guru:

His followers called him Mahasamatman and said he was a god. He preferred to drop the maha- and the -atman, however, and called himself Sam. He never claimed to be a god. But then, he never claimed not to be a god. Circumstances being what they were, neither admission could be of any benefit. Silence, though could.

Therefore, there was mystery about him (p.1).

Sam cultivates this mystery as he plays the part of a holy man, trying to introduce Buddhism into this world and thus weaken the hold of the Hindu-style "gods." He is at first, simply acting. Later, it becomes more than that. Laughing, he tells a friend: "I'm very gullible when it comes to my own words. I believe everything I say, though I know I'm a liar" (p.33). What he preaches is the impermanence of words, but above all the necessity of breaking out of limiting conceptions of self and existence:

"Therefore, I charge you—forget the names you bear, forget the words I speak as soon as they are uttered. Look, rather, upon the Nameless within yourselves, which arises as I address it. It hearkens not to my words, but to the reality within me, of which it is part. This is the *atman*, which hears *me* rather than my words. All else is unreal. To define is to lose. The essence of all things is the Nameless. The Nameless is unknowable, mightier even than Brahma. Things pass, but the essence remains" (p.30).

Sam tries to break men out of their confining faith so they can live up the human necessity of acting effectively, not wasting energy on shadow contests.

"The answer, the justification [of action] is the same for men as it is for gods. Good or ill, say the sages, mean nothing for they are of Samsara. Agree with the sages, who have taught our people for as far as the memory of man may reach. Agree, but consider also a thing of which the sages do not speak. This thing is 'beauty.' which is a word—but look behind the word and consider the Way of the Nameless. And what is the Way of the Nameless? It is the Way of Dream. And why does the Nameless dream: This thing is not known to any dweller within Samsara. So ask, rather, *what* does the Nameless dream?

"The Nameless, of which we are all a part, does dream form. And what is the highest attribute any form may possess? It is beauty. The Nameless, then, is an artist. The problem, therefore, is not one of good or evil, but one of esthetics. To struggle against those who are mighty among dreamers and are mighty for ill, or ugliness, is not to struggle for that which the sages have taught us to be meaningless in terms of Samsara or Nirvana, but rather it is to struggle for the symmetrical dreaming of a dream, in terms of the rhythm and the point, the balance and the antithesis which will make it a thing of beauty. Of this, the sages say nothing. This truth is so simple that they have obviously overlooked it. For this reason, I am bound by the esthetics of the situation to call it to your attention. To struggle against the dreamers who dream ugliness, be they men or gods, cannot but be the will of the Nameless" (pp.31-32).

Sam does not lead a purely ascetic life—it is likely that he does not consciously believe the words quoted above while he is saying them. He is willing to bargain with demons, and when his body is possessed by one who does great evil as Sam's consciousness looks on, he unwillingly comes to recognize that the demon's acts reflect his own selfish desires. But even so, fully aware of his own limitations, he is willing to cooperate with misguided or evil forces in order to win a victory that will set the people free. He is ready to take help wherever he finds it because he embodies Zelazny's confidence in man's ability to *grow*, to meet unexpected dilemmas successfully. He believes that good ultimately will develop out of free growth.

As with Conrad in *This Immortal,* Sam's personal development is reflected in a political debate that pops up throughout the novel. In *This Immortal,* Conrad must outargue *and* outfight the Returnists, who want to hold on to a narrow vision of Earth's past. In *Lord of Light,* the debate is between the Deicrats, the gods' party, and the Accelerationists, represented by Sam. The gods rationalize their rigid control by declaring that man must be protected from premature technological or social developments; the Accelerationists are willing to take a chance on man's ability to handle anything he devises. In the novel's action, the gods maintain power by concentrating on some part of themselves and clinging to it forever, world without end, but in doing so they become so wrapped up in themselves as they were that they cannot cope with the present. Trying to preserve a static, peaceful society, they organize increasingly cataclysmic battles. Their accomplishment, finally, is folly. Sam does not take himself so seriously—except when he is overcome by *hubris* during the battle for Keenset—but he practices more wisdom. He is not sure exactly who he is or what he can do; however, he is free to improvise brilliantly on new opportunities and new abilities he finds in himself. The novel's overall action demonstrates the deadly sterility of refusing to change, and the ultimate viability of accepting natural growth. Sam's way finally works.

Within the overall action, too, the characters work out this principle in their experience. Perhaps the most interesting example of growth, for our study, is Sam's conversion of Rild, an assassin sent by Heaven to silence the "Buddha." Rild falls ill before he can approach Sam in the guise of a pilgrim. Instead, after Sam nurses him back to health, he becomes a true disciple because he has "held [Sam's] words within [himself] and felt the truth which they contain" (p.82). Rild becomes a magnetic holy man in his own right, taking the name Sugata, but he renounces nonviolent holiness to fight Yama, the death god, also sent to kill Sam. Having grown into and through a new role, the man continues on; as he tells Yama: "By opposing you now and in this manner, I . . . betray the teachings of my new master. But I must follow the dictates of my heart. Neither my old name nor my new do therefore fit me, nor are they deserved—

so call me by no name!" (p.88). The man fails to defeat the god. But Sam recognizes that Rild/Sugata could not really have believed he could win against Yama. And Sam tells Yama that Rild was thus a success, not a failure: "I have listened too often to his sermons, to his subtle parables, to believe that he would do a thing such as this without a purpose. You have slain the true Buddha, deathgod. You know what *I* am" (p.103). Still later in the story, Sam thinks back on Sugata:

the strange one...whose hands had held both death and benediction. Over the years, their names would merge and their deeds would be mingled. He had lived too long not to know how time stirred the pots of legend. There had been a real Buddha, he knows that now. The teaching he had offered, no matter how spuriously, had attracted this true believer, this one who had somehow achieved enlightenment, marked man's minds with his sainthood, and then gone willingly into the hands of Death himself. Tathagatha [Sam's alias at that time] and Sugata would be part of a single legend, he knew, and Tathagatha would shine in the light shed by his disciple (p.135).

As with Rild, so it is with Sam himself. He too has become something new—or revealed something unsuspected in himself—by playing a role. Taraka, lord of demons, recognizes him before Sam realizes what has happened:

"Mortals call you Buddha."

"That is only because they are afflicted with language and ignorance."

"No. I have looked upon your flames [true nature] and name you Lord of Light. You bind them as you bound us, you loose them as you loosed us. Yours was the power to lay a belief upon them. You are what you claimed to be."

"I lied. I never believed in it myself, and I still don't...My choice was based upon calculation, not inspiration, and I am nothing."

"You are the Lord of Light" (pp.239-240).

Typically, Sam vanishes mysteriously at the end of the novel. Zelazny leaves the reader with profound uncertainty about the fate of his main characters, but with this reminder: "Death and light are everywhere, always, and they begin, end, strive, attend, into and upon the Dream of the Nameless that is the world, burning words within Samsara, perhaps to create a thing of beauty" (p.257).

This summary of the novel leaves out *much*. In particular, I have left out the theme of love, which is as close to an unchanging force as Sam can conceive (pp.156-157) and which transfigures the end of this novel (and of other works, including *Isle of the Dead*). But I believe that much of the force of this great novel is its striking depiction of the unfinished, unlimitable process of human growth, Zelazny's great theme. If the parts of the novel seem broken, the effect is to force the reader to experience something of the disorientation and growth that Zelazny's characters learn to accept. And when the parts do come together in the reader's mind, the impact is great.

Since *Lord of Light*, Zelazny has written several novels. They have not been so successful as *Lord of Light*, but then they have not been much *like* that novel. One of the easiest things for a writer to do, once he has discovered a vein of material that sells well and feels comfortable, is to settle down and exploit it. Zelazny has never done that. Perhaps part of his attitude is expressed by Sam, who plays dice with a demon to the limit of his luck; another character comments: "It must have been the only way he could call upon his life-will, to bind him again to his task—by placing himself in jeopardy, by casting his very existence with each roll of the dice" (p.20). Or perhaps more mundanely, Zelazny is taking the risks an artist must, as he has described his early practice as a writer, "When I decide to write a story I make a quick mental checksheet of all the items I consider myself capable of handling with impunity; I then think about the debit entries and consider the best ways to cover over the majority—and always I pick one, usually the one I deem my most egregrious current failing, and I force myself to write it through."[20]

Or perhaps the two are the same, and it *is* aesthetic impulses that lead us into battle with life. In any case, in the novels written since *Lord of Light*, Zelazny has been working with different combinations of action and fragmentary suggestion, ritual vs. emotional weight. *Damnation Alley* (1969) is concentrated pretty directly on action, due to the nature of its motorcycle outlaw hero,[21] while *Nine Princes in Amber (1970), The Guns of Avalon (1972),* and *Sign of the Unicorn (1975)* are somewhat limited by the conventions of super-science and sorcery adventure (though the tale they tell is as yet unfinished, and Zelazny certainly has room to take the story anywhere he wishes).[22] *To Die in Italbar* (1973) uses the hero of *Isle of the Dead* as a supporting character in a hard-driving tale of interstellar intrigue and superhuman conflict—another story that calls for a continuation. On the other hand, *Creatures of Light and Darkness* (1969) takes Egyptian mythology much further than *Lord of Light* did Hindu; both the background and foreground are more obscure than in the earlier novel, and though *Creatures* is a satisfying aesthetic construct, it remains cryptically unmoving otherwise. And *Jack of Shadows* is another cryptic parable, this time removed from any familiar system of myth—and yet fascinating and haunting.[22] Finally, *Today We Choose Faces* (1973) is an intricate tale of a plot to reshape humanity over many generations; the main character is an especially clear presentation of Zelazny's pattern of development, though the novel's conclusion becomes less emotionally satisfying than usual when, before he goes off on his own, the hero coldly rejects a chance to communicate with the force that has manipulated him earlier. Of course it should go without saying that all those novels are rich, impressive works in their own right. It's just that they aren't the stunning successes that *Lord of Light* was. The last two, in particular, strike one as easier to comprehend than much of Zelazny's earlier work, but with some loss of power. The confrontation of deities in *To Die in Italbar,* for example, is less directly presented—safer—than in *Isle of the Dead.* And Sam would not have held himself aloof from listening to a message from his opponent, as does the hero of *Today We Choose Faces.*

Zelazny's latest novel is *Doorways in the Sand* (1976). In some ways it probably is his lightest-weight, most accessible novel. The form is taken more or less straight from a very familiar vein of mass entertainment, the espionage suspense novel. Also the tone is predominantly light, and Zelazny gets off some fine comic scenes— and some gloriously awful gags. Still, the reader's comfortable approach to just-another-mystery whodunit is deliberately short-circuited several times, and the humor is balanced by dialogue that is Zelazny's best sustained natural, or only slightly heightened, style. And the onrushing action is countered by some of the most fragmented narrative he has ever done—including repeated use of the reverse cliffhanger, chapters that *begin* with the hero dangling in the middle of a disaster, and only later reveal the buildup. Within the action, Zelazny is doing some extremely interesting things, and his overall point is serious enough to stir deeper interest. The book is at once enormously easy to read and a formidable challenge to grasp. The paradigm set forth above fits, however. So does the basic point. Fred Cassidy, Zelazny's hero, is acrophiliac—he loves to climb the outside walls and roofs of buildings. This trait is a key to his underlying nature, although he must be shaken rudely out of a comfortable niche and is reluctant to take a chance to go off into the unknown. Early in the story, a building-climbing friend asks him:

"...tell me what it feels like when you reach the top."

"An elation, I guess. A sense of accomplishment, sort of."

"Up here the view is less obstructed. You can see farther, take in more of the features of the landscape. Is that it, I wonder? A better perspective?"

"Part of it, maybe. But there is always one other thing I feel when I reach the top: I always want to go just a little bit higher, and I always feel that I almost can, that I am just about to."[24]

And this, I think, illustrates the basis of Zelazny's success. He has already produced some truly fine stories, including at least one outstandingly fine novel, *Lord of Light.* He has awesome natural gifts, and he has invested considerable effort in developing them. But he has not been content to rest easily with his success. He has tried to live up to his own ideal of deliberate experimentation. It is not simply what he had done already but what he *might* do that makes Zelazny important. And that is why, since his first few appearances in *Amazing* and *Fantastic,* readers have regarded each new Zelazny story as Zelazny regards his characters: with wonder, affection--and anticipation.

Notes

The Fictions of Robert Silverberg

¹Russell Letson, "The Worlds of Philip Jose' Farmer," *Extrapolation, 18 (May* 1977), 124-130.

²Robert Silverberg, "Some Notes from the Pre-Dynastic Epoch," in *Unfamiliar Territory* (New York: Charles Scribner's Sons, 1973), p. 37.

³Silverberg, "Ms. Found in an Abandoned Time Machine," in *Capricorn Games* (New York: Random House, 1976), pp. 40,51.

⁴Silverberg, "Breckenridge and the Continuum," in *Capricorn Games,* pp.78-80.

⁵Silverberg, "Introduction," *Next Stop the Stars* (New York: Ace Books, 1977), p. xv.

⁶Silverberg, "Introduction," *Valley Beyond Time* (New York: Dell, 1973), [p.ii].

⁷Silverberg, "Introduction to 'To See the Invisible Man,'" in *The Best of Robert Silverberg* (New York: Pocket Books, 1976), p. 47.

⁸Russell Letson, "Introduction," *To Open the Sky* (Boston: Gregg Press, 1977), pp. v, x.

⁹Silverberg, "The Road to Nightfall," in *The Best of Robert Silverberg,* p. 20.

¹⁰Ibid., p. 10.

¹¹Silverberg, "Warm Man," in *The Best of Robert Silverberg,* p.41.

¹²Silverberg, *The Seed of Earth* (New York: Ace Books, 1977), p. 157.

¹³Silverberg, "Flies," in *The Best of Robert Silverberg,* p. 83.

¹⁴Silverberg, *Thorns* (New York: Ballantine Books, 1967), p. 12.

¹⁵Silverberg, *The Man in the Maze* (New York: Avon Equinox Books, n.d.), p. 52.

¹⁶Silverberg, "The Fangs of the Trees," in *Parsecs and Parables* (New York: Doubleday & Company, Inc., 1970), p. 202.

¹⁷Silverberg, *The Stochastic Man* (Greenwich, Cn.: Fawcett Publications, 1975), p. 5.

¹⁸Silverberg, "Schwartz Between the Galaxies," in *The Feast of St. Dionysus* (New York: Charles Scribner's Sons, 1975), p. 85.

¹⁹Silverberg, "A Sea of Faces," in *Capricorn Games,* p. 115.

²⁰Silverberg, "The Man Who Came Back," in Lester del Rey, ed., *Best Science Fiction Stories of the Year* (New York: E.P. Dutton, 1975), pp. 181, 188. Originally published in *New Worlds* (February 1961), it was published a second time in *Galaxy* (December 1974).

²¹Silverberg, *The Silent Invaders* (New York: Ace Books, 1977), pp. 116, 118.

²²Silverberg, *Collision Course* (New York: Ace Books, 1977), p. 154.

²³Silverberg, *Across a Billion Years* (New York: Dial Press, Inc., 1969), p. 247.

²⁴Silverberg, "Push No More," in *Unfamiliar Territory,* p. 132.

²⁵Silverberg, *The Time Hoppers* (New York: Avon Books, 1967), p. 9.

²⁶Silverberg, *Nightwings* (New York: Avon Books, 1969), p. 97.

²⁷Silverberg, *Downward to the Earth* (New York: Nelson Doubleday, 1970), p. 15.

²⁸Silverberg, "Sundance," in Robert Silverberg, ed., *Aliens* (New York and Nashville: Thomas Nelson Inc., Publishers, 1976), p. 180.

²⁹Silverberg, *Recalled to Life* (New York: Doubleday & Company, 1972), pp. 183-184.

³⁰Silverberg, *Son of Man* (New York: Ballantine Books, 1971), pp. 210-211.

³¹Silverberg, *Dying Inside* (New York: Charles Scribner's Sons, 1972), p. 17.

³²Barry Malzberg, "Robert Silverberg," *The Magazine of Fantasy and Science Fiction,* 46 (April 1974), 71.

³³Silverberg, *The Book of Skulls* (New York: Charles Scribner's Sons), p. 25.

³⁴Silverberg, "Born with the Dead," in *Born with the Dead: Three Novellas about the Spirit of Man* (New York: Vintage Books, 1975), p. 5.

³⁵Silverberg, "Thomas the Proclaimer," in *Born with the Dead,* p. 128.

[36]Silverberg, *Tower of Glass* (New York: Bantam Books, 1971), pp. 40-41.

[37]Silverberg, *Shadrach in the Furnace* (Indianapolis, New York: The Bobbs-Merrill Company, Inc., 1977), p. 8.

Philip Jose' Farmer: The Trickster as Artist

[1]Ted White, Review of *Image of the Beast*, in *Amazing*, 43 (July 1969), 122.

[2]James Blish, *More Issues at Hand* (Chicago: Advent, 1970), pp. 122, 133.

[3]Alfred Bester, "Books," *The Magazine of Fantasy and Science Fiction*, 20 (March 1961), 80.

[4]Theodore Sturgeon, "Science Fiction, Morals, and Religion," in Reginald Bretnor, ed., *Science Fiction, Today and Tomorrow* (Baltimore: Penguin, 1975), p. 106.

[5]Norman Spinrad, *Modern Science Fiction* (Garden City, N.Y.: Anchor, 1974), pp. 267, 273. Something of that economic and emotional cost is suggested by the primarily biographical sketch of Farmer by Sam Moskowitz in *Seekers of Tomorrow: Masters of Modern Science Fiction* (Westport, Cn.: Hyperion Press, 1974), pp. 392-409; this study extends only to the early 1960's. For further biographical information, see David Kraft and Mitch Scheele, "An Interview with Philip Jose' Farmer," with additional comments on the transcript by Farmer and Richard Geis, *Science Fiction Review*, 4 (August 1975), 721.

[6]Leslie Fiedler, originally a book review in the Los Angeles *Times* (23 April 1972), reprinted as "Thanks for the Feast: Notes on Philip Jose' Farmer," in *The Book of Philip Jose'©* Farmer (New York: DAW, 1973), pp. 233-239.

[7]Franz Rottensteiner, "Playing Around with Creation: Philip Jose' Farmer," *Science-Fiction Studies*, 1 (1973), 96, 98.

[8]Russell Letson, "The Worlds of Philip Jose' Farmer," *Extrapolation*, 18 (May 1977), 124-130; see also Letson's, "The Face of a Thousand Heroes: Philip Jose' Farmer," *Science-Fiction Studies*, 4 (1977), 35-41. Subsequent references to Letson in the text will be to the *Extrapolation* article.

[9]Paul Radin, *The Trickster: A Study in American Indian Mythology* (London: Philosophical Library, 1956); see especially the appended essay by C. G. Jung, "On the Psychology of the Trickster Figure."

[10]Warwick Wellington, *The Confidence Game in American Literature* (Princeton, N.J.: Princeton University Press, 1975).

[11]Farmer, *Tarzan Alive* (New York: Popular Library, [1973]), p. 64.

[12]Farmer, "Extracts from the Memoirs of Lord Greystoke," in *Mother Was a Lovely Beast: A Feral Man Anthology* (Radnor, Pa.: Chilton, 1974), pp. 45-46.

[13]For a discussion and list of the major Farmer series and a full bibliography of Farmer's works, see my "Speculative Fiction, Bibliographies, and Philip Jose' Farmer," *Extrapolation*, 18 (December 1976), 59-72.

[14]Farmer, *The Maker of Universes* (London: Sphere, 1970), p. 108: the Wolff-Kickaha series has been for some time available only in this edition, a condition Ace is finally correcting this year, with planned reprints of all four novels.

[15]"Philip Jose' Farmer: An Interview Conducted by Paul Walker," *Luna*, No. 54 (September 1974), 6.

[16]Ibid., p. 6.

[17]Farmer, "After King Kong Fell," in Roger Elwood, ed., *Omega* (New York: Fawcett, 1974), pp. 50-51.

[18]Farmer, *Doc Savage: His Apocalyptic Life* (Garden City, N.Y.: Doubleday & Company, 1973), p. 4.

[19]John Layard, Review of Radin's *The Trickster*, in *Journal of Analytical Psychology*, 2 (1957), 107.

[20]Farmer, *The Lovers* (New York: Ballantine Books, 1961, p. 109.

²¹See especially "The Spiritual Problem of Modern Man," most conveniently available in Joseph Campbell, ed., *The Portable Jung* (New York: Viking, 1971), pp. 456-479.

²²Farmer, "The Captain's Daughter," in *The Alley God* (London: Sphere, 1972), p. 58.

²³Farmer, "My Sister's Brother," in *Strange Relations* (New York: Avon Books, 1974), p. 156.

²⁴The discussion here of archaic phallic gods and warriors is based on H.R. Hays, *In the Beginnings: Early Man and His Gods* (New York: G. P. Putnam's Sons, 1963), pp. 136-149.

²⁵Farmer, *A Feast Unknown* (North Hollywood, Ca.: Fokker DLXIX Press, 1975), p. 152.

²⁶Richard Slotkin, *Regeneration through Violence: The Mythology of The American Frontier, 1600-1860* (Middletown, Cn.: Wesleyan University Press, 1973) p. 6.

²⁷See David Samuelson, "The Frontier Worlds of Robert A. Heinlein," in Thomas D. Clareson, ed., *Voices for the Future* Bowling Green, Ohio: Bowling Green Popular Press, 1976), 1:104-152.

²⁸Farmer, *Night of Light* (New York: Berkley Medallion Books, 1972), p. 51.

²⁹Farmer, *Dare* (London: Quartet, 1974), p. 154.

³⁰Farmer, "Down in the Black Gang," in *Down in the Black Gang and Other Stories* (New York: Signet, 1971), p. 27.

³¹Farmer, *To Your Scattered Bodies Go* (New York: Berkley Medallion Books, 1971), p. 212.

³²Farmer, *The Other Log of Phileas Fogg* (New York: DAW, 1973), p. 179.

³³Gunnar Gallmo, "Oversattarens Efterskrift," in *Phileas Foggs hemliga dagbok* (Vanersborg, Sweden: Delta Forlags AB, 1974); I am indebted for this note to Farmer, who added, "Sam Lundwall told me Eyvind Johnson wrote it, so I suppose that Gunnar Gallmo is either Johnson's real name or pen name."

³⁴Farmer, *Behind the Walls of Terra* (New York: Ace Books, 1970), p. 136.

³⁵Farmer, "Osiris on Crutches," in Robert Silverberg, ed., *New Dimensions 6* (New York: Harper & Row, 1976), pp. 199-209.

³⁶Farmer, "Stations of the Nightmare, Part I," in Roger Elwood, ed., *Continuum 1* (New York: Berkley, 1975), p. 24.

³⁷Farmer, "Fundamental Issue," listed in my bibliography as forthcoming in 1977, saw print a bit earlier than expected: *Amazing*, 51 (December 1976), 6-23, 35.

³⁸Karl Kerenyi, "The Trickster in Relation to Greek Mythology," in Radin, p. 185.

The Lost Canticles of Walter M. Miller, Jr.

¹Miller's first published story, "MacDougal's Wife," *American Mercury* (March 1950), 313-320, is not science fiction, though it invokes religious and scientific imagery, in keeping with his science fiction, to magnify the significance of the biological sterility and assumed infidelity of the titular character.

²Anthony Boucher, "The Publishing of Science Fiction," in Reginald Bretnor, ed., *Modern Science Fiction: Its Meaning and Its Value* (New York: Coward McCann, 1953), p. 33. His observation is supported in "Science Fiction Rockets into Big Time," *Business Week*, 20 October 1951, pp. 82-84, 89; and in Bradford M. Day, ed.,*The Complete Checklist of Science-Fiction Magazines*, pamphlet (New York: Science Fiction and Fantasy Publication [*sic*], 1961. Data on anthologies has been compiled from W. R. Cole, ed., *A Checklist of Science Fiction Anthologies* (New York: W.R. Cole, 1964) and Frederick Siemon, ed., *Science Fiction Story Index, 1950-1968* (Chicago: American Library Association, 1971).

³A political article, "Bobby and Jimmy" (concerning Kennedy and Hoffa),

identifying its author as the writer of *A Canticle for Leibowitz*, appeared in *Nation*, 7 April 1962, pp. 300-303. But I have been unable to find any other stories or articles by Miller outside of the science fiction magazines.

[4]William F. Nolan, in the headnote to "The Lineman" in his anthology, *A Wilderness of Stars* (Los Angeles: Sherbourne Press, 1971) states simply: "For good and valid reasons of his own, Walter Miller, Jr., has retired as a storyteller."

[5]See Robert S. Chapman, "Science Fiction and the Fifties: Billy Graham, McCarthy and the Bomb," *Foundation 7 & 8* (March 1975), pp. 38-52, about which editor Peter Nicholls comments: "It is excerpted from a paper he wrote for the Department of History, while a student at the University of California at Berkeley." He adds: "The whole subject of social attitudes as manifested in science fiction...is rapidly becoming, and with good reason, one of the most popular themes among students doing their Ph.D. theses on science fiction, especially in Europe."

[6]Leslie Fiedler, *Love and Death in the American Novel* (Cleveland: World Publishing Company, 1962), p. 478.

[7]At least one anthology, May Mohs, ed., *Other Worlds, Other Gods* (Garden City: Doubleday and Company, 1971) has been built out of stories that combine religion and science fiction, and that seem to me to bear out my contention, despite the editor's sentiments as expressed in his introductory essay. For other brief mentions of the topic, see William Atheling, Jr. [James Blish], *The Issue at Hand: Studies in Contemporary Magazine Science Fiction* (Chicago: Advent, 1964), pp. 49-61; and Sam Moskowitz, *Seekers of Tomorrow: Masters of Modern Science Fiction* (Cleveland: World Publishing Company, 1966), pp. 410-414.

[8]Review articles on the novel's original publication appeared in the following publications: *Analog* (November 1960); *Chicago Sunday Tribune*, 6 March 1960; *Christian Century*, 25 May 1960; *Commonweal*, 4 March 1960; *Galaxy* (February 1961); *Manchester Guardian Weekly*, 7 April 1960; *New York Herald Tribune Book Review*, 13 March 1960; *New York Times Book Review*, 27 March 1960; *New Yorker*, 2 April 1960; *San Francisco Chronicle*, 8 March 1960; *Saturday Review*, 4 June 1960; *Spectator*,25 March 1960, and *Time*, 22 February 1960. At least seven subsequent revaluations have also been published: Martin Green, *Science and the Shabby Curate of Poetry* (New York: W. W. Norton, 1965); Edward Ducharme, "A Canticle for Miller," *English Journal*, 55 (November 1966), 1042-1044; R.A. Schroth, "Between the Lines," *America*, 20 January 1968, p. 79; Hugh Rank, "Song out of Season: *A Canticle for Leibowitz*," *Renascence*, 21 (Summer 1969), 213-221; Michael Alan Bennett, "The Theme of Responsibility in *A Canticle for Leibowitz*," in David Madden, ed., *Rediscoveries* (New York: Crown, 1971); Russell Griffin, "Medievalism in *A Canticle for Leibowitz*," *Extrapolation*, 14 (May 1973), 112-125. The Catholic journals were most parochial in dismissing the science fiction in the book, but the reviewers for the *Herald-Tribune*, *Manchester Guardian*, and *Spectator* were also remiss.

[9]The only treatment of these aspects of the book of which I am aware is my 1969 U.S.C. dissertation, now published as *Visions of Tomorrow: Six Journeys from Outer to Inner Space* (New York: Arno Press, 1975), pp. 221-279.

[10]Robert P. Mills, ed. *The Worlds of Science Fiction* (New York: Dial Press, 1963), p. 86.

What Are We to Make of J.G. Ballard's Apocalypse?

[1]A perfect display of the shift in attitudes is presented in Orson Welles's 1976 film adaptation of *The Food of the Gods;* Welles leaves out altogether the main message about superhuman scientific achievement and thus converts Wells's paean to triumph science into a horror story of nature in disastrous rebellion against science.

[2]See Manfred Nagl, *Science Fiction in Deutschland: Untersuchungen zur Soziographie und Ideologie der phantastischen Massenliteratur* (Tubingen: Tubinger Vereinigung fur Volkskunde, 1972).

³Originally published as *The Burning World* (New York: Fawcett Medallion Books, 1964). The British version, greatly rewritten and expanded from fifteen chapters to 42, was published as *The Drought* by Jonathan Cape in 1965. I have used *The Drought* because it is more fully developed and more readily available.

⁴Ballard, *The Wind from Nowhere* (New York: Berkley Medallion Books, 1962), p. 48.

⁵Ballard, *The Crystal World* (New York: Berkley Medallion Books, 1967), p. 75.

⁶Ballard, *The Drought* (Middlesex, England: Penguin Books, 1974), pp. 31-32.

⁷I shall for convenience refer to this book as a novel, though its structure and intentions are clearly those of an anti-novel. Subsequently I shall cite, and therefore use the title of, the American edition, because it is far more readily available in this country and because interested readers ought to look at William Burroughs' preface to this edition.

⁸For a general statement and application of this theory, see my article entitled (by the editors) "Chic Bleak in Fantasy Fiction," *Saturday Review: The Arts,* 15 July 1972, pp. 42-45.

⁹Ballard, "The Overloaded Man," in *The Voices of Time* (New York: Berkley Medallion Books, 1962), p. 72.

¹⁰Ballard, "Deep End," in *Chronopolis* (New York: G.P. Putnam's Sons, 1971), p. 312.

¹¹Ballard, *The Drowned World* (New York: Berkley Medallion Books, 1962), p. 44.

¹²Ballard, "The Waiting Grounds," in *The Voices of Time*, p. 144.

¹³Brian Aldiss, "The Wounded Land: J.G. Ballard," in Thomas D. Clareson, ed., *SF: The Other Side of Realism* (Bowling Green, Ohio: Bowling Green University Popular Press, 1971), p. 122.

¹⁴Ballard, "The Killing Ground," in *The Day of Forever* (London: Panther Books, 1971), p. 140.

¹⁵Ballard, *Crash* (New York: Farrar, Straus and Giroux, 1973), p. 13.

¹⁶Ballard, *Love and Napalm: Export U.S.A.* (New York: Grove Press, 1972), p. 73.

¹⁷Ballard, "The Subliminal Man," in Robert Silverberg, ed., *The Mirror of Infinity* (New York: Harper & Row, 1970), pp. 246-247. The following discussion of "The Subliminal Man" follows the lines of my introduction to that story in the Silverberg anthology.

¹⁸Ballard, "The Subliminal Man," in *The Mirror of Infinity*, p. 261.

¹⁹San Francisco *Chronicle*, 12 July 1970.

²⁰Andre van Dam, "The Limits of Waste," *The Futurist*, 6 (February 1975), 20.

²¹Bradford C. Snell, "American Ground Transport," *Hearings before the Subcommittee on Antitrust and Monopoly of the Committee of the Judiciary, United States Senate, 93rd Congress, Second Session on S. 1167* (Washington: U.S. Government Printing Office, 1974), p. A-1.

²²Snell, p. A-2 and *passim,* pp. A-1 to A-103.

²³Snell, pp. A-2, A-3.

²⁴Ballard, *Concrete Island* (New York: Farrar, Straus and Giroux, 1974), p. 162.

²⁵Ballard, "Preface," *Vermilion Sands* (Frogmore, St. Albans: Panther Books, 1975), p. 7.

The Development of John Brunner

¹For an overview of Brunner's career and a fairly complete bibliography of his work, see Joe DeBolt, ed., *The Happening Worlds of John Brunner* (Port Washington, N.Y.: Kennikat Press, 1975).

²By science fiction-mainstream hybrid, I mean a story with traditional science fiction trappings plus some combination of the following: an increased concern with character development; a contemporary or near future setting; the use of narrative

techniques developed in the mainstream but rarely applied in science fiction; a focus on the inner psychological workings of characters rather than on their environments. Brunner consciously decided to produce such works, as he points out in his major autobiographical statement to date:

'More and more I have become concerned with what might be called borderline SF, that is to say fiction which, while incorporating some element of the standard SF *canan*, is nonetheless primarily of the present and relates very closely to discernible current trends. In some cases this has led me completely out of the field (tenuous though its frontier may be), as in *The Gaudy Shadows* (1970), which appeared as a murder mystery although its plot revolves around the discovery of a group of so far nonexistent hallucinogenic drugs. Contrastingly, I feel that some of my recent output may be said to have extended SF, rather than trespassed over its edge; the use in such novels as *Quicksand* and *The Productions of Time* (1967) of science-fiction elements in an otherwise wholly contemporary novel constitutes for me a kind of topological inversion that—like the image in a mirror—does not alter the thing perceived, but leads to a new appreciation of it.' John Brunner, "The Development of a Science Fiction Writer," *Foundation 1* (March 1972), 10.

[3]Actually, of course, Brunner had been writing for some time before the date of his first publication. But since we do not know, except in a few significant cases, when a work was actually written, the date of publication is used to place a work in its appropriate period. Brunner was writing for a living, and this living depended upon sales; hence, we assume that he generally got a work into print as soon after its completion as he could.

[4]Brunner, "Thou Good and Faithful," *Astounding,* 51 (March 1953), 20.

[5]Brunner, "Brainpower," *Nebula,* 1 (Spring 1953), 106.

[6]Brunner, "Tomorrow Is Another Day," *Authentic,* (March 1954).

[7]Brunner, "Armistice," *Astounding,* 54 (January 1955), 76.

[8]Brunner, "By the Name of Man," in Donald A. Wollheim, ed., *More Adventures on Other Planets* (New York: Ace Books, 1963), p. 83.

[9]Brunner, "Puzzle for Spacemen," *No Future in It* (New York: Curtis Books, 1969), p. 41.

[10]Brunner, "No Future in It," *No Future in It,* p. 14.

[11]Fantasy as used here refers to that branch of imaginative literature whose premises rest on supernatural or nonempirical grounds and includes tales of sorcery, ghosts, folk legends, and the mystical. Conversely, science fiction must be empirically grounded, and even though the elements of a story are not known at the time to be empirically possible, the author's premise must be that they are based on actual, albeit fictional, empirical principles ultimately knowable by science. The above are working definitions limited in application to this essay and are not offered as definitive definitions of science fiction and fantasy.

[12]Brunner had actually published an earlier novel under a publishing house's pseudonym, but its quality was so poor that he refuses to reveal its identity.

[13]Brunner, *The 100th Millenium* (New York: Ace Books, 1959), p. 19.

[14]In *The Happening Worlds of John Brunner*, I have called it his "Ace" period because of his large output of novels more than two dozen—for Ace Books.

[15]Brunner, *The World Swappers* (New York: Ace Books, 1959), p.150.

[16]Brunner, *Echo in the Skull* (New York: Ace Books, 1959), p. 65.

[17]Brunner, *The World Swappers,* p. 86.

[18]Brunner, "Round Trip," in *Out of My Mind* (New York: Ballantine Books, 1967), p. 213.

[19]"City of the Tiger" was originally published in *Science Fantasy* for December 1958. It was then published in *Fantastic Universe* for November 1959 so that it would precede "The Curative Telepath" in the December issue.

[20]Brunner, *The Squares of the City* (New York: Ballantine Books, 1965), p. 315.

[21]DeBolt, *The Happening Worlds of John Brunner,* p. 21.

[22]Brunner, *The Crutch of Memory* (London: Barrie and Rockliff, 1964), p. 9.

[23]Brunner, *Wear the Butcher's Medal* (New York: Pocket Books, 1965), p. 229.

[24]Brunner, "Dread Empire," *Fantastic Stories*, 20 (April 1971), 128.

[25]Brunner, *The Atlantic Abomination* (New York: Ace Books, 1960), p. 128.

[26]Brunner, *Born Under Mars* (New York: Ace Books, 1967), p. 127.

[27]Brunner, *Sanctuary in the Sky* (New York: Ace Books, 1960), p. 116.

[28]Brunner, "The Totally Rich," *Worlds of Tomorrow*, 1 (June 1963), 104.

[29]Brunner, "Nobody Axed You," in *Time-Jump* (New York: Dell, 1973), p. 160.

[30]The nine revised science fiction novels are: *The Hundredth Millenium* (1959) to *Catch a Falling Star* (1968); *Slavers of Space* (1960) to *Into the Slave Nebula* (1968); *Times Without Number* (1962) to *Times Without Number* (1969); *Secret Agent of Terra* (1962) to *The Avengers of Carrig* (1969); *Listen! the Stars!* (1963) to *The Stardroppers* (1972); *The Astronauts Must Not Land* (1963) to *More Things in Heaven* (1973); *Day of the Star Cities* (1965) to *Age of Miracles* (1973); *Castaways' World* (1963) to *Polymath* (1974); *Echo in the Skull* (1959) to *Give Warning to the World* (1974).

[31]Brunner, *Bedlam Planet* (New York: Ace Books, 1968), p. 146.

[32]Brunner, *The Dramaturges of Yan* (New York: Ace Books, 1971), p. 153.

[33]Brunner, "Web of Everywhere," *Galaxy*, 34 (April 1974), 175.

[34]Brunner, *A Plague on Both Your Causes* (London: The Thriller Book Club, 1970), p. 186.

[35]Brunner, *Good Men Do Nothing* (New York: Pyramid Books, 1971), p. 204.

[36]Brunner, *Honky in the Woodpile* (London: Constable, 1971), pp. 32-33.

[37]Most of the essays in my book, *The Happening Worlds of John Brunner*, focus on these three major dystopias. For a more traditional literary analysis, see Stephen H. Goldman, "The Polymorphic Worlds of John Brunner: How Do They Happen?" *Science-Fiction Studies*, 3 (July 1976), 103-111; and Michael Stern, "From Technique to Critique: Knowledge and Human Interests in Brunner's *Stand on Zanzibar, The Jagged Orbit,* and *The Sheep Look Up,*" *SFS*, 3 (July 1976), 112-129.

[38]Norman Spinrad, "*Stand on Zanzibar:* The Novel as Film," in Thomas D. Clareson, ed., *SF: The Other Side of Realism* (Bowling Green, Ohio: Bowling Green University Popular Press, 1971), pp. 181-185; Judith Merril, "Books," *The Magazine of Fantasy and Science Fiction*, 36 (February 1969), 24-25.

[39]DeBolt, p. 47.

[40]In a personal communication, Brunner has informed me that the genesis of *The Wrong End of Time* occured several years ago during a hotter period in the Cold War. This may explain why it is somewhat atypical of Brunner's works of the 1970s.

[41]Brunner, *The Shockwave Rider* (New York: Harper & Row, 1975), p. 288.

[42]Brunner, "The Suicide of Man," *Isaac Asimov's Science Fiction Magazine*, 2 (July-August, 1978), 176.

[43]DeBolt, pp. 36-37.

[44]Robert Scholes, "Science Fiction as Conscience: John Brunner and Ursula K. Le Guin," *The New Republic*, 30 October 1976, p. 38.

Mack Reynolds: The Future as Socio-economic Possibility

[1]Brian W. Aldiss, *Billion Year Spree* (New York: Schocken Books, 1974), p. 303.

[2]Private letter from Mack Reynolds dated December 18, 1975.

[3]Private letter from Mack Reynolds dated December 18, 1975.

[4]Reynolds, commentary on his "Retaliation," in Harry Harrison, ed., *SF: Author's Choice* (New York: Berkley Books, 1968), p. 221.

[5]I have corresponded with Reynolds, who has been helpful in confirming (and slightly expanding) my proposed categories.

[6]Reynolds, "What Do You Mean—Marxism?" *Science-Fiction Studies*, 1 (Fall 1974), 271.

[7]Reynolds, *Time Gladiator* (New York: Lancer Books, 1969), p. 155.

[8]Reynolds, *Time Gladiator*, p. 187.

[9]Reynolds, *The Five Way Agent* (New York: Ace Books, 1969), p. 18.

[10]Reynolds, *The Five Way Agent*, p. 56.

[11]Dennis Livingston, "Science Fiction Models for World Order Systems," *International Organization*, 25 (Spring 1971), 269.

[12]Virgil L. Lokke, "The American Utopian Anti-Novel," in Ray Browne, ed., *Frontier of American Culture* (West Lafayette, Indiana: Purdue University Press, 1968), p. 127. Reynolds is not the first to borrow from Bellamy. Other utopian thinkers have freely mined Bellamy's future world for ideas in designing their ideal societies. One of the most recent is B.F. Skinner in *Walden II*. A long list of earlier novelists, including Arthur D. Vinton in *Looking Further Backward* (1890) and Conrad Wilbrandt in *Mr. East's Experiences in Mr. Bellamy's World* (1891), have made use of his plot and characters.

[13]Arthur E. Morgan, *Edward Bellamy* (New York: Columbia University Press, 1944), p. xxiii.

[14]Reynolds, *Looking Backward from the Year 2000* (New York: Ace Books, 1973), p. 83.

[15]Vernon Louis Parrington, Jr., *American Dreams* (New York: Russell and Russell, Inc., 1964), p. 72.

[16]Reynolds, "Freedom," in *The Best of Mack Reynolds* (New York: Pocket Books, 1976), p. 51.

[17]Reynolds, "Utopian," in *The Best of Mack Reynolds*, p. 347.

[18]Reynolds, "Pacifist," in *The Best of Mack Reynolds*, p. 153.

[19]Irving Howe, *Politics and the Novel* (New York: Horizon Press, 1957), p. 21.

Discovering Worlds: The Fiction of Ursula K. Le Guin

[1]Ursula K. Le Guin, *Rocannon's World* (New York: Ace Books, 1972); *Planet of Exile* (New York: Ace Books, 1971); *City of Illusions* (New York: Ace Books, 1967); *A Wizard of Earthsea* (New York: Parnassus, 1968); *The Left Hand of Darkness* (New York: Walker and Company, 1969); *The Tombs of Atuan* (New York: Atheneum, 1971); *The Lathe of Heaven* (New York: Charles Scribner's Sons, 1971); *The Farthest Shore* (New York: Berkley, 1976); *The Dispossessed* (New York: Harper & Row, 1974); *The Wind's Twelve Quarters* (New York: Harper & Row, 1975). All references in the text are to the editions cited here.

For a more complete bibliography to 1975, see Jeff Levin, "Ursula K. Le Guin: A Select Bibliography," *Science-Fiction Studies*, 2 (1975), 204-208. It appears as part of an issue (volume 2, part 3; whole number 7) devoted entirely to Le Guin's work.

[2]Ursula K. Le Guin, "Dreams Must Explain Themselves," *Algol 21* (November 1973), p. 8. This article and other Le Guin material, including the National Book Award Acceptance Speech, were collected as *Dreams Must Explain Themselves* (New York: Algol Press, 1975).

[3]See Douglas Barbour, "Wholeness and Balance in the Hainish Novels of Ursula K. Le Guin," *SFS*, 1 (1973), 164-173; and his "Wholeness and Balance: An Addendum," *SFS*, 2 (1974), 248-249.

[4]Le Guin, "A Citizen of Mondath," *Foundation 4* (July 1973), pp. 20-24.

[5]The Nebula Award of the Science Fiction Writers of America was presented to Ursula K. Le Guin for *The Left Hand of Darkness* (best novel, 1970); "The Day Before the Revolution" (best short story, 1974); and *The Dispossessed (best novel, 1974)*. The ⎫ Awards of the World Science Fiction Convention were awarded to *The Left ⎭ of Darkness*: "The Word for World Is Forest" (best novella, 1973); "The Ones Walk Away from Omelas" (best short story, 1973) and *The Dispossessed*.

Le Guin, "Foreword," in *The Wind's Twelve Quarters*, pp. vii-viii.

[7]Le Guin, *The Dispossessed,* p. 303.

[8]Le Guin, *Planet of Exile,* p. 83.

[9]Le Guin, *The Lathe of Heaven,* p. 173.

[10]Ian Watson, "Le Guin's *Lathe of Heaven* and the Role of Dick: The False Reality as Mediator," *SFS,* 2 (1975), 67-75.

[11]Le Guin, "Vaster Than Empires and More Slow," in *The Wind's Twelve Quarters,* p. 182.

[12]Le Guin, *The Dispossessed,* pp. 306-307.

[13]Donald Wollheim, *The Universe Makers* (New York: Harper & Row, 1971), pp. 42-44.

[14]Le Guin, "The Word for World Is Forest," in Harlan Ellison, ed., *Again, Dangerous Visions* (Garden City, N.Y.: Doubleday & Company, Inc., 1972), p. 93.

[15]Northrop Frye, *The Educated Imagination* (Toronto: CBC Publications, 1963), p. 2.

[16]Le Guin, "Is Gender Necessary?" in Vonda N. McIntyre and Susan Janice Anderson, eds., *Aurora: Beyond Reality* (Greenwich, Cn.: Fawcett, 1976), p. 137. This essay sums up the problems, shortcomings, and potentials of her human experiment.

An early criticism of Le Guin's use of Gethenian sexuality is Stanislaw Lem's "Lost Opportunities," *SF Commentary 24* (November 1971), pp. 22-24. Le Guin's reply, a letter in which she discusses the problems of readers' perceptions and her own rejections of a created ambisexual pronoun, appears in *SF Commentary 26* (April 1972), pp. 90-92. The exchange is reprinted in Pamela Sargent, ed., *Women of Wonder* (New York: Vintage, 1974), pp. xxxii-xxxvi.

[17]David Ketterer, *New Worlds for Old* (New York: Anchor Book , 1974), pp. 79-80.

[18]See David Barbour, "*The Lathe of Heaven:* Taoist Dream," *Algol 21* (November 1973), pp. 22-24.

[19]Le Guin, "The Day Before the Revolution," in *The Wind's Twelve Quarters,* p. 291.

[20]George Turner, "Paradigm and Pattern: Form and Meaning in *The Dispossessed,*" *SF Commentary 41/42* (February 1975), p. 71. For a study of *The Dispossessed* as a utopian novel by a scholar outside the science fiction field, see Robert C. Elliott, "A New Utopian Novel," *The Yale Review,* 65 (December 1975), 256-261.

[21]Le Guin, *From Elfland to Poughkeepsie* (Portland: Pendragon, 1973), pp. 22-24.

[22]Le Guin, "Foreword," in *The Wind's Twelve Quarters,* p. viii.

[23]Peter Nicholls, "Showing Children the Value of Death," *Foundation 5* (Jaunuary 1974), p. 75.

[24]Le Guin, *The Farthest Shore,* p. 196.

[25]Le Guin, *A Wizard of Earthsea,* pp. 189-190.

[26]Le Guin, "National Book Award Acceptance Speech," *Algol 21* (November 1973), p. 14.

[27]Le Guin, "A Citizen of Mondath," *Foundation 4,* p. 24.

Roger Zelazny: Unfinished Business

[1]Personal letter dated October 4, 1974. Zelazny's early stories sometimes appear two in an issue, one under the penname Harrison Denmark.

[2]Today Zelazny disowns the excessive whimsy of that first autobiography. For the sake of interested readers, however, he supplies the following information in vita form:

Born May 13, 1937, Euclid, Ohio. B.A., Western Reserve University, 1959; M.A., Columbia University, 1962. Ohio National Guard, 1960-1963; Army Reserve, 1963-1966. Employed, Social Security Administration, Cleveland, Ohio, and Baltimore, Maryland, 1962-1969; claims representative, 1962-1965, Cleveland; claims policy specialist, 1965-1969, Baltimore. Married to Judith Alene Callahan, 1966; one son, Devin Joseph, b. 1971.

Began writing professionally, 1962; began writing fulltime, 1969. Approximately 70 short stories published in *Amazing, Analog, Fantastic Adventures, Galaxy, If, The Magazine of Fantasy and Science Fiction, New Worlds, Worlds of Tomorrow*. [Interesting on the start of Zelazny's career is a transcript of an interview published in *If*, 19 (January 1969), 159-161.]

The same vita records that he was Guest of Honor at the 1974 World Science Fiction Convention, Washington D.C., and that a collection of his manuscripts is maintained at Syracuse University. What the vita cannot show is that, as I found out in researching this essay, he is one of the most courteous and helpful of human beings.

[3]Zelazny's nominations for major awards include "Damnation Alley" (1967), Hugo; "For a Breath I Tarry" (1966), Hugo; "This Moment of the Storm (1966), Hugo; "Now Comes the Storm" (1966/1967), Hugo; "The Engine at the Heartspring's Center (1974), Nebula. His fiction has been anthologized so often that he literally has lost count of how many times quoted from the dust jacket of *The Doors of His Face, The Lamps of His Mouth and Other Stories* (Garden City, N.Y.: Doubleday & Company, 1971)

[4]Commentaries include Samuel R. Delany, "Faust and Archimedes," *The Science Fiction Writers of America Forum* (August 1969), pp. 15-26; and Banks Mebane, "Gunpowder: the Court, Wildfire at Midnight," *Algol 13* (January 1968), pp. 39-45.

[5]Zelazny, "Horseman!" *Fantastic Adventures*, 11 (August 1962), 109.

[6]Zelazny, "Passion Play," *Amazing Stories*, 36 (August 1962), 31.

[7]Zelazny, *Jack of Shadows* (New York: Walker and Company, 1971), pp. 147-148. True, the Colonel Who Never Died will be reborn, like all natives of Darkside, thus slightly lessening death's sting. But the process of returning to life is highly unpleasant, the sensation of dying is still more dreadful—as Jack has shown earlier, and the Colonel's own name suggests how he really views the matter.

[8]Zelazny, "The Keys to December," in *The Doors of His Face, the Lamps of His Mouth*, p. 36.

[9]Zelazny, *Lord of Light* (Garden City, N.Y.: Doubleday & Company, 1967), p. 209.

[10]Zelazny, *Lord of Light*, p. 65.

[11]Zelazny, "A Museum Piece," in *The Doors of His Face, the Lamps of His Mouth*, p. 77.

[12]Thomas Monteleone, "Science Fiction as Literature: Selected Stories and Novels of Roger Zelazny," M.A. thesis, University of Maryland, 1973. Monteleone's analyses of several of Zelazny's best stories and novels, utilizing several long conversations with Zelazny, are extremely valuable.

[13]Zelazny, "A Rose for Ecclesiastes," in *The Doors of His Face, the Lamps of His Mouth*, p. 77.

[14]Zelazny, "A Rose for Ecclesiastes," p. 71. One important part of Zelazny's work is his use of literary allusions. Although they do not control the action, Gallinger's reference to his perception of himself as Hamlet charged by his father's ghost to perform a mission he cannot—enriches our emotional reaction to his behavior. In the same way, Zelazny uses the Book of Job and Coleridge's "The Rime of the Ancient Mariner" in "For a Breath I Tarry"; Hamlet and Othello in *Today We Choose Faces; and* Noh drama in *Damnation Alley*. Replying to a query on this last work, he has explained his purpose as follows: "I somewhat subscribe to the notion of a resonance-effect in literature. I think that if someone has had even a brief exposure to a particular medium, something that later mimes it will strike a chord of familiarity, even if he does not know why... A sense of familiarity is always a good thing to stir in a reader, as I see it, perhaps especially if he doesn't know why. It makes a thing seem somewhat more important if it nags him a bit." From a personal letter dated August

29, 1971, quoted by Carl B. Yoke, in "Zelazny's *Damnation Alley:* Hell Noh," *Extrapolation,* 15 (December 1973), 6.

¹⁵"For a Breath I Tarry" was published in garbled form in *New Worlds* (March 1966), and a corrected version in *Fantastic Adventures* (September 1966). It is Zelazny's personal favorite of all of his short fiction. From a personal letter dated January 11, 1975.

¹⁶Zelazny, *Isle of the Dead* (New York: Ace Books, 1969), p. 188).

¹⁷As a beginning novelist, Zelazny developed a large cast of characters primarily because he wanted to have enough things to write about, and threw in action sequences primarily to add suspense at the breaks necessary to serial publication. From a taped interview dated August 7, 1973; quoted by Monteleone, pp. 58, 60.

¹⁸Zelazny, *This Immortal* (New York: Ace Books, 1966), p. 129.

¹⁹Monteleone, p. 63.

²⁰Zelazny, as quoted by Bill Mallardi and Bill Bowers, eds., *The Double: Bill Symposium* (Akron, Ohio: D:B Press, 1969), p. 21. Originally published in the fanzine *Double: Bill,* written in the middle/late 1960's.

²¹Zelazny has described *Damnation Alley* as "primarily a bang-bang odyssey"; from a personal letter dated August 29, 1971; quoted by Yoke, p. 6.

²²For example, Alexei and Cory Panshin are very enthusiastic about the direction the Amber series is taking. The Panshins have disliked most of Zelazny's recent work, but they are pleased that in *Sign of the Unicorn* Zelazny "has launched himself into a life or death improvisation. He is in honest pursuit of true reality of whole nature and worthwhile action. He has probed his old familiar too-ready answers...and seen beyond them... In view of the daring magnificence of the undertaking, clumsiness and crudity become secondary. The pursuit is all"; "Books," *The Magazine of Fantasy and Science Fiction,* 49 (August 1975), 162.

²³Early in his career, Zelazny deliberately tried to satisfy Northrop Frye's prescription for literature's use of myths in the "Mythic or High Mimetic" modes (noted by Monteleone, pp. 12-13; see also Zelazny's essay, "Some Science Fiction Parameters: A Biased View," *Galaxy,* 36 (July 1975), 6-11). However, Tolkien's comments in "On Fairy-Stories" are more relevant to Zelazny's more recent works, like *Jack of Shadows,* which are truly independent of known myths, but are instead "plainly not primarily concerned with possibility, but with desirability. If they awakened desire, satisfying it while often whetting it unbearably, they succeeded": Tolkien, in *Tree and Leaf* (London: Allen Unwin, 1964), p. 40. Stories like *Jack of Shadows* and *Creatures of Light and Darkness* deliberately alternate between whetting and straight-arming desire. Their hints of powerful emotion under inhuman restraint create a rather different feeling from that which Tolkien suggests, at times resembling Zelazny's own description of Tourneur's *The Revenger's Tragedy:* "A universe denuded of spiritual significance may be horrible--it may also be a comic universe": Zelazny, "Two Traditions and Cyril Tourneur: An Examination of Morality and Comedy Conventions in *The Revenger's Tragedy*" (M.A. Thesis, Columbia University, 1962), p. 44.

²⁴Zelazny, *Doorways in the Sand* (New York: Avon Books, 1977), p. 30.

Contributors

Thomas D. Clareson received the 1977 Pilgrim Award (named for J.O. Bailey's pioneering book) given by the Science Fiction Research Association (SFRA) to individuals who have made a career-long contribution to the study of science fiction. He chaired the first M.L.A Seminar on Science Fiction in 1958, has edited the journal *Extrapolation* since 1959, and was the first president of SFRA from 1970 through 1976. His most recent book is *Many Futures, Many Worlds* (Kent State University Press, 1977). He is General Editor for the Greenwood Press microform reprint series of science fiction magazines and is currently working on a bibliography and critical study of Robert Silverberg. In 1976 he received an N.E.H. summer grant to work at the Huntington Library while completing research for a history of early American science fiction.

Joe DeBolt of the Sociology Department at Central Michigan University has edited *The Happening Worlds of John Brunner* (1975), and his *Ursula K. Le Guin: Voyager to Inner Lands and to Outer Space* will be released early in 1979. He is the new president of SFRA.

H. Bruce Franklin of the Department of English at Rutgers University--Newark is best known for his early anthology, *Future Perfect: American Science Fiction of the Nineteenth Century* (1966).

David N. Samuelson of the Department of English at the University of California-Long Beach contributed the essay on Heinlein to the first volume of *Voices for the Future*. A student of futurology as well as literary criticism, his *Visions of Tomorrow: Six Journeys from Outer to Inner Space* was included in the Arno Press Science Fiction Collection (1975).

Joe Sanders of the Department of Communications at Lakeland Community College (Mentor, Ohio) has reviewed science fiction for the Cleveland *Plain Dealer*. He is at work on a critical study of fantasist, Mervyn Peake.

Patricia Warrick of the Department of English at the University of Wisconsin—Fox Center has co-edited a series of anthologies with Martin Greenberg and Joseph Olander. Her recent essay "Images of the Man-Machine Intelligence Relationship in Science Fiction" was published in *Many Futures, Many Worlds*.

Susan Wood of the Department of English at the University of British Columbia, has won the Hugo award for her popular criticism in the field of science fiction. Her essay, "A City of Which the Stars Are Suburbs," was included in *SF: The Other Side of Realism* (1971).

Thomas L. Wymer of the Department of English at Bowling Green University has contributed an essay on Kurt Vonnegut to the first volume of *Voices for the Future* and the essay, "Perception and Value in Science Fiction," to *Many Futures, Many Worlds*. He has been one of the organizers of the science fiction sections in the Popular Culture Association.